VOL. 30
VIZ Media Edition

Story and Art by
RUMIKO TAKAHASHI

English Adaptation by Gerard Jones

Translation/Mari Morimoto
Touch-up Art & Lettering/Bill Schuch
Cover and Interior Graphic Design/Yuki Ameda
Editor/Ian Robertson

Editor in Chief, Books/Alvin Lu
Editor in Chief, Magazines/Marc Weidenbaum
VP of Publishing Licensing/Rika Inouye
VP of Sales/Gonzalo Ferreyra
Sr. VP of Marketing/Liza Coppola
Publisher/Hyoe Narita

Printed in the U.S.A.

Published by VIZ Media, LLC
P.O. Box 77010
San Francisco, CA 94107

VIZ Media Edition
10 9 8 7 6 5 4 3 2 1
First printing, July 2007

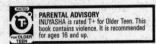

www.viz.com

store.viz.com

INUYASHA

VOL. 30

VIZ Media Edition

STORY AND ART BY
RUMIKO TAKAHASHI

CONTENTS

Long ago, in the "Warring States" era of Japan's Muromachi period (*Sengoku-jidai*, approximately 1467-1568 CE), a legendary dog-like half-demon called "Inuyasha" attempted to steal the Shikon Jewel—or "Jewel of Four Souls"—from a village, but was stopped by the enchanted arrow of the village priestess, Kikyo. Inuyasha fell into a deep sleep, pinned to a tree by Kikyo's arrow, while the mortally wounded Kikyo took the Shikon Jewel with her into the fires of her funeral pyre. Years passed.

Fast-forward to the present day. Kagome, a Japanese high school girl, is pulled into a well one day by a mysterious centipede monster and finds herself transported into the past—only to come face to face with the trapped Inuyasha. She frees him, and Inuyasha easily defeats the centipede monster.

The residents of the village, now 50 years older, readily accept Kagome as the reincarnation of their deceased priestess Kikyo, a claim supported by the fact that the Shikon Jewel emerges from a cut on Kagome's body. Unfortunately, the jewel's rediscovery means that the village is soon under attack by a variety of demons in search of this treasure. Then, the jewel is accidentally shattered into many shards, each of which may have the fearsome power of the entire jewel.

Although Inuyasha says he hates Kagome because of her resemblance to Kikyo, the woman who "killed" him, he is forced to team up with her when Kaede, the village leader, binds him to Kagome with a powerful spell. Now the two grudging companions must fight to reclaim and reassemble the shattered shards of the Shikon Jewel before they fall into the wrong hands...

THIS VOLUME Kagura and the demonic baby Hakudoshi are killing off priests in order to find the border between the afterworld and this world, where it is said that the last of the Shikon Jewel shards lies. Inuyasha and the others are also doing everything they can to recover this last shard. Could it be that Inuyasha and Kagome...

INUYASHA
Half-demon hybrid, son of a human mother and demon father. His necklace is enchanted, allowing Kagome to control him with a word.

KAGOME
Modern-day Japanese schoolgirl who can travel back and forth between the past and present through an enchanted well.

NARAKU
Enigmatic demon-mastermind behind the miseries of nearly everyone in the story.

MIROKU
Lecherous Buddhist priest cursed with a mystical "hellhole" in his hand that's slowly killing him.

KOGA
Leader of the Wolf Clan, Koga is himself a Wolf Demon and, because of several Shikon shards in his legs, possesses super speed. Enamored of Kagome, he quarrels with Inuyasha frequently.

SANGO
"Demon Exterminator" or slayer from the village where the Shikon Jewel was first born.

SCROLL 1
HALL OF THE BODHISATTVA

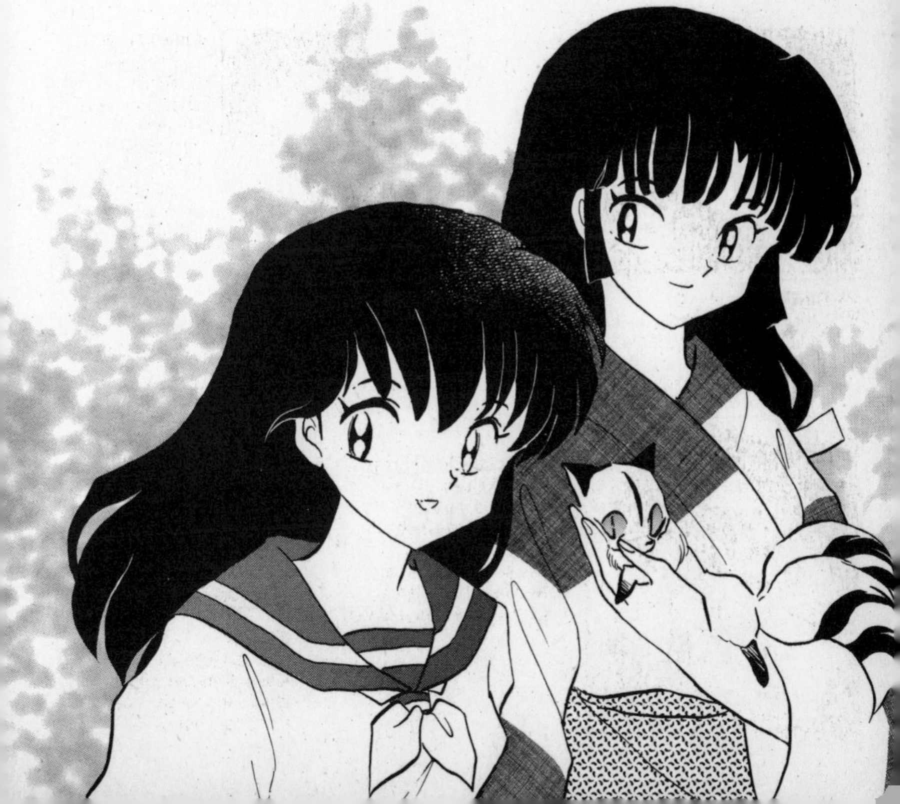

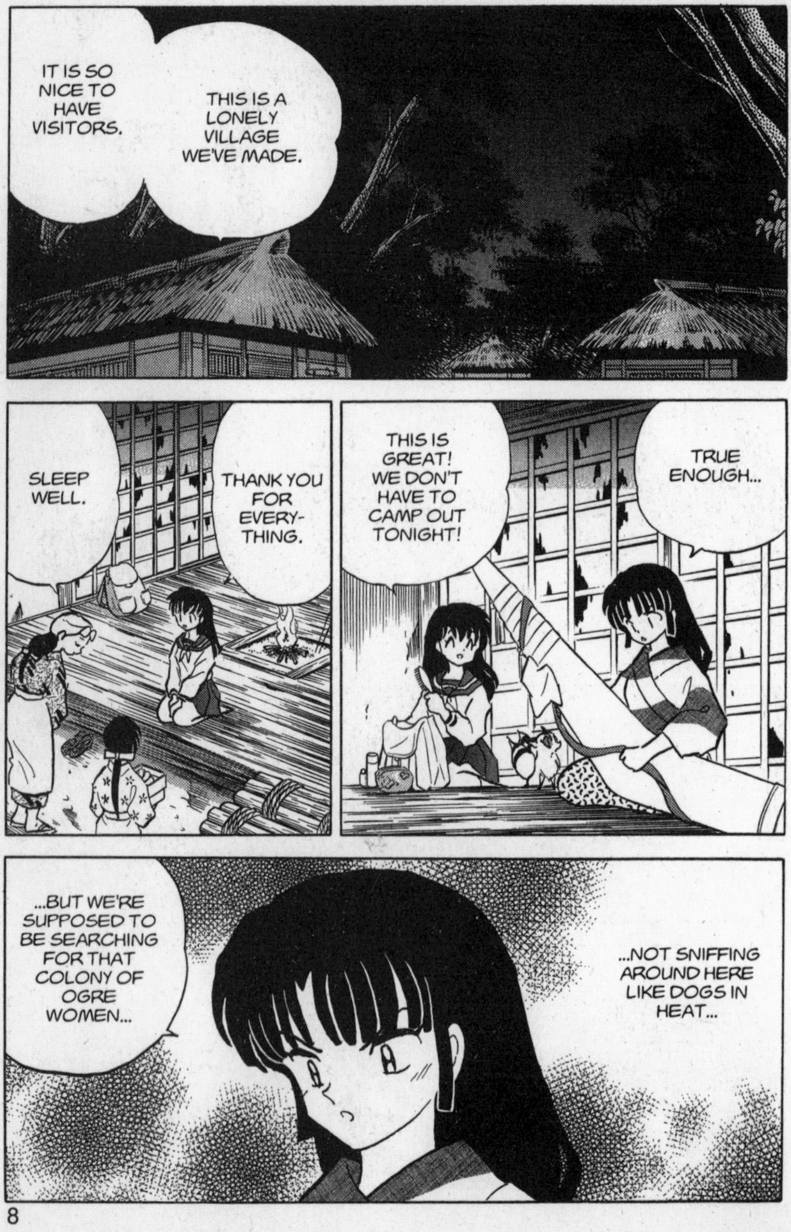
IT IS SO NICE TO HAVE VISITORS.
THIS IS A LONELY VILLAGE WE'VE MADE.
SLEEP WELL.
THANK YOU FOR EVERY-THING.
THIS IS GREAT! WE DON'T HAVE TO CAMP OUT TONIGHT!
TRUE ENOUGH...
...BUT WE'RE SUPPOSED TO BE SEARCHING FOR THAT COLONY OF OGRE WOMEN...
...NOT SNIFFING AROUND HERE LIKE DOGS IN HEAT...

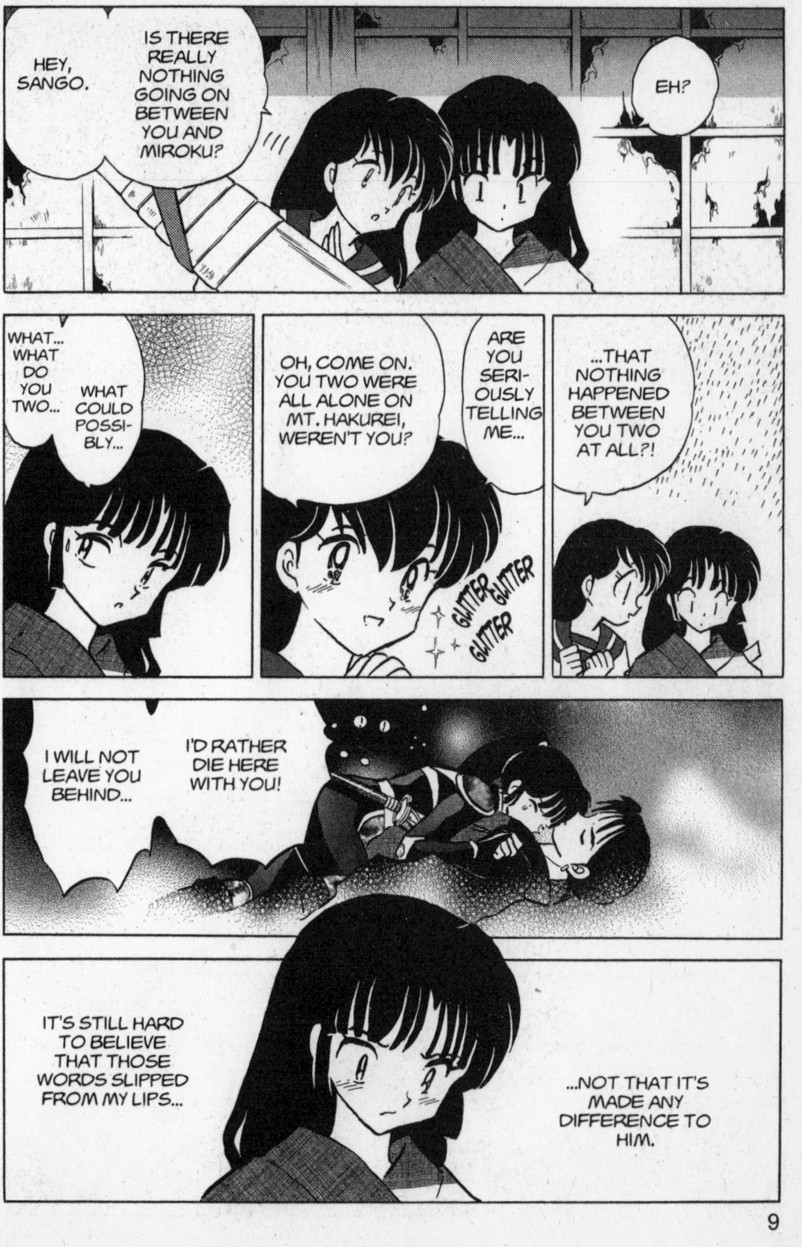
HEY, SANGO.
IS THERE REALLY NOTHING GOING ON BETWEEN YOU AND MIROKU?
EH?
WHAT... WHAT DO YOU TWO...
WHAT COULD POSSIBLY...
OH, COME ON. YOU TWO WERE ALL ALONE ON MT. HAKUREI, WEREN'T YOU?
ARE YOU SERIOUSLY TELLING ME...
GLITTER GLITTER GLITTER GLITTER
...THAT NOTHING HAPPENED BETWEEN YOU TWO AT ALL?!
I WILL NOT LEAVE YOU BEHIND...
I'D RATHER DIE HERE WITH YOU!
IT'S STILL HARD TO BELIEVE THAT THOSE WORDS SLIPPED FROM MY LIPS...
...NOT THAT IT'S MADE ANY DIFFERENCE TO HIM.

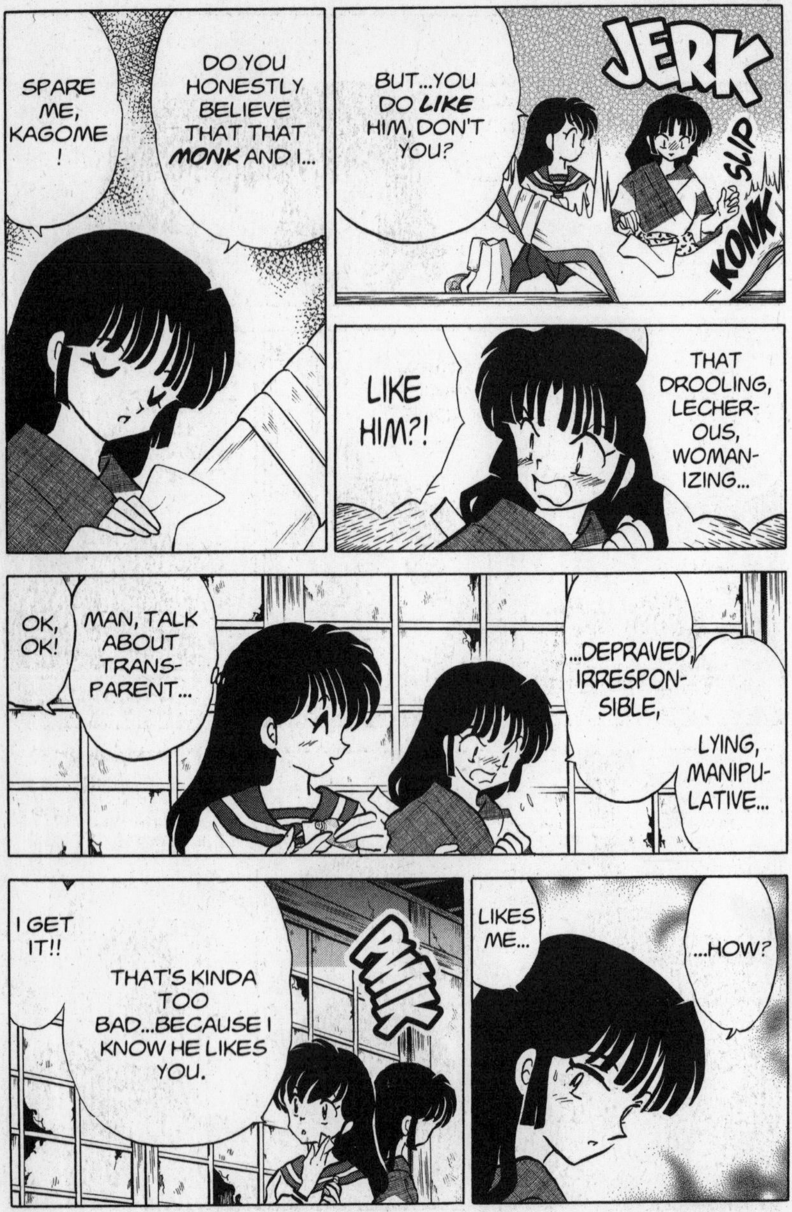
SPARE ME, KAGOME!
DO YOU HONESTLY BELIEVE THAT THAT MONK AND I...
BUT...YOU DO LIKE HIM, DON'T YOU?
JERK
SLIP
KONK
LIKE HIM?!
THAT DROOLING, LECHEROUS, WOMANIZING...
OK, OK!
MAN, TALK ABOUT TRANSPARENT...
...DEPRAVED, IRRESPONSIBLE,
LYING, MANIPULATIVE...
I GET IT!!
THAT'S KINDA TOO BAD...BECAUSE I KNOW HE LIKES YOU.
PWIK
LIKES ME...
...HOW?

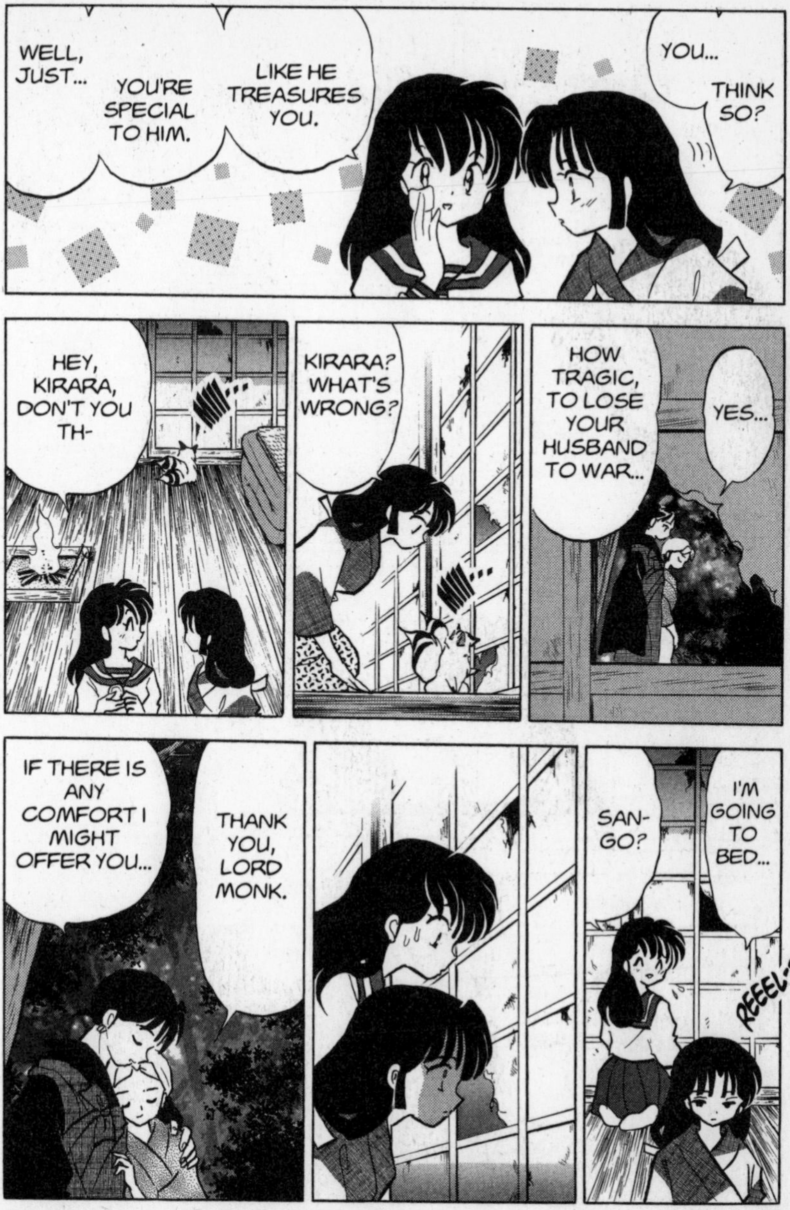
WELL, JUST...
YOU'RE SPECIAL TO HIM.
LIKE HE TREASURES YOU.
YOU... THINK SO?
HEY, KIRARA, DON'T YOU TH-
KIRARA? WHAT'S WRONG?
HOW TRAGIC, TO LOSE YOUR HUSBAND TO WAR...
YES...
IF THERE IS ANY COMFORT I MIGHT OFFER YOU...
THANK YOU, LORD MONK.
SAN-GO?
I'M GOING TO BED...
REEEL...

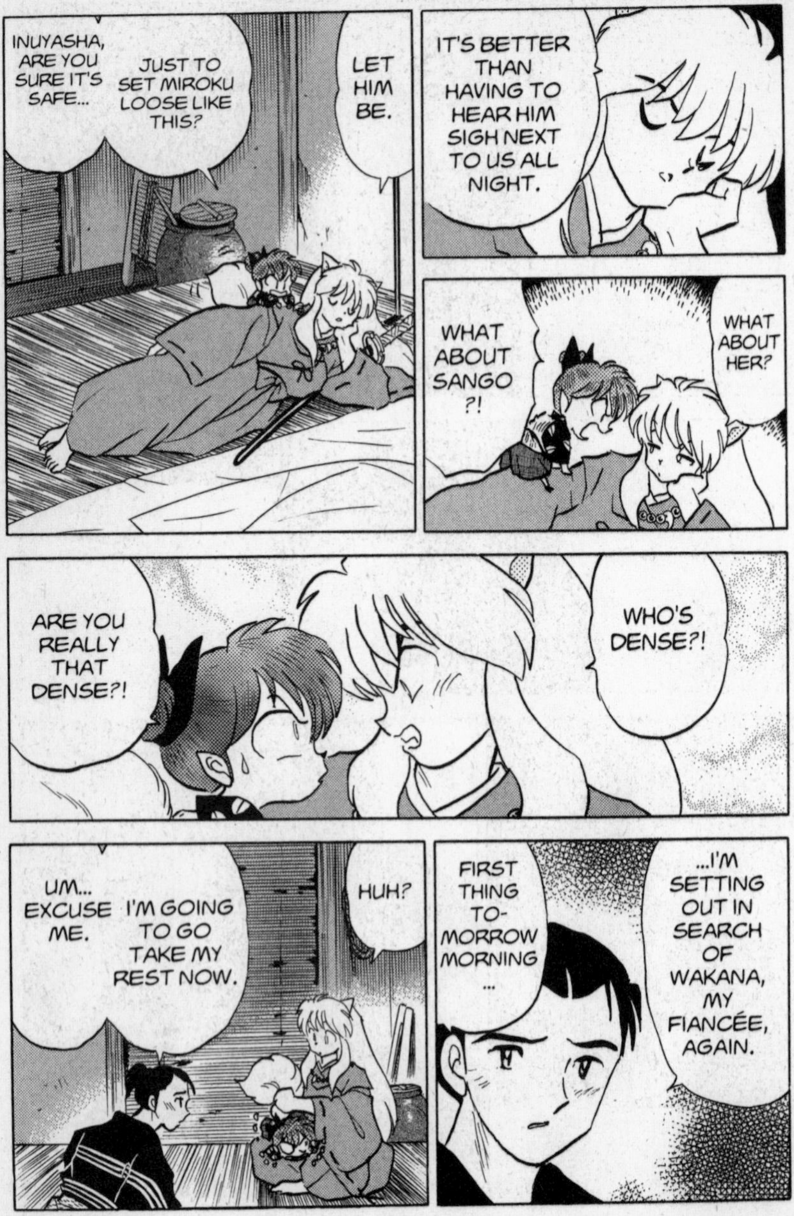
INUYASHA, ARE YOU SURE IT'S SAFE...
JUST TO SET MIROKU LOOSE LIKE THIS?
LET HIM BE.
IT'S BETTER THAN HAVING TO HEAR HIM SIGH NEXT TO US ALL NIGHT.
WHAT ABOUT SANGO?!
WHAT ABOUT HER?
ARE YOU REALLY THAT DENSE?!
WHO'S DENSE?!
UM... EXCUSE ME.
I'M GOING TO GO TAKE MY REST NOW.
HUH?
FIRST THING TO-MORROW MORNING...
...I'M SETTING OUT IN SEARCH OF WAKANA, MY FIANCÉE, AGAIN.

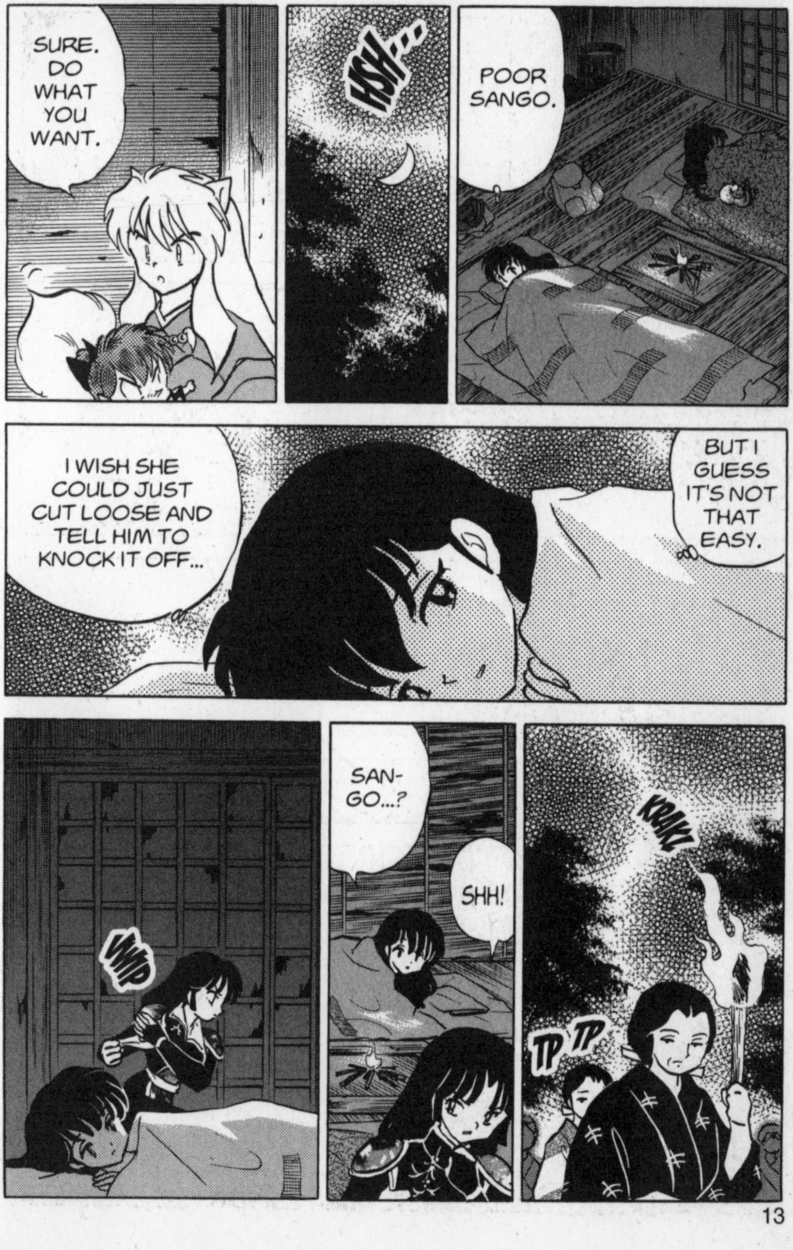
SURE. DO WHAT YOU WANT.
HSH...
POOR SANGO.
I WISH SHE COULD JUST CUT LOOSE AND TELL HIM TO KNOCK IT OFF...
BUT I GUESS IT'S NOT THAT EASY.
WMP
SAN-GO...?
SHH!
KRAK!
TP TP

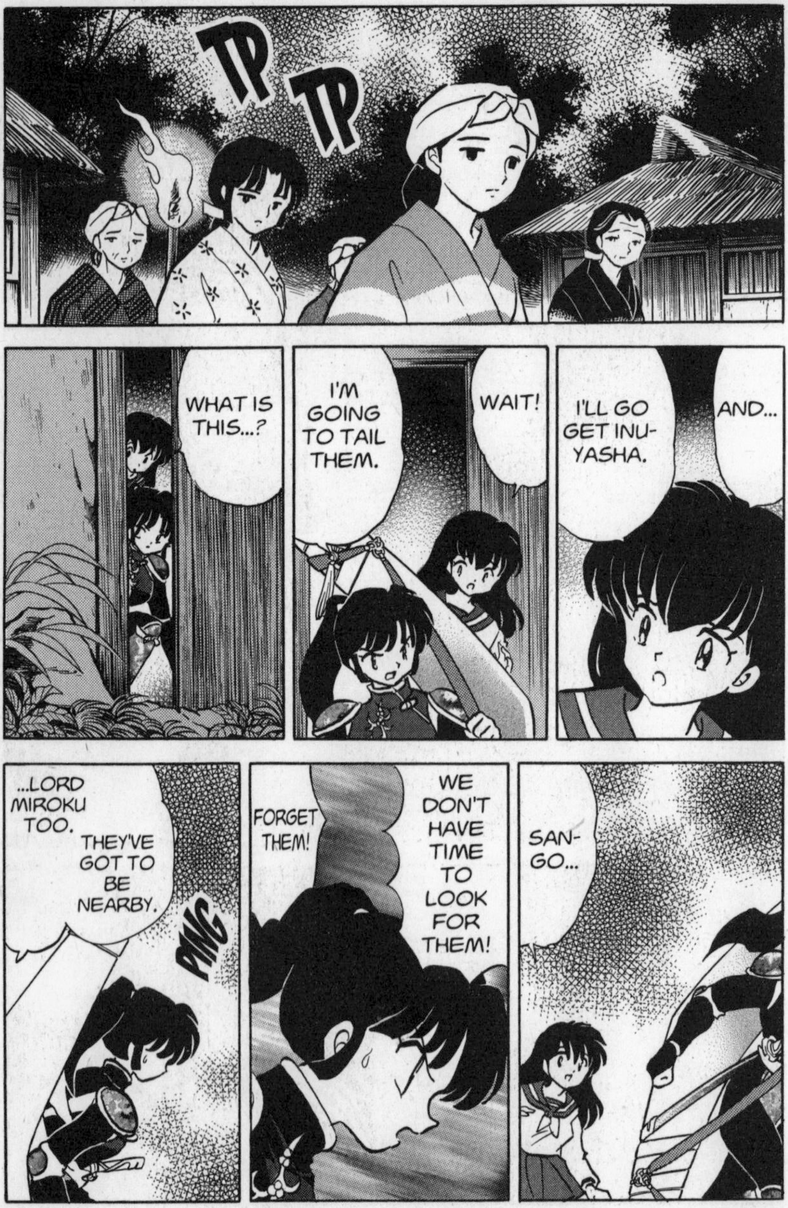
TP
TP
WHAT IS THIS...?
I'M GOING TO TAIL THEM.
WAIT!
I'LL GO GET INU-YASHA.
AND...
...LORD MIROKU TOO.
THEY'VE GOT TO BE NEARBY.
PING
FORGET THEM!
WE DON'T HAVE TIME TO LOOK FOR THEM!
SAN-GO...

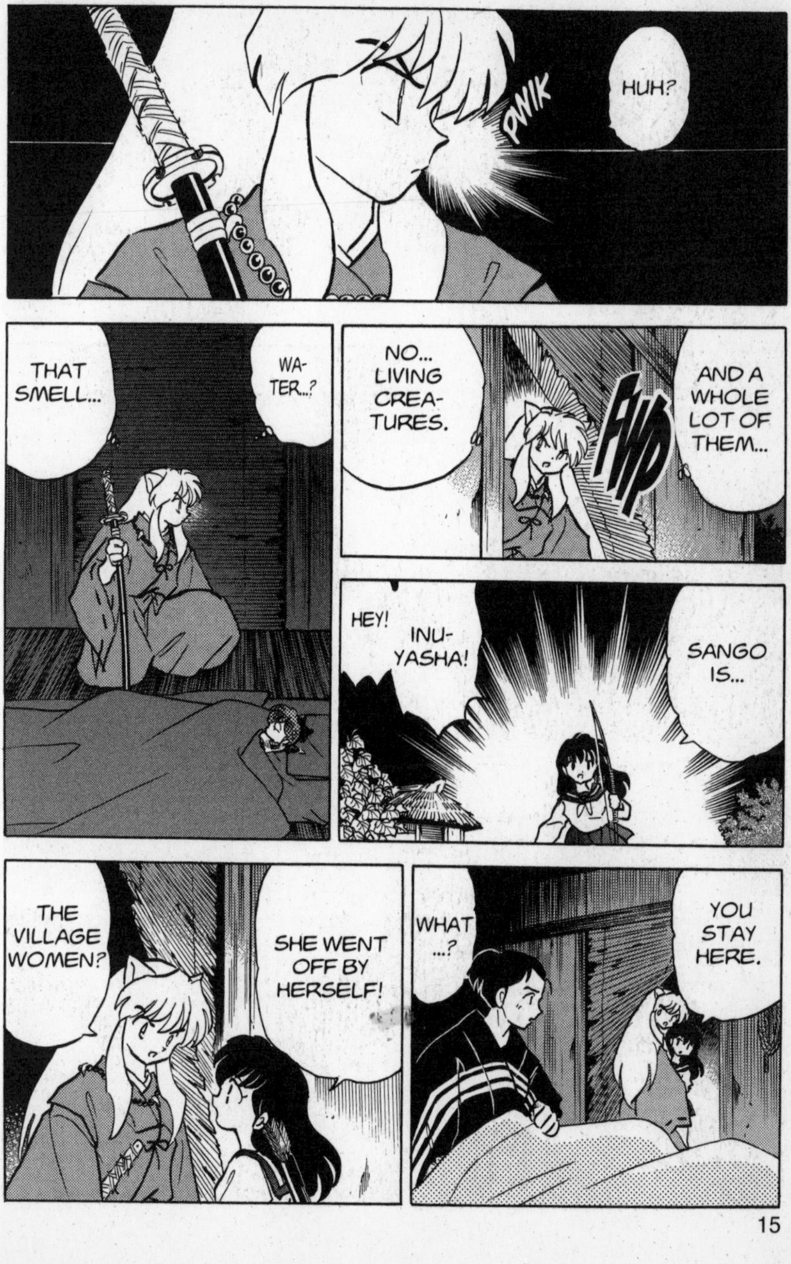
PWIK
HUH?
THAT SMELL...
WA-TER...?
NO... LIVING CREA-TURES.
FWP
AND A WHOLE LOT OF THEM...
HEY!
INU-YASHA!
SANGO IS...
THE VILLAGE WOMEN?
SHE WENT OFF BY HERSELF!
WHAT ...?
YOU STAY HERE.

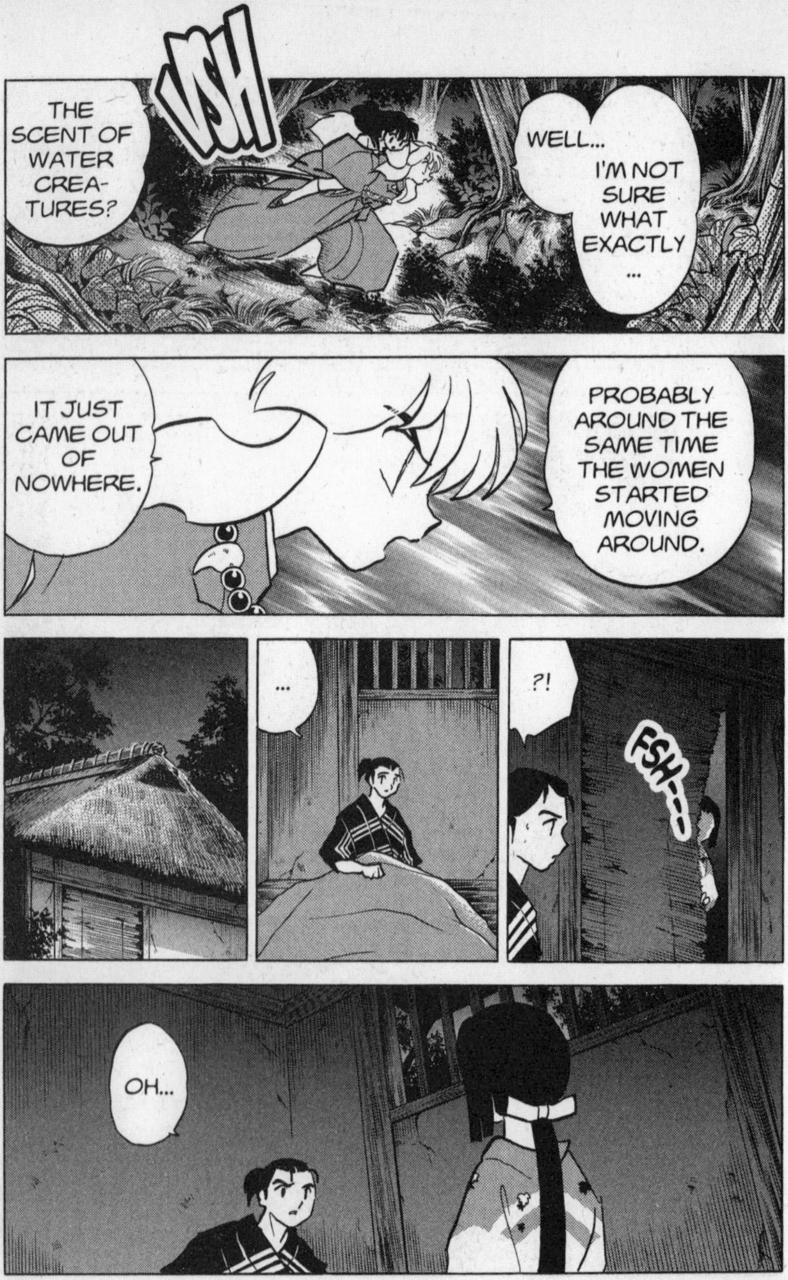
THE SCENT OF WATER CREA-TURES?
VSH
WELL... I'M NOT SURE WHAT EXACTLY ...
IT JUST CAME OUT OF NOWHERE.
PROBABLY AROUND THE SAME TIME THE WOMEN STARTED MOVING AROUND.
...
?!
FSH---
OH...

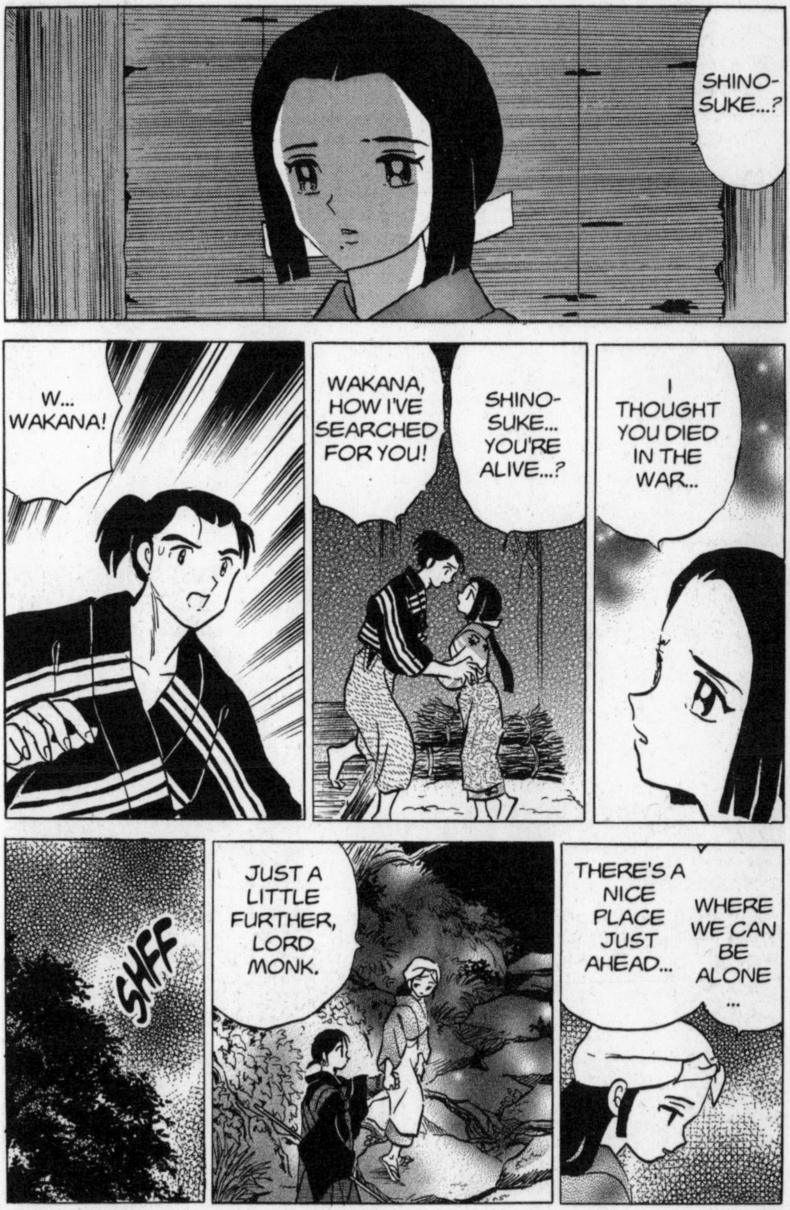
SHINO-SUKE...?
W... WAKANA!
WAKANA, HOW I'VE SEARCHED FOR YOU!
SHINO-SUKE... YOU'RE ALIVE...?
I THOUGHT YOU DIED IN THE WAR...
SHFF
JUST A LITTLE FURTHER, LORD MONK.
THERE'S A NICE PLACE JUST AHEAD...
WHERE WE CAN BE ALONE ...

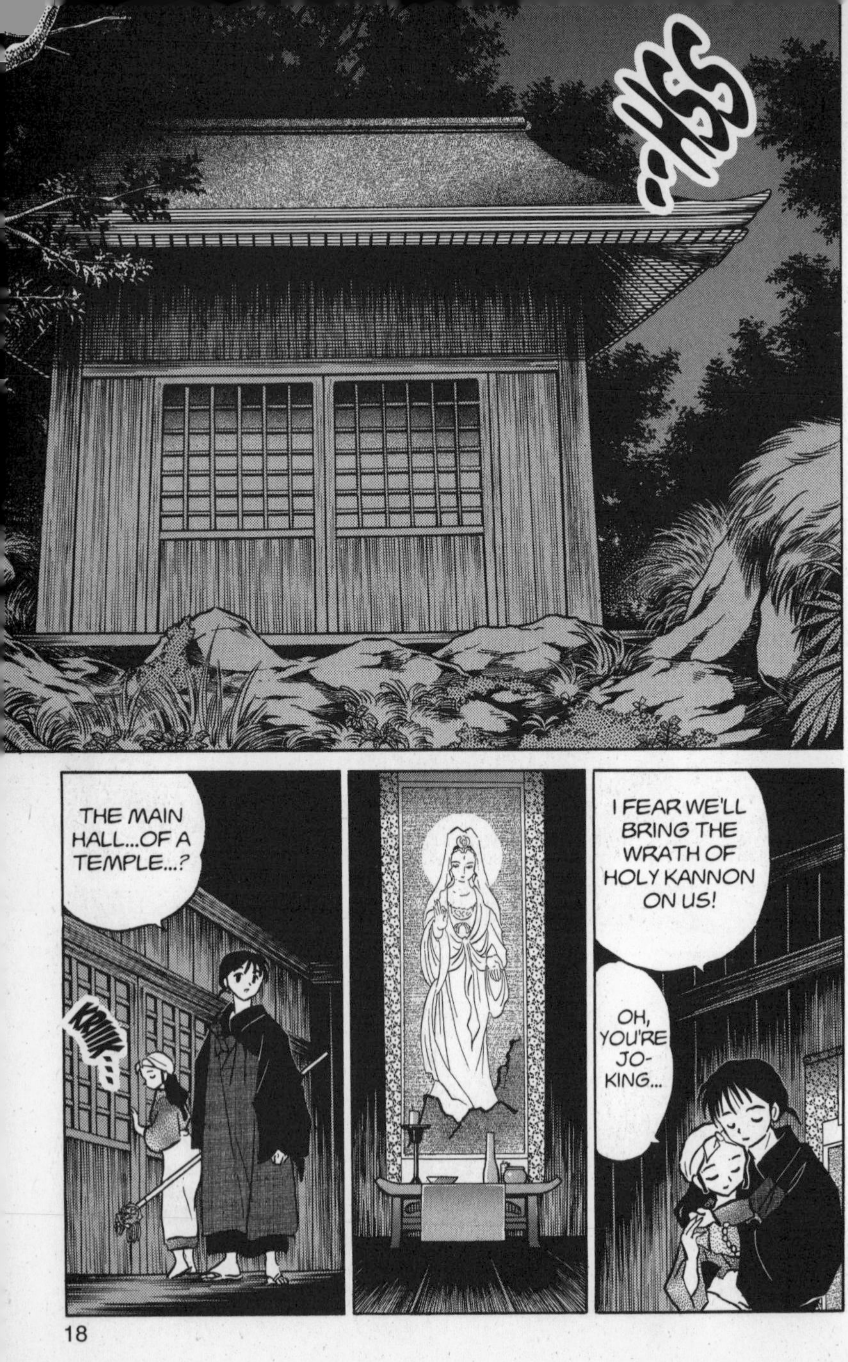
SSH...
THE MAIN HALL...OF A TEMPLE...?
KRUNK...
I FEAR WE'LL BRING THE WRATH OF HOLY KANNON ON US!
OH, YOU'RE JO-KING...

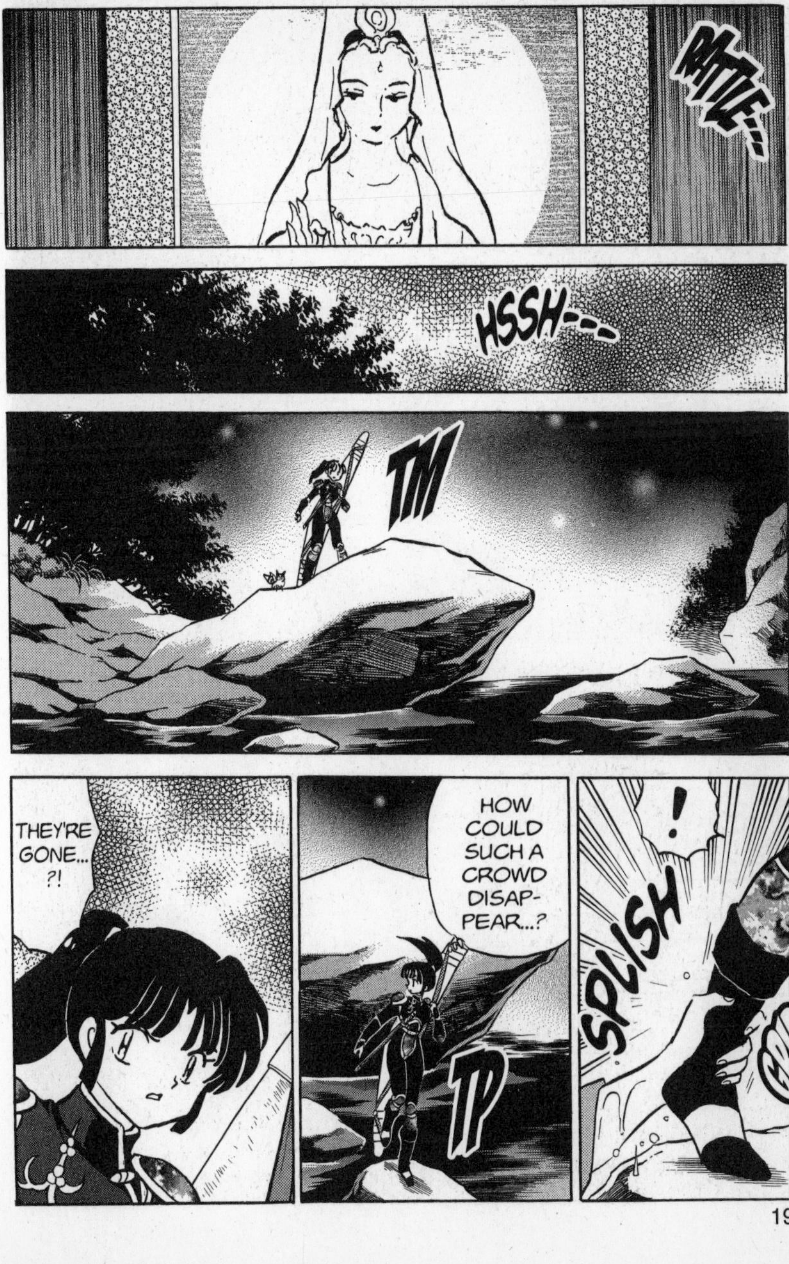
RATTLE...
HSSH---
TM
THEY'RE GONE... ?!
HOW COULD SUCH A CROWD DISAP- PEAR...?
TP
!
SPLISH
GRIP

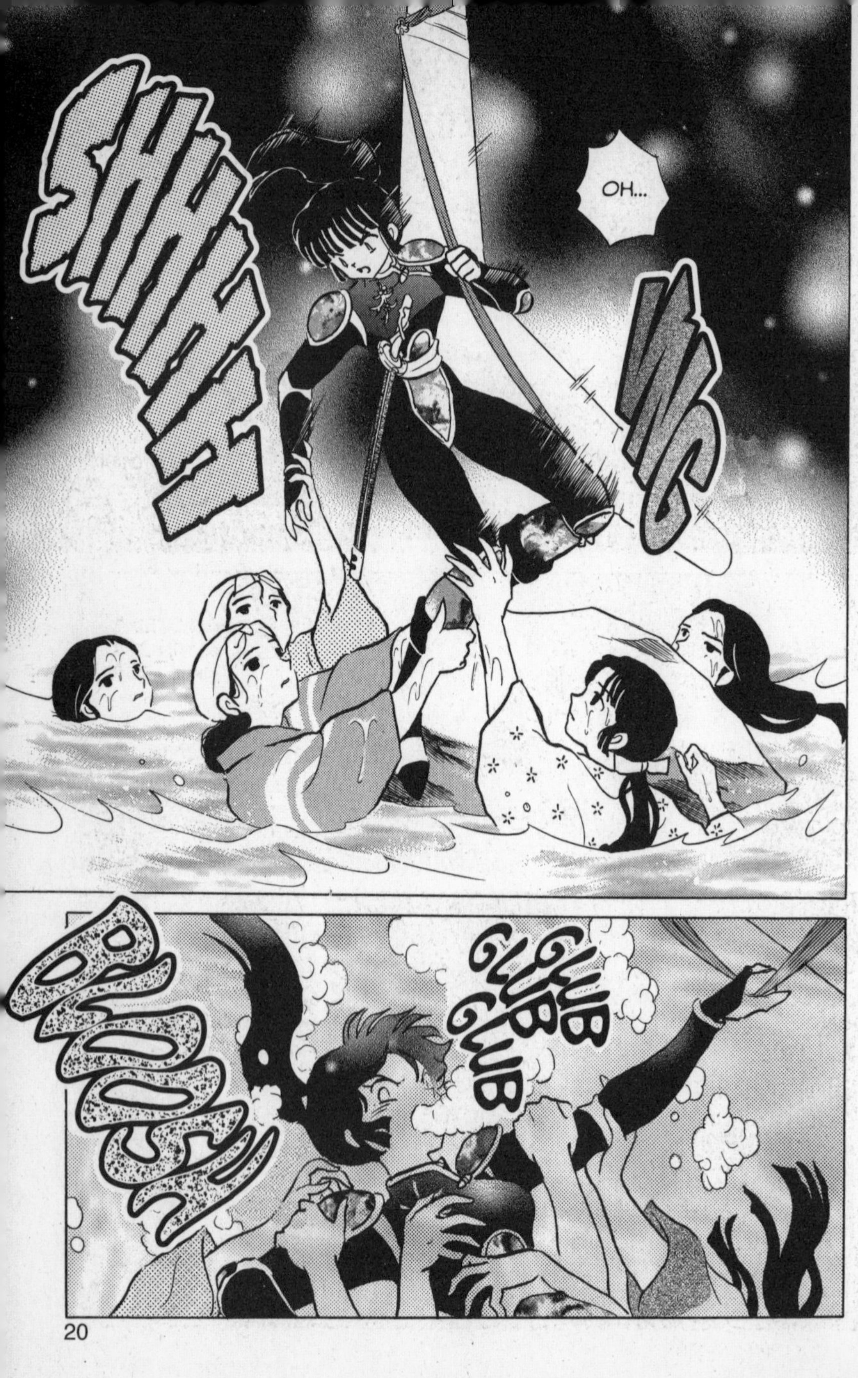
SHHHH
OH...
WHNG
GLUB GLUB GLUB
BLOOOSH

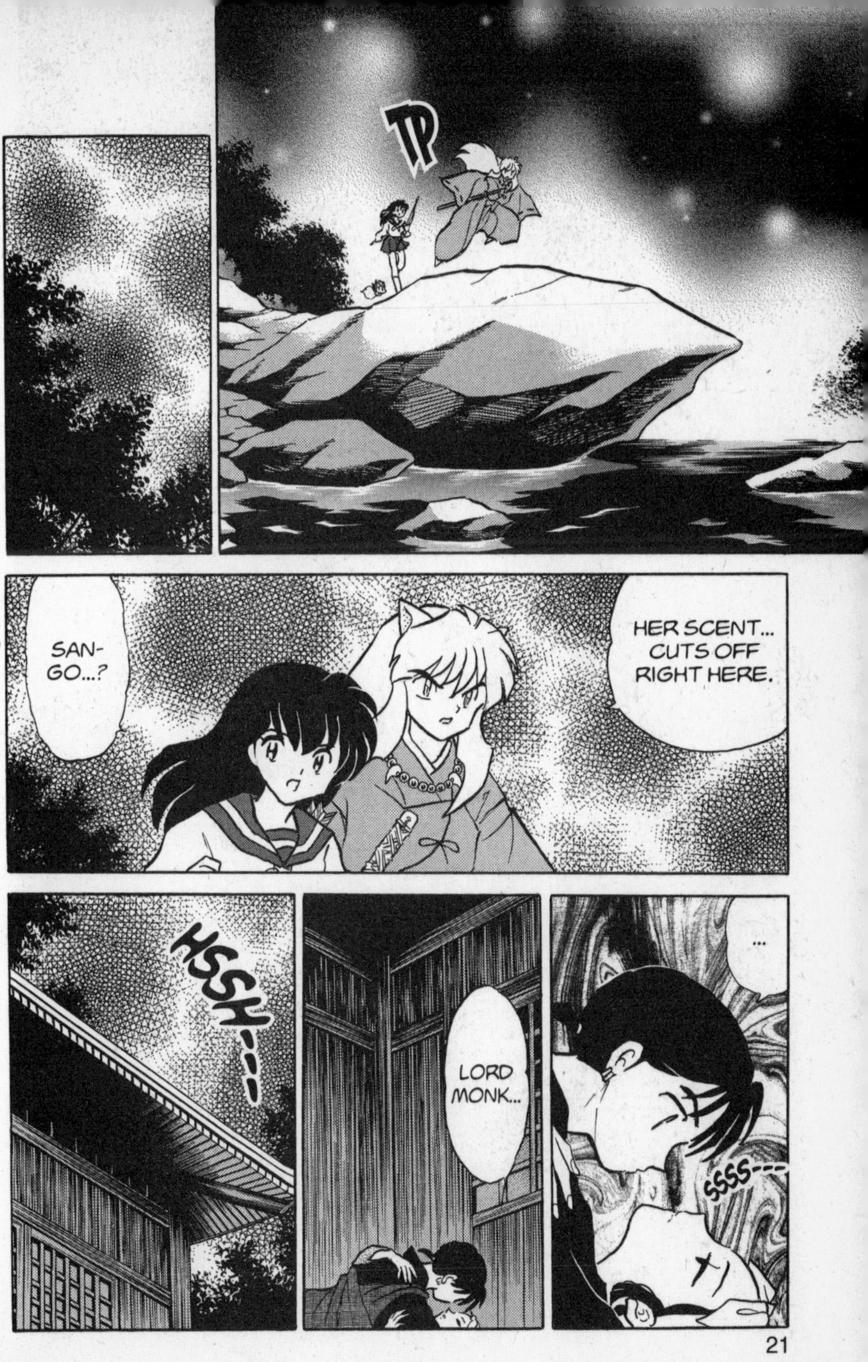
TP
SAN-GO...?
HER SCENT... CUTS OFF RIGHT HERE.
HSSH---
LORD MONK...
...
SSSS---

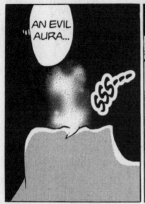

AN EVIL
AURA...

SSS...

SOME-
THING
LURKING...
IN HER
BELLY?

DEAR
BUDDHA
...

SIIIGH

WHY IS IT
ALWAYS
LIKE
THIS?

IS
SOME-
THING
WRONG...
?

DON'T
WOR-
RY.

I KNOW
YOU'RE
JUST THE
PUPPET.

AND MY
REAL
ENEMY
IS...

WSHK

SSS

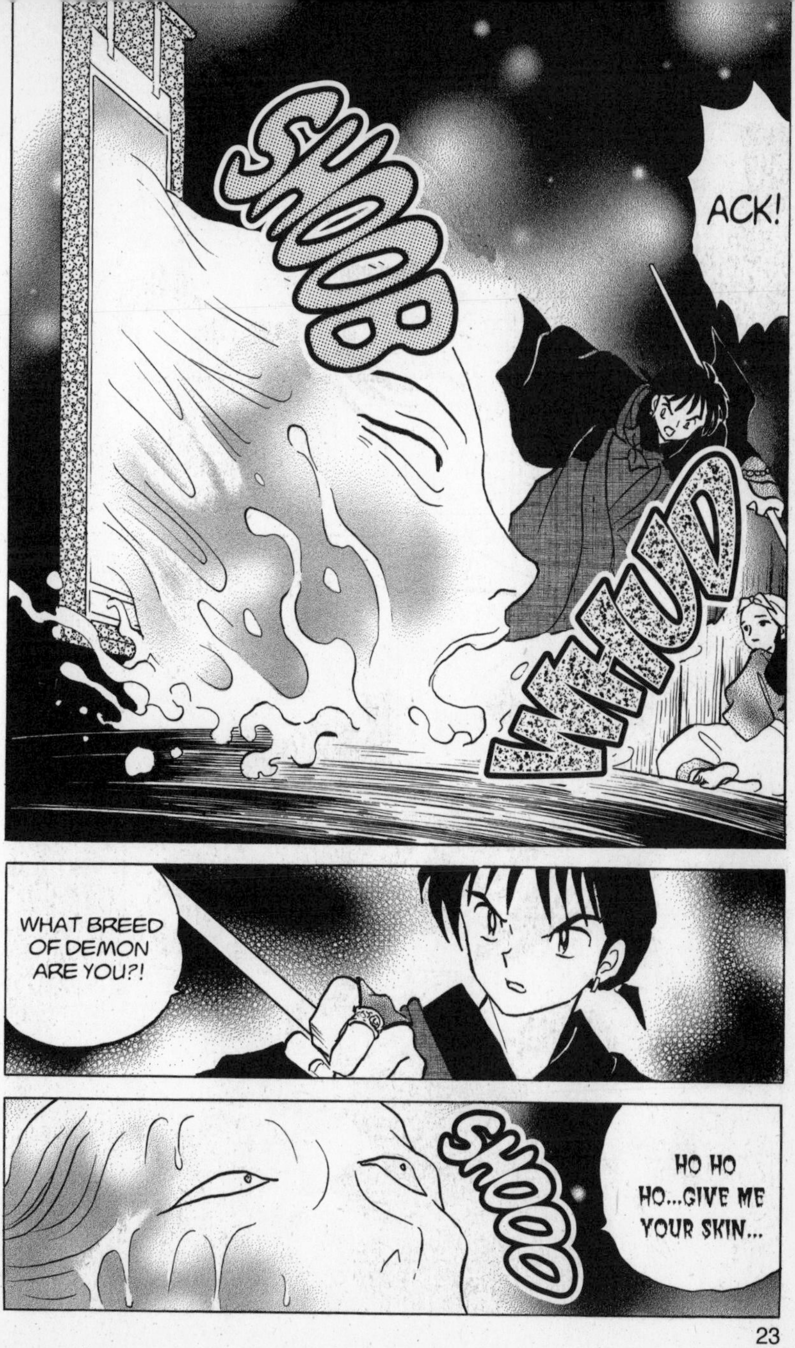
SHOOB
ACK!
WHUD
WHAT BREED OF DEMON ARE YOU?!
HO HO HO...GIVE ME YOUR SKIN...
SHOOO

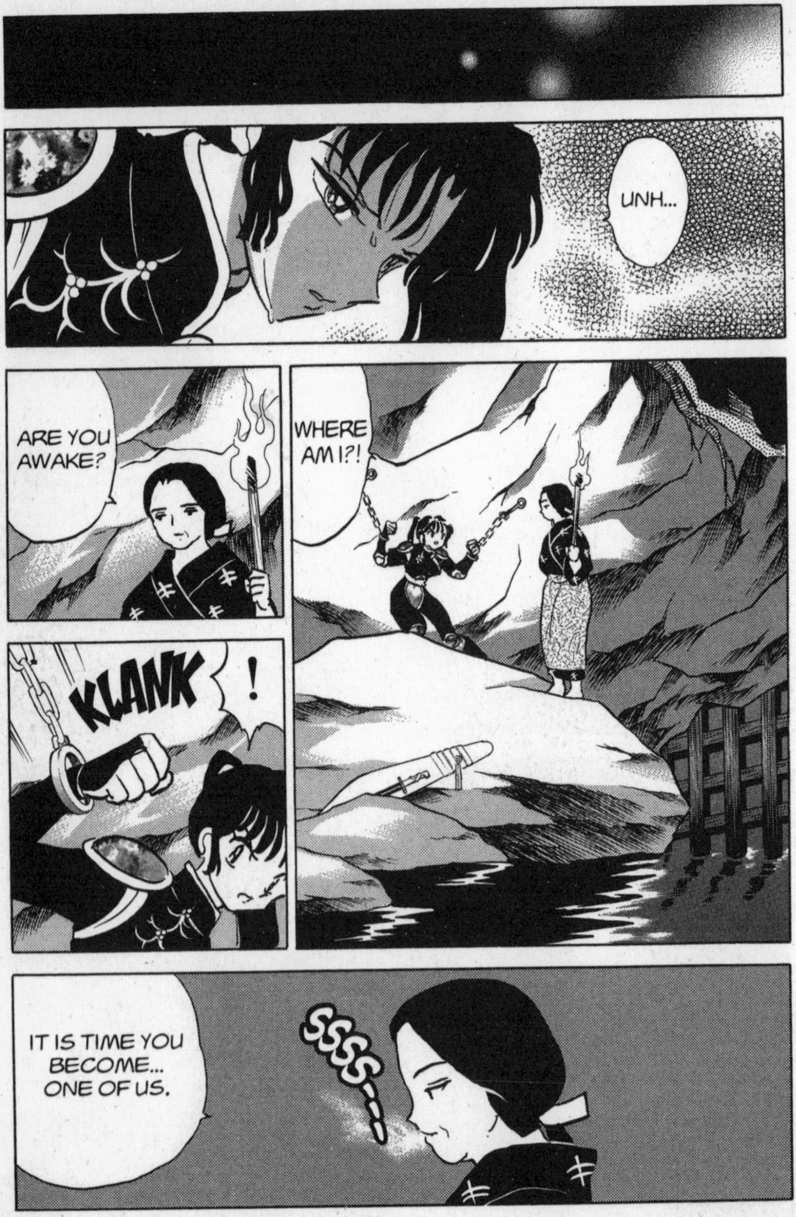
UNH...
ARE YOU AWAKE?
KLANK
!
WHERE AM I?!
IT IS TIME YOU BECOME... ONE OF US.
SSSS

SCROLL 2
A DEMON IN THE BELLY

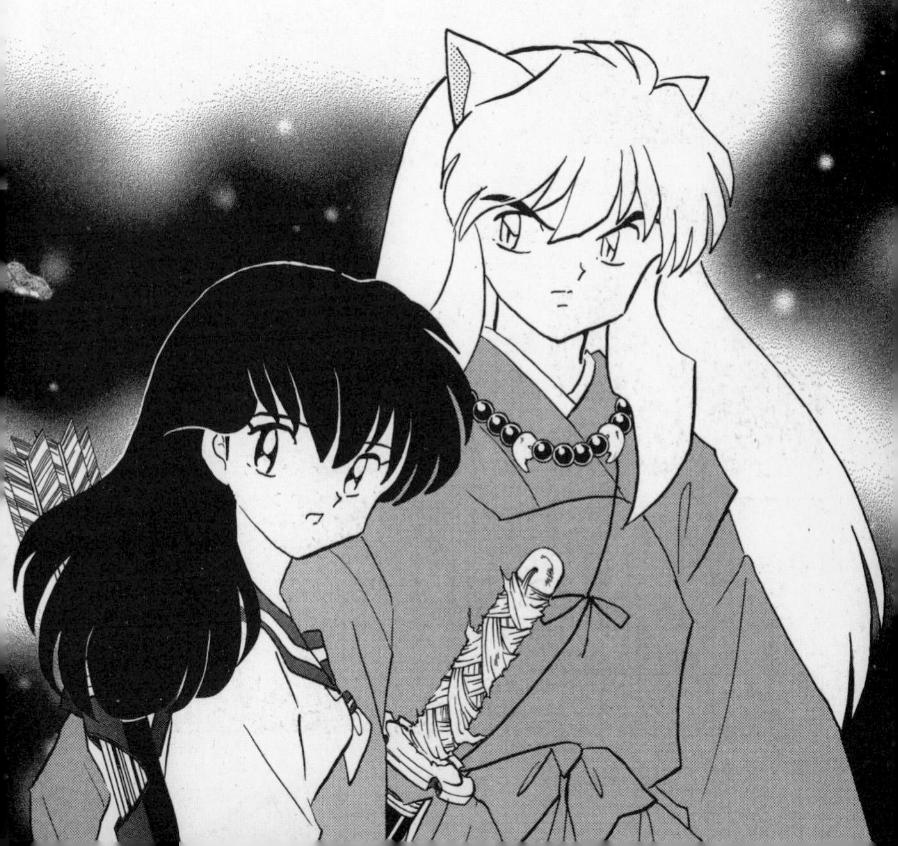

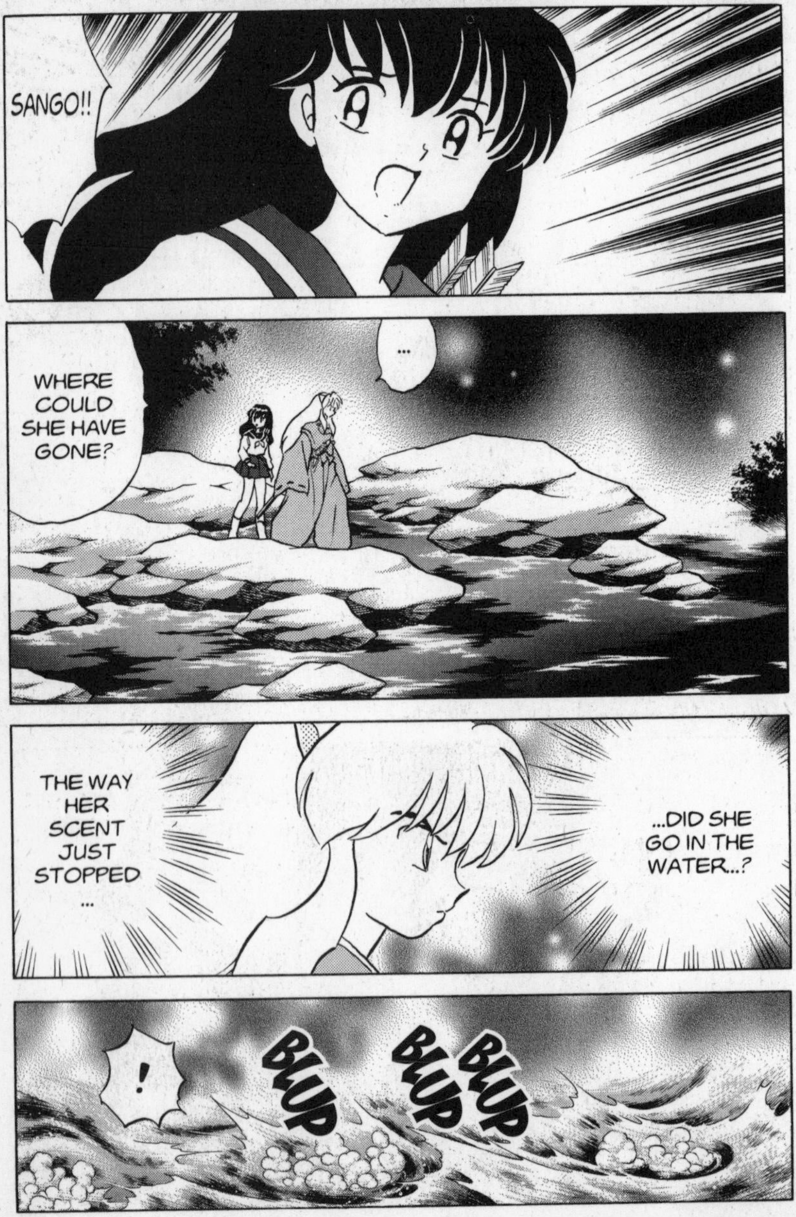
SANGO!!
WHERE COULD SHE HAVE GONE?
...
THE WAY HER SCENT JUST STOPPED ...
...DID SHE GO IN THE WATER...?
!
BLUP
BLUP
BLUP
BLUP

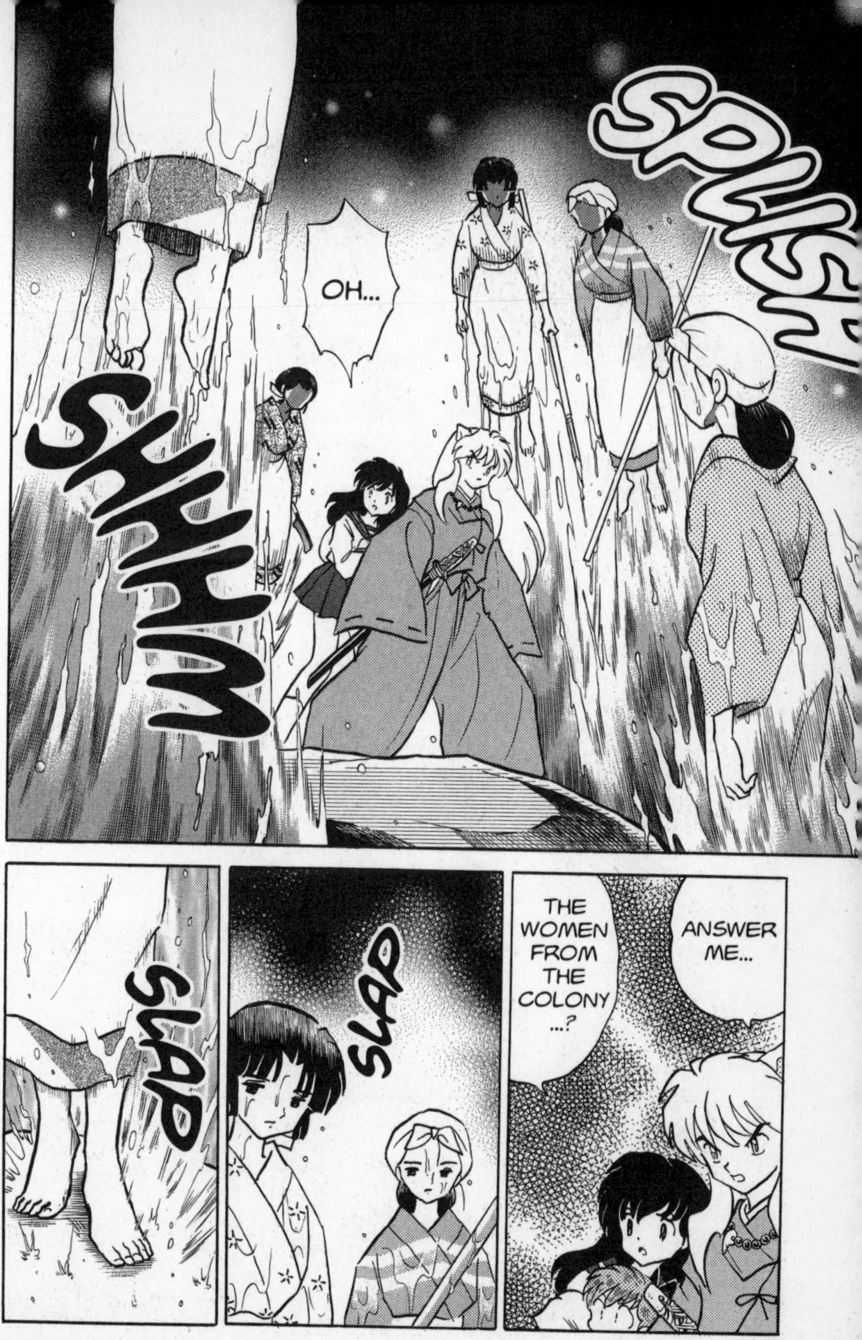
OH...
SHHHM
SPLISH!
SLAP
SLAP
THE WOMEN FROM THE COLONY ...?
ANSWER ME...

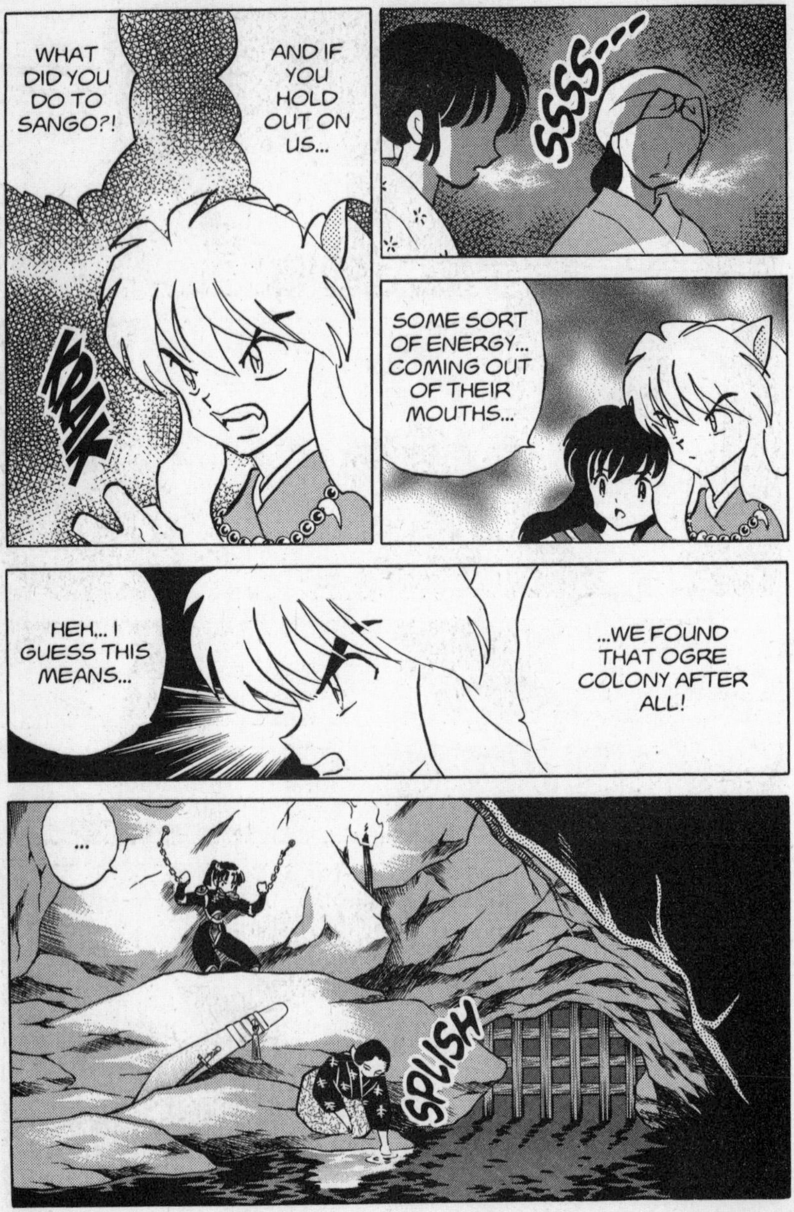
WHAT DID YOU DO TO SANGO?!
AND IF YOU HOLD OUT ON US...
KRAK
SSSS---
SOME SORT OF ENERGY... COMING OUT OF THEIR MOUTHS...
HEH... I GUESS THIS MEANS...
...WE FOUND THAT OGRE COLONY AFTER ALL!
...
SPLISH

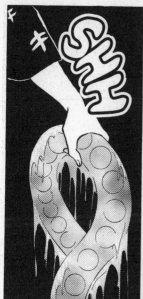

WHAT IS THAT?

SOME CREA-TURE'S EGGS?!

SWAL-LOW IT.

LET IT HATCH WITHIN YOUR BELLY...

SSS

...AND MAKE YOURSELF JUST LIKE US.

GWIP

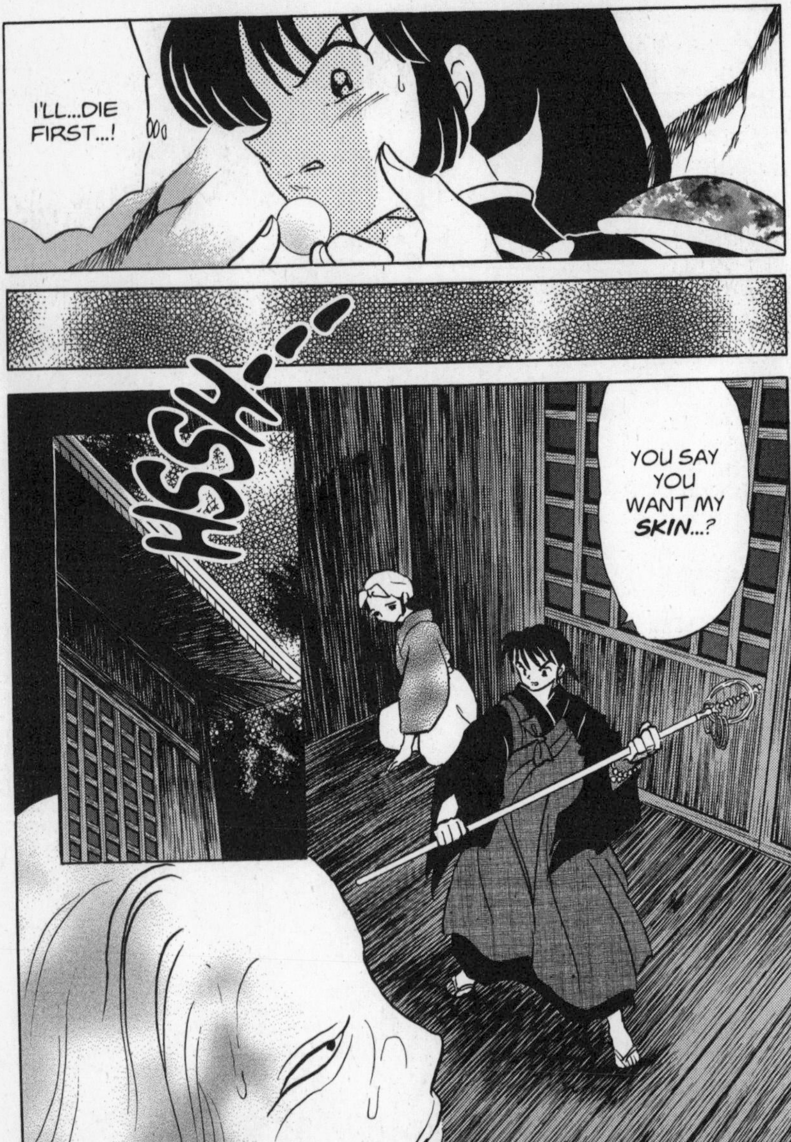
I'LL...DIE FIRST...!
HSSH...
YOU SAY YOU WANT MY **SKIN**...?

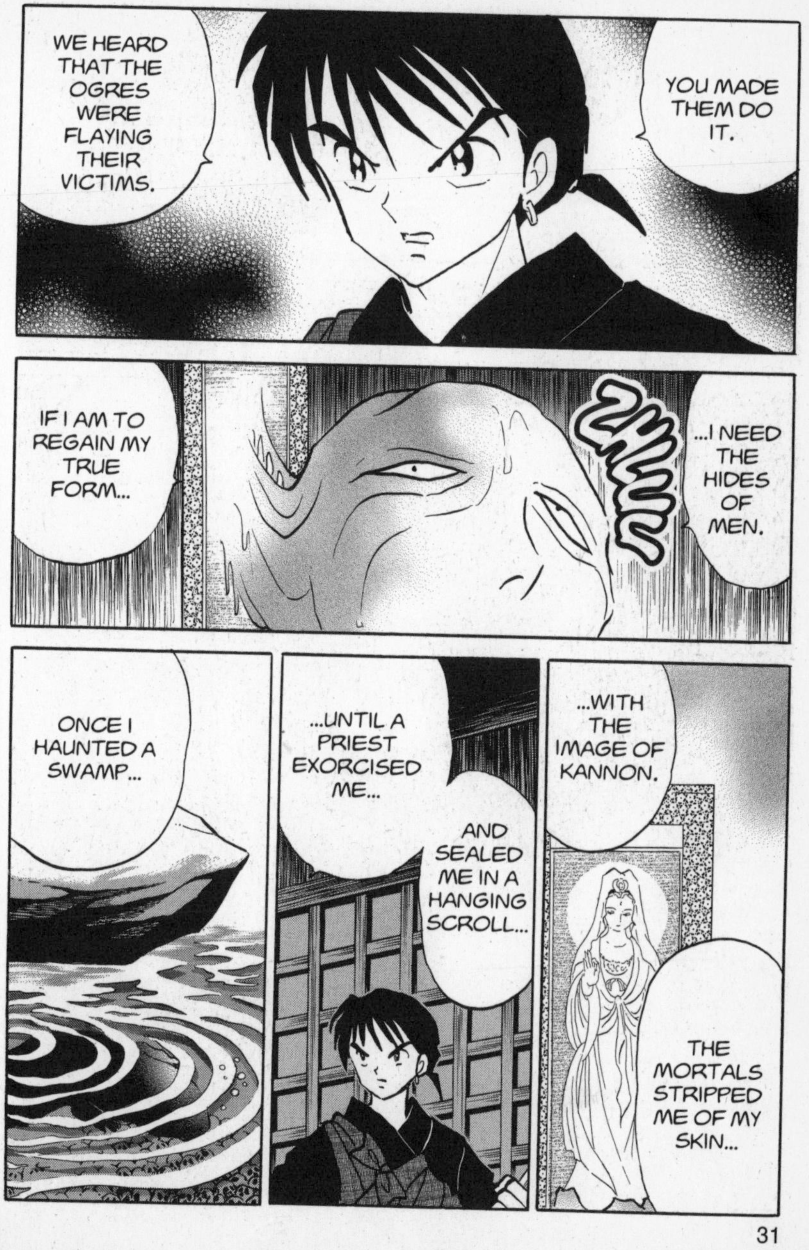
WE HEARD THAT THE OGRES WERE FLAYING THEIR VICTIMS.
YOU MADE THEM DO IT.
IF I AM TO REGAIN MY TRUE FORM...
...I NEED THE HIDES OF MEN.
ONCE I HAUNTED A SWAMP...
...UNTIL A PRIEST EXORCISED ME...
AND SEALED ME IN A HANGING SCROLL...
...WITH THE IMAGE OF KANNON.
THE MORTALS STRIPPED ME OF MY SKIN...

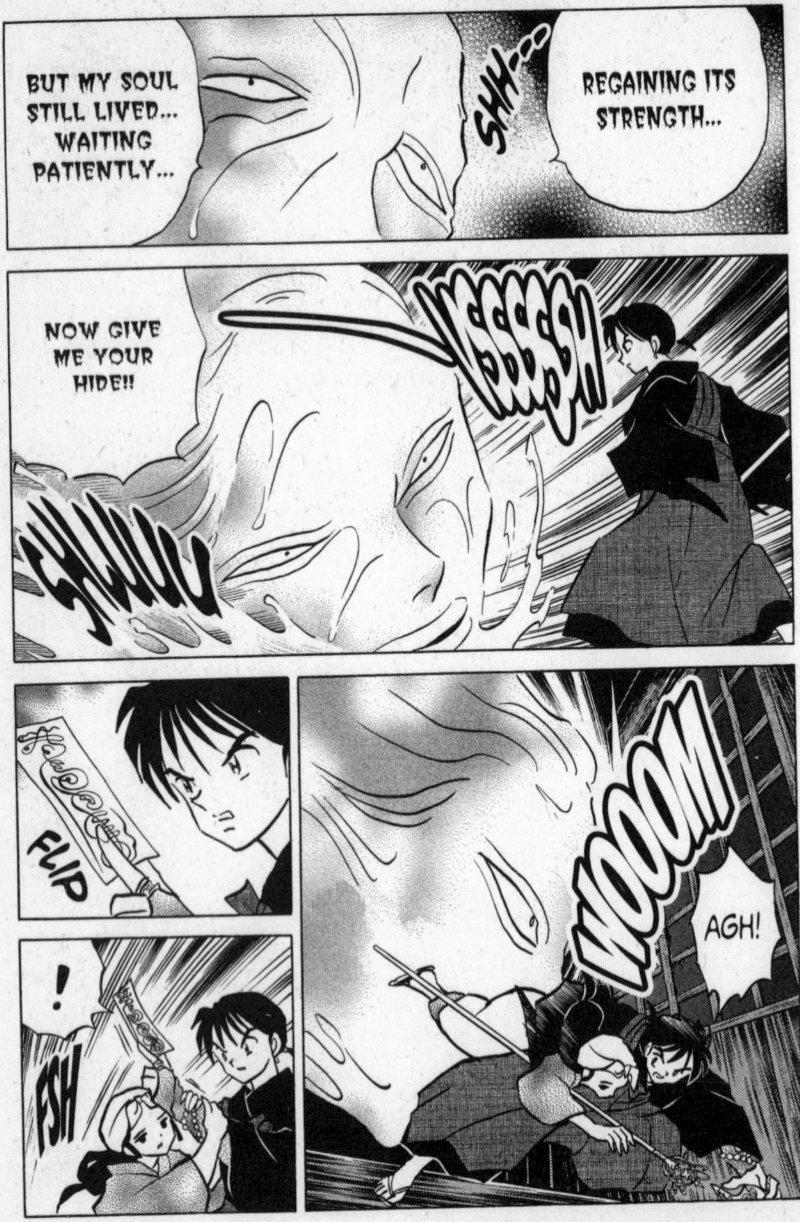

BUT MY SOUL STILL LIVED... WAITING PATIENTLY...
SHH---
REGAINING ITS STRENGTH...
NOW GIVE ME YOUR HIDE!!
VSSSSH
SHUUU
FLIP
!
FSH
WOOOM
AGH!

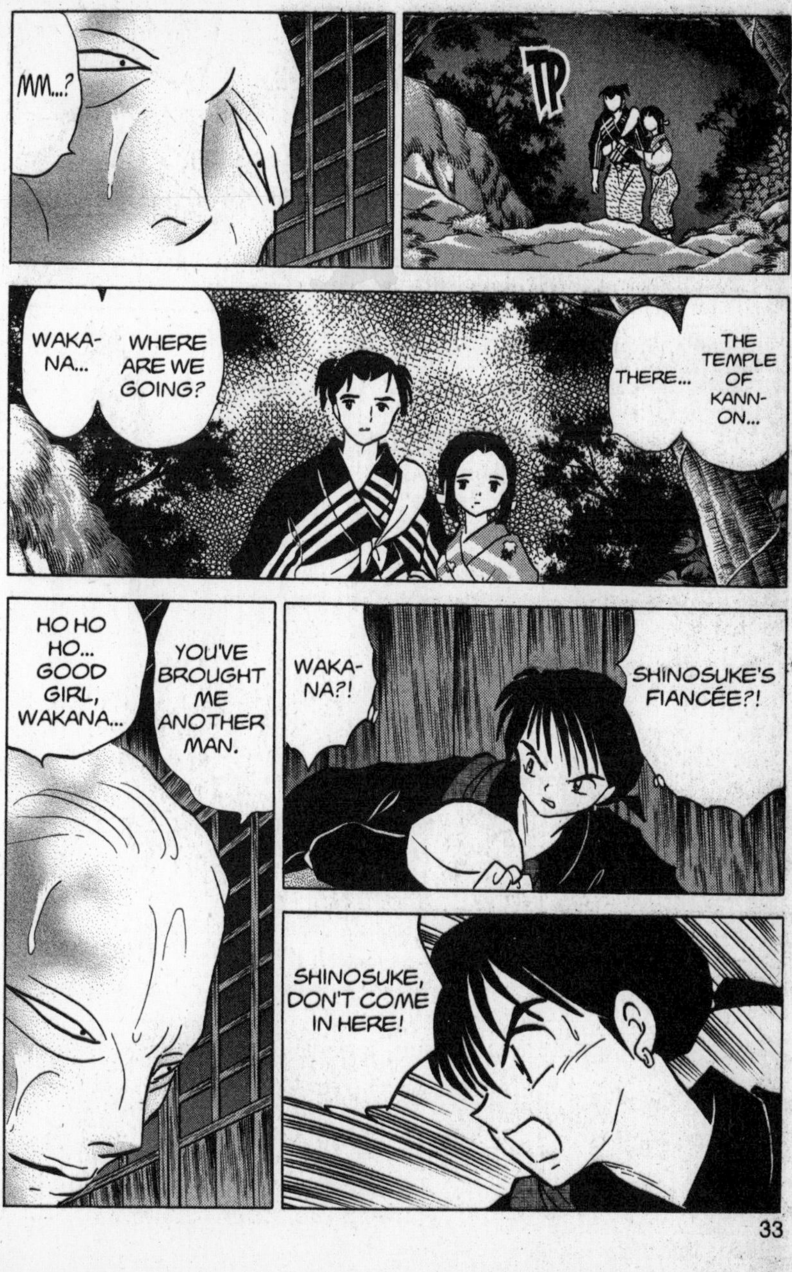
MM...?
TP
WAKA-NA...
WHERE ARE WE GOING?
THERE...
THE TEMPLE OF KANN-ON...
HO HO HO... GOOD GIRL, WAKANA...
YOU'VE BROUGHT ME ANOTHER MAN.
WAKA-NA?!
SHINOSUKE'S FIANCÉE?!
SHINOSUKE, DON'T COME IN HERE!

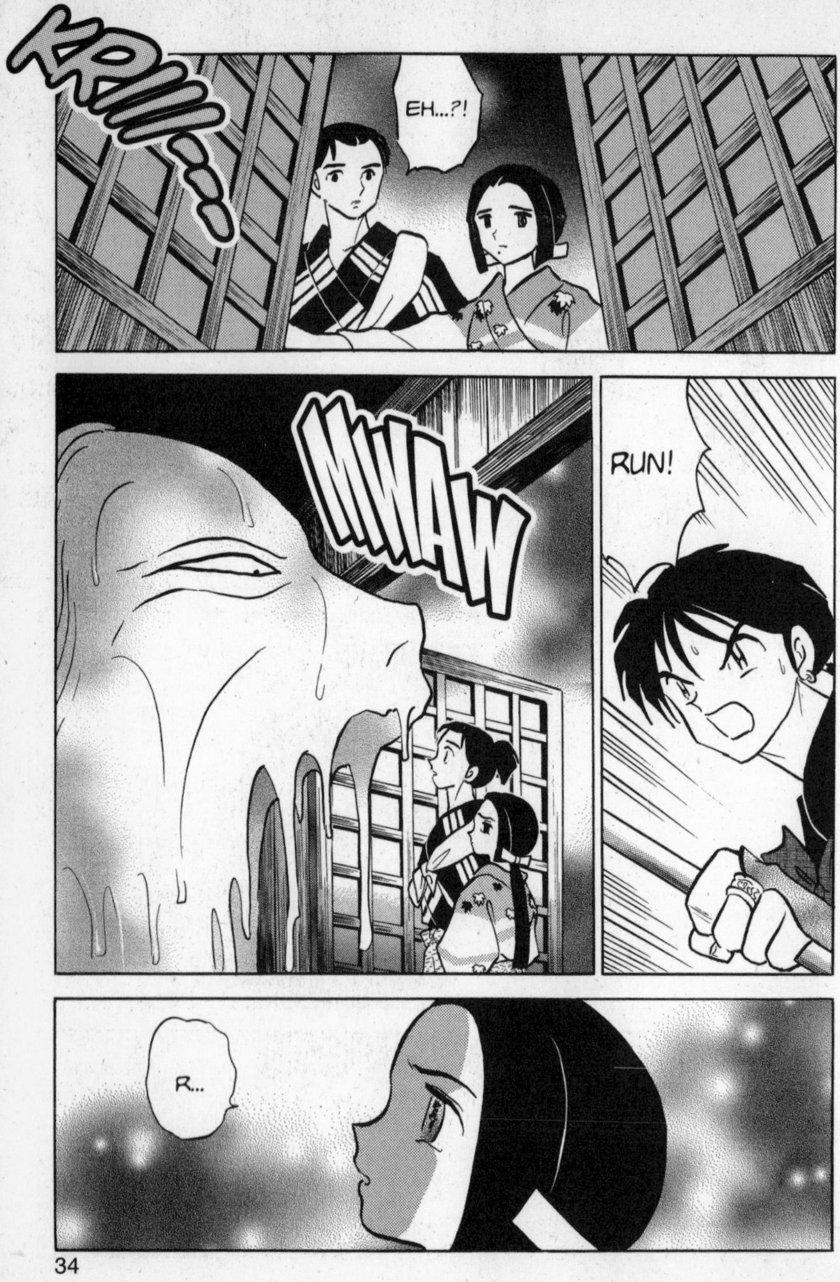
KRIII....
EH...?!
MIWAW
RUN!
R...

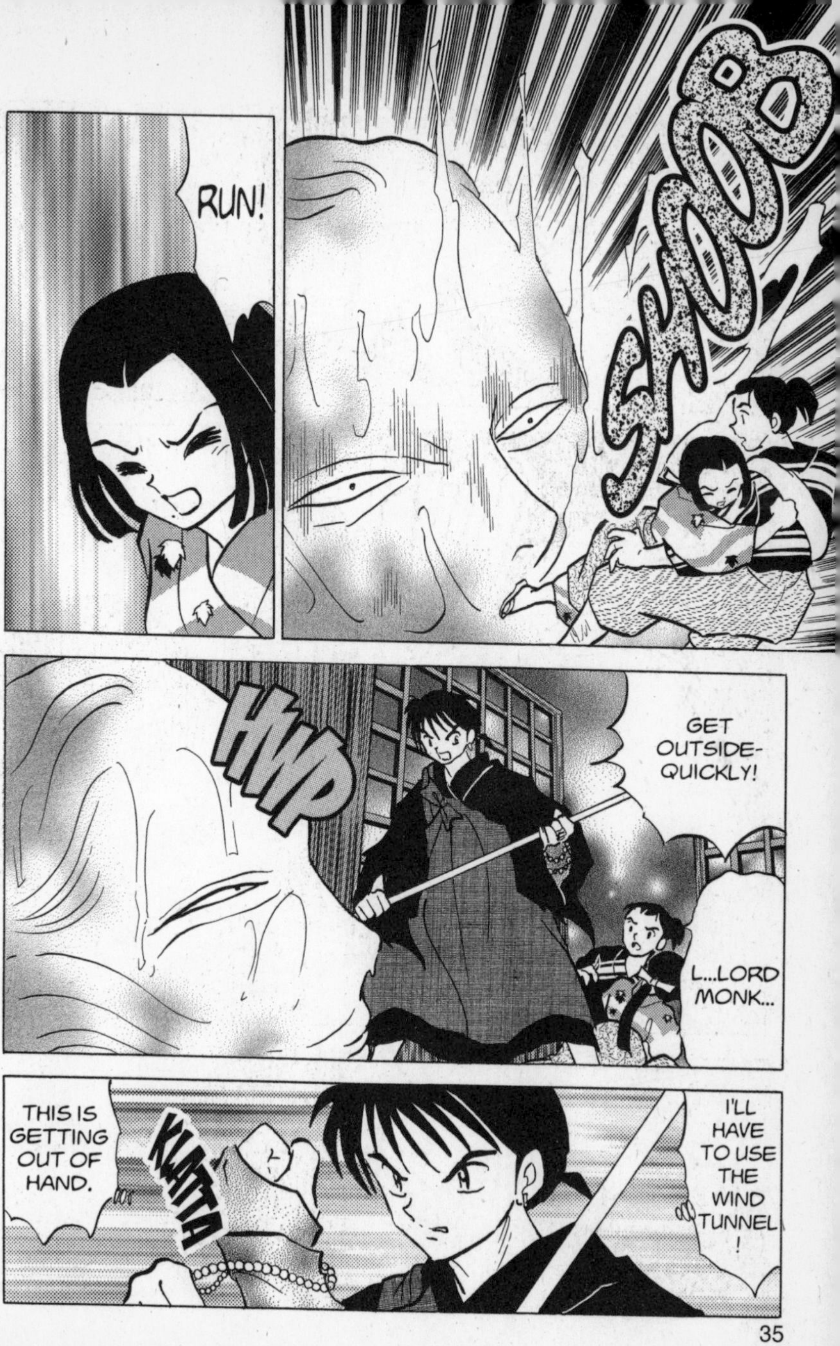
RUN!
SHOOOB
HWP
GET OUTSIDE-QUICKLY!
L...LORD MONK...
THIS IS GETTING OUT OF HAND.
I'LL HAVE TO USE THE WIND TUNNEL!

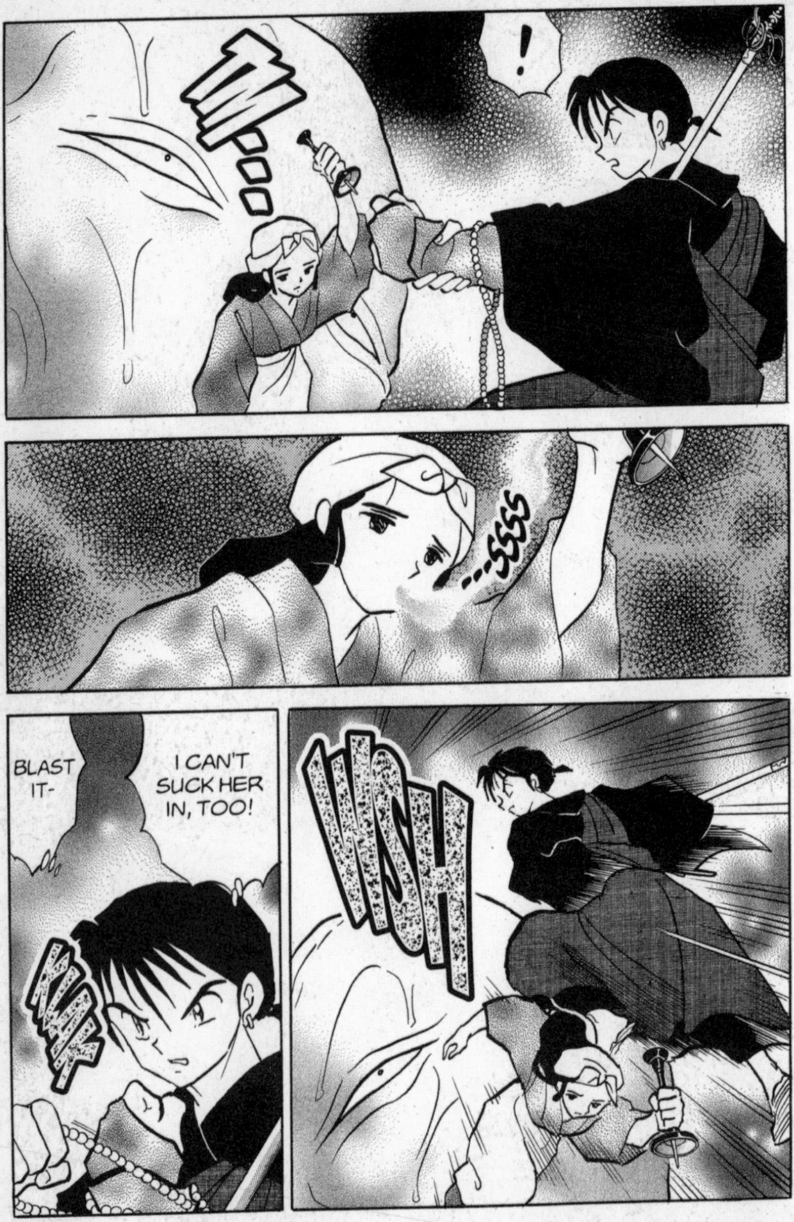
!
...SSSS
BLAST IT-
I CAN'T SUCK HER IN, TOO!
WSH

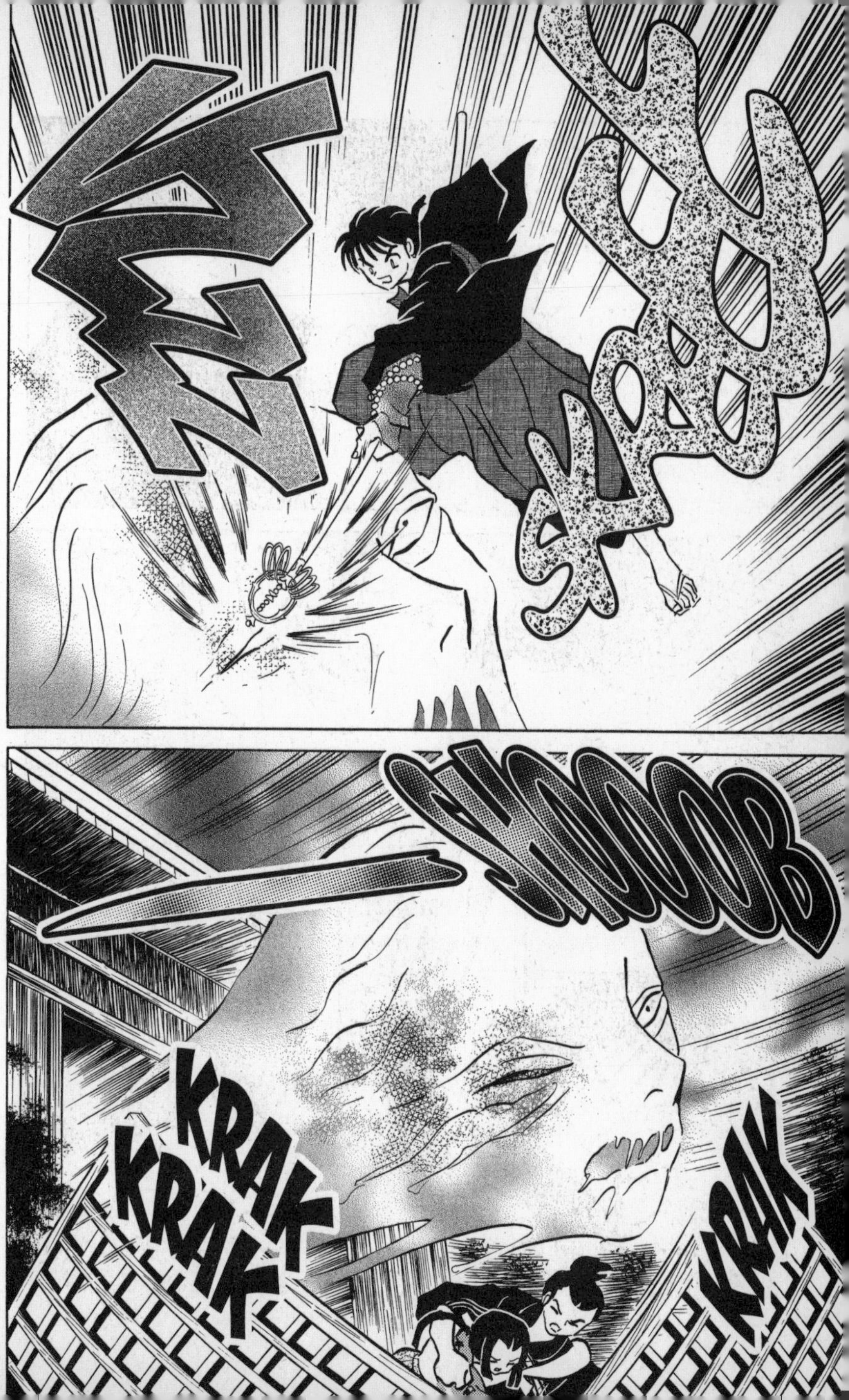
KRAK
KRAK
KRAK

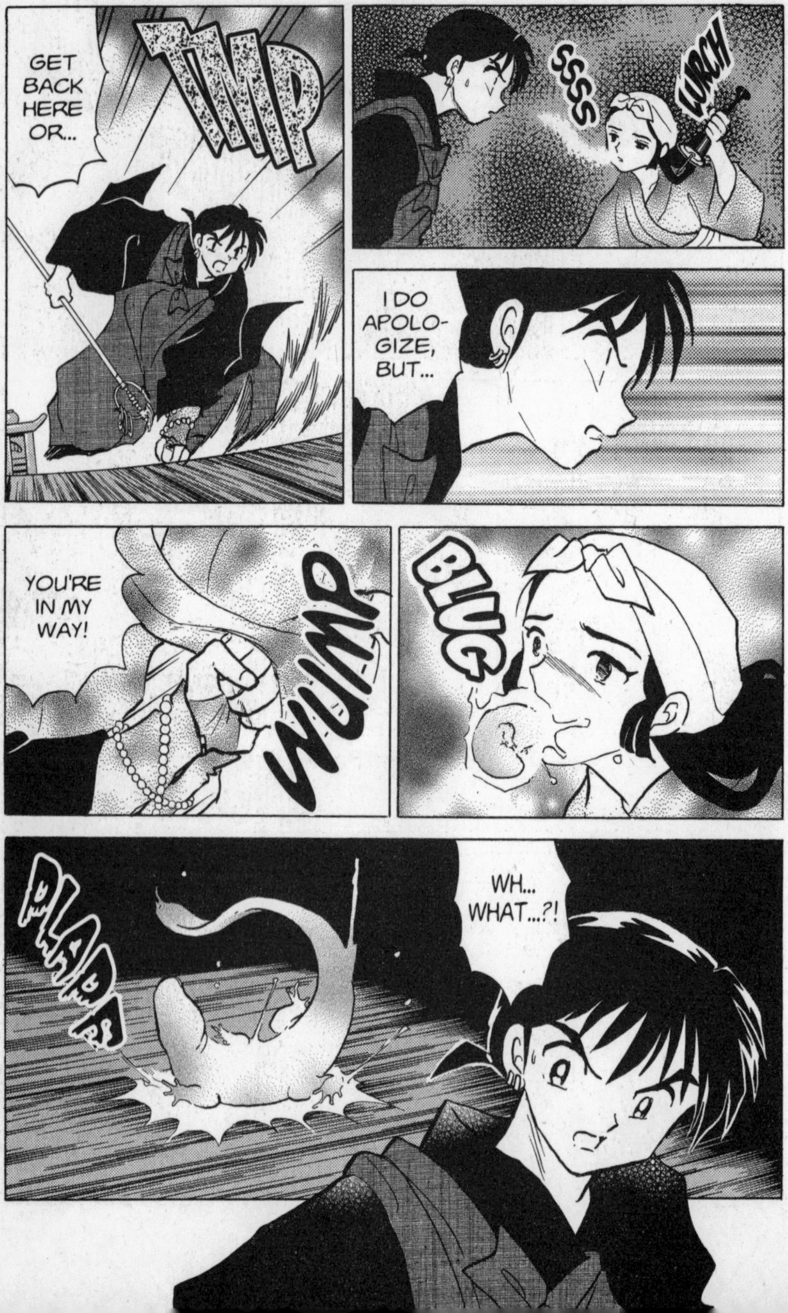
GET BACK HERE OR...
TMP
SSSS
LURCH
I DO APOLOGIZE, BUT...
YOU'RE IN MY WAY!
WUMP
BLUG
PLAP
WH... WHAT...?!

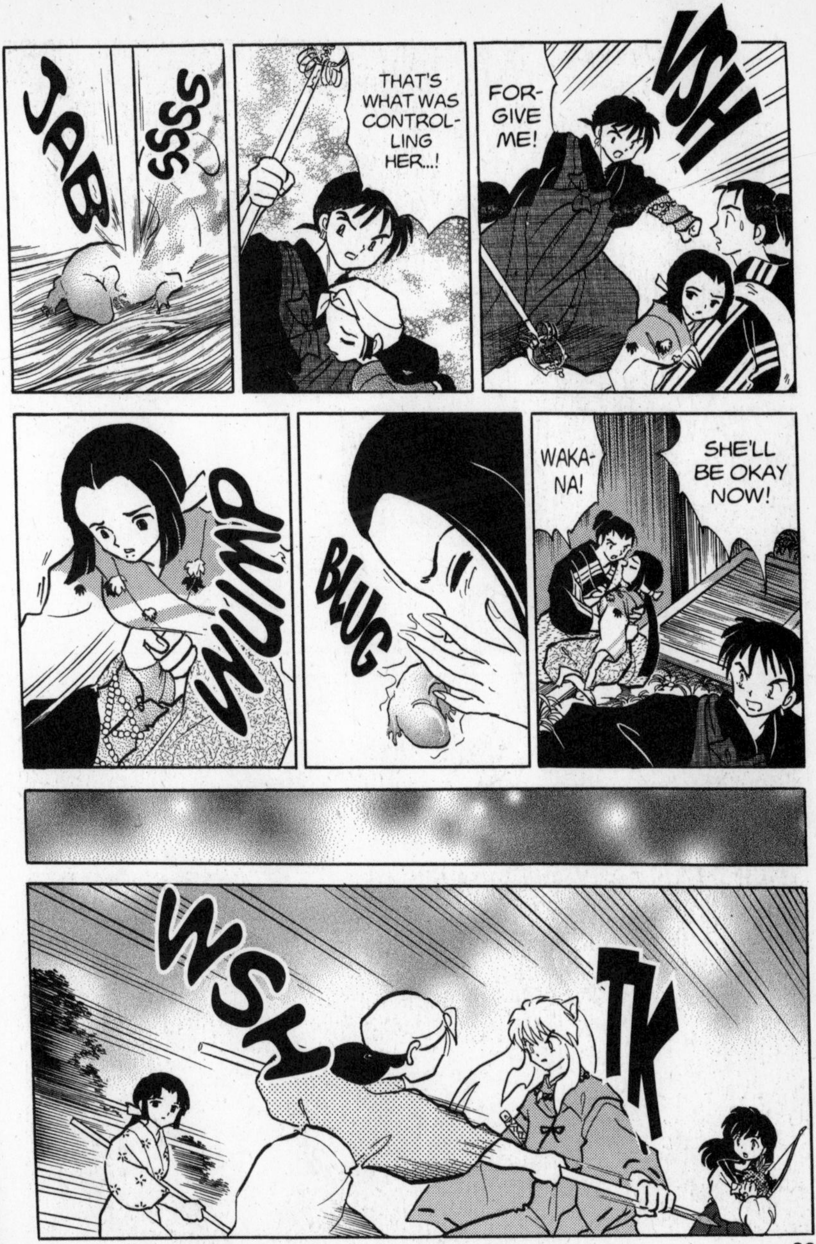
JAB
SSSS
THAT'S WHAT WAS CONTROL-LING HER...!
FOR-GIVE ME!
VSH
WUMP
BLUG
WAKA-NA!
SHE'LL BE OKAY NOW!
WSH
TK

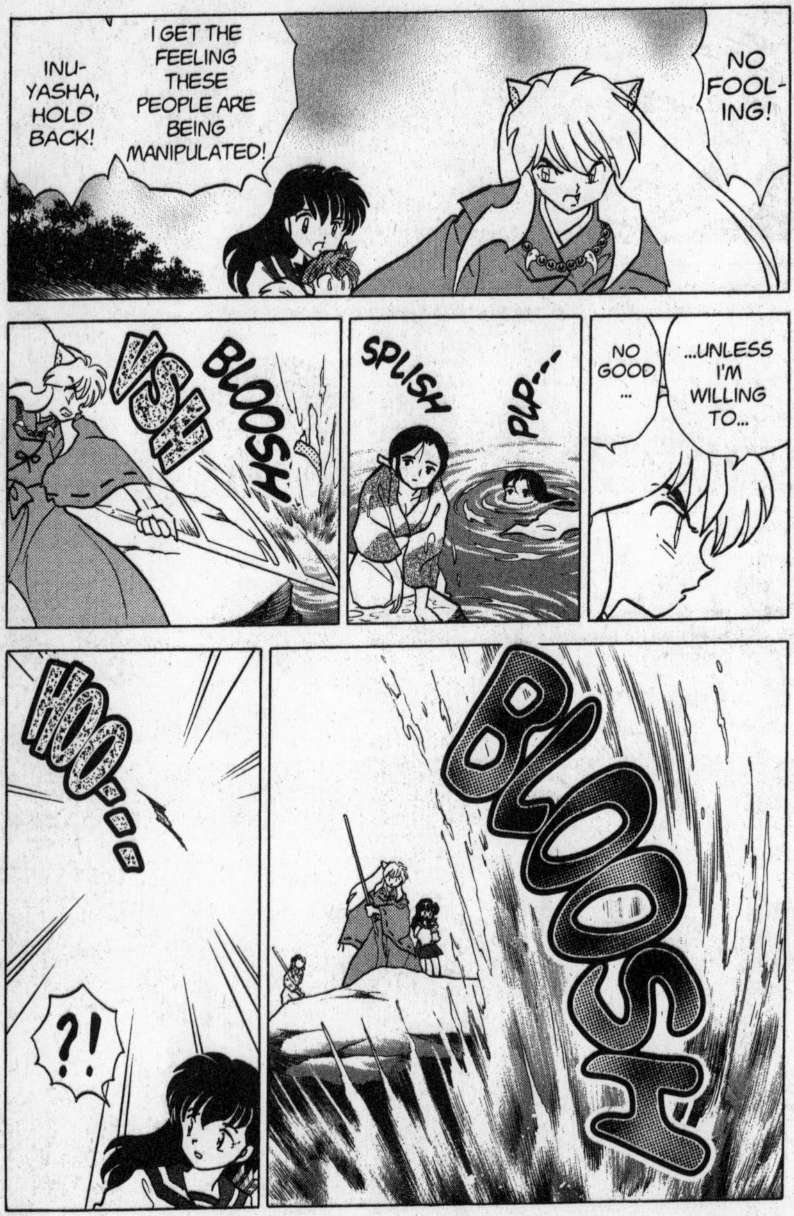
INU-YASHA, HOLD BACK!
I GET THE FEELING THESE PEOPLE ARE BEING MANIPULATED!
NO FOOLING!
VSH!
BLOOSH
SPLISH
PLIP...
NO GOOD...
...UNLESS I'M WILLING TO...
HOO...
?!
BLOOOSH

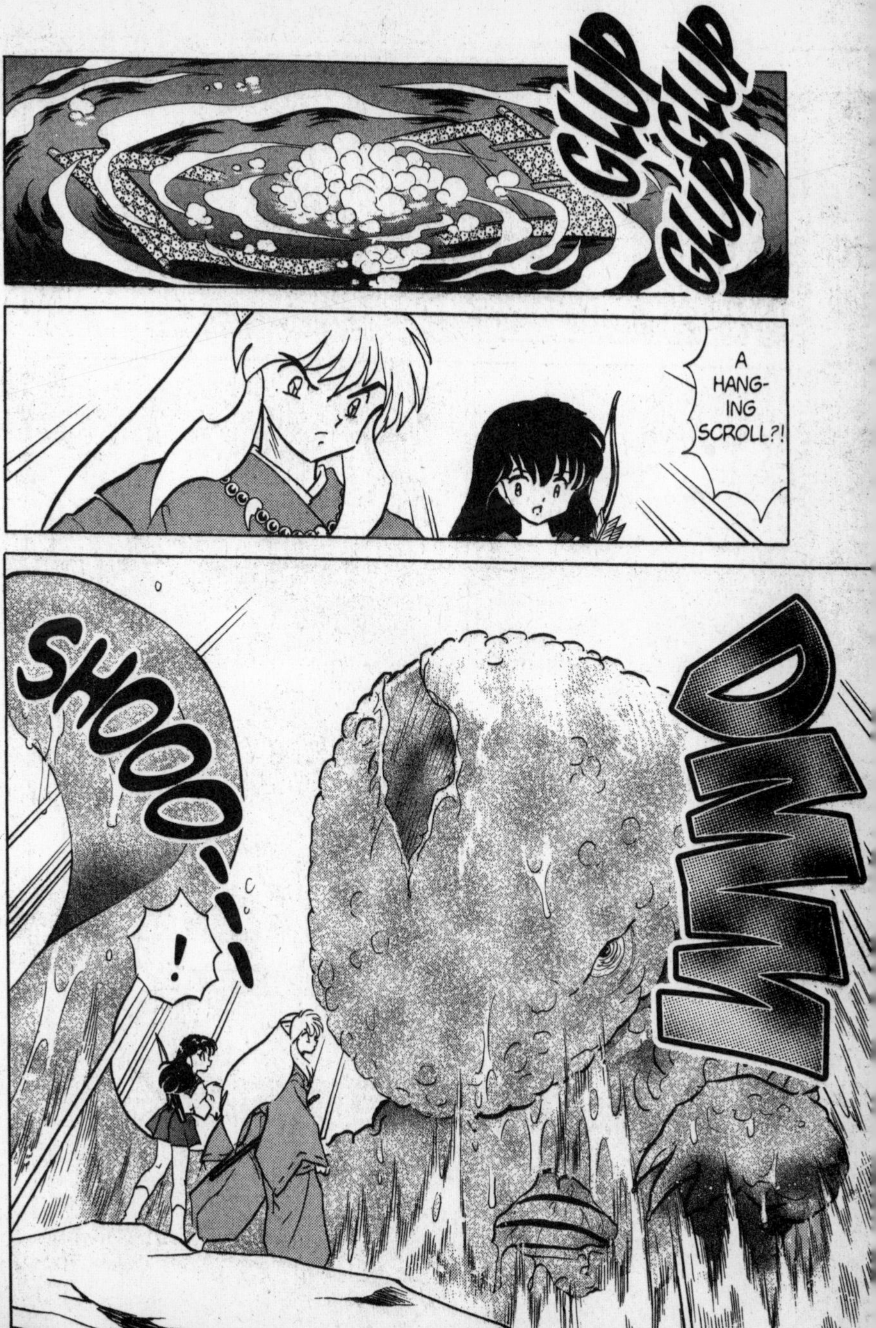
GLUP
GLUP GLUP
A HANG-ING SCROLL?!
SHOOO...
!
DMMM

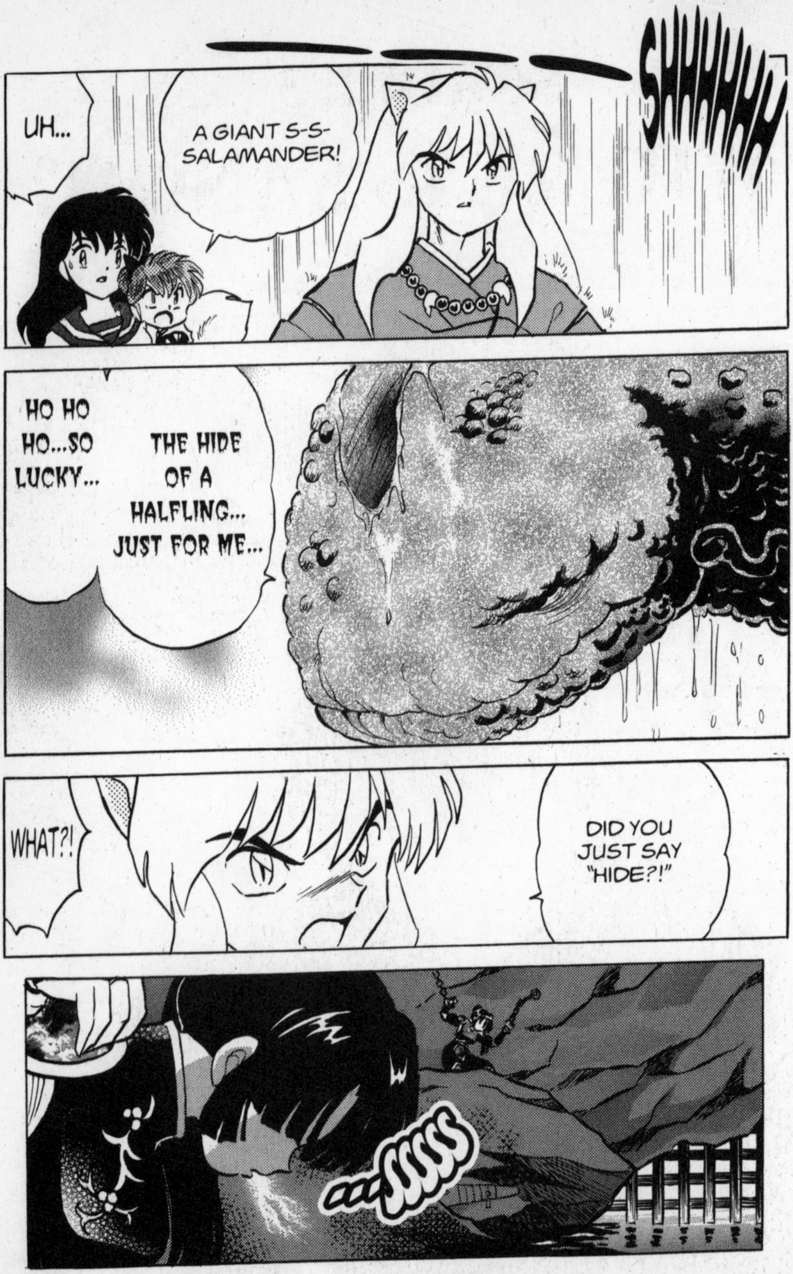
SHHHHH
UH...
A GIANT S-S-SALAMANDER!
HO HO HO...SO LUCKY...
THE HIDE OF A HALFLING... JUST FOR ME...
WHAT?!
DID YOU JUST SAY "HIDE?!"
...SSSSS

SCROLL 3
WHERE IS SANGO?

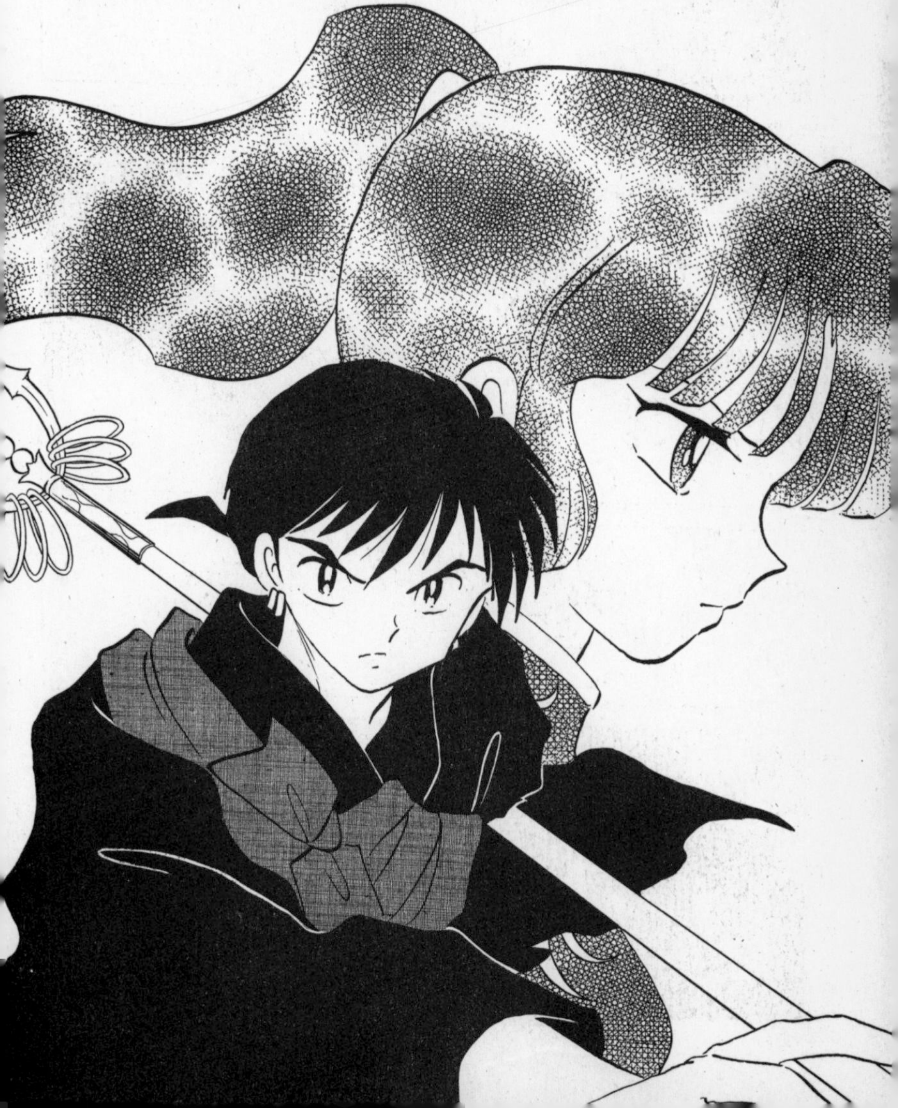

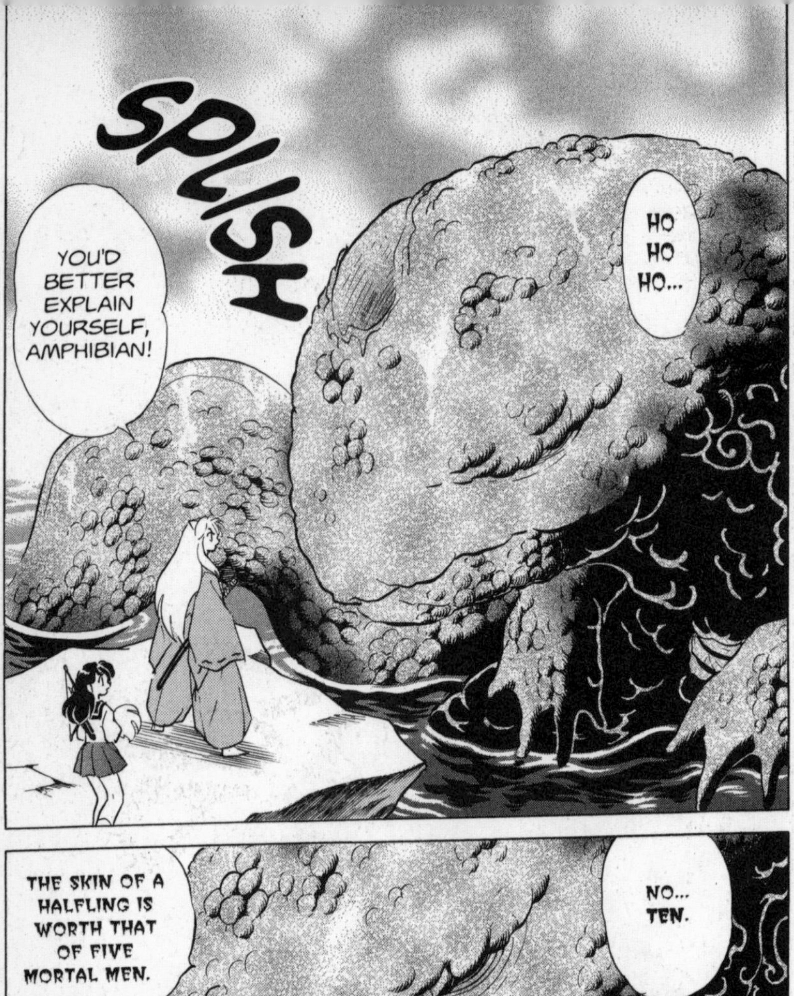
SPLISH
YOU'D BETTER EXPLAIN YOURSELF, AMPHIBIAN!
HO HO HO...

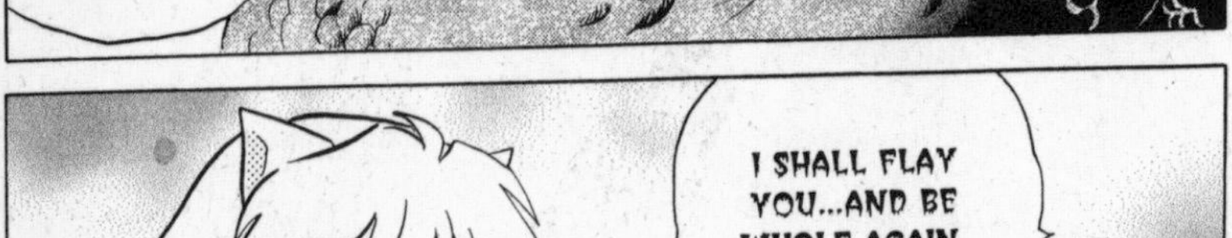
THE SKIN OF A HALFLING IS WORTH THAT OF FIVE MORTAL MEN.
NO... TEN.

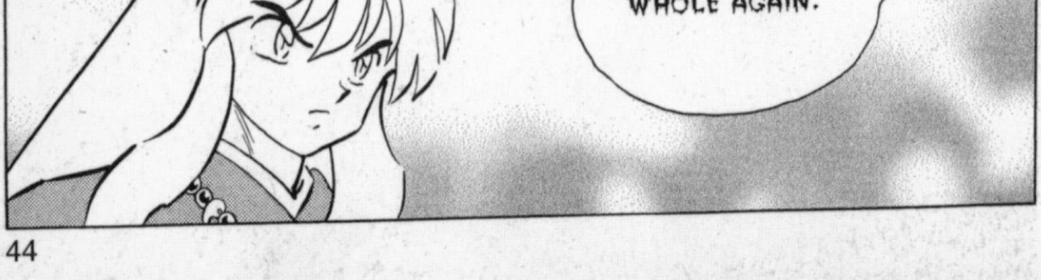
I SHALL FLAY YOU...AND BE WHOLE AGAIN.

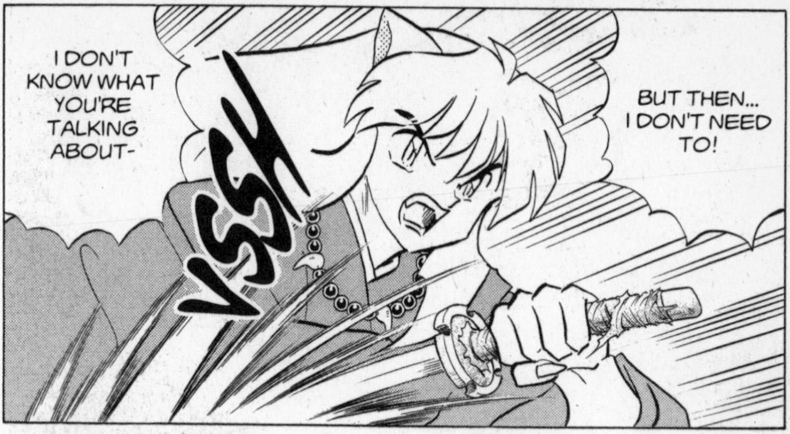
I DON'T KNOW WHAT YOU'RE TALKING ABOUT-
VSSH
BUT THEN... I DON'T NEED TO!

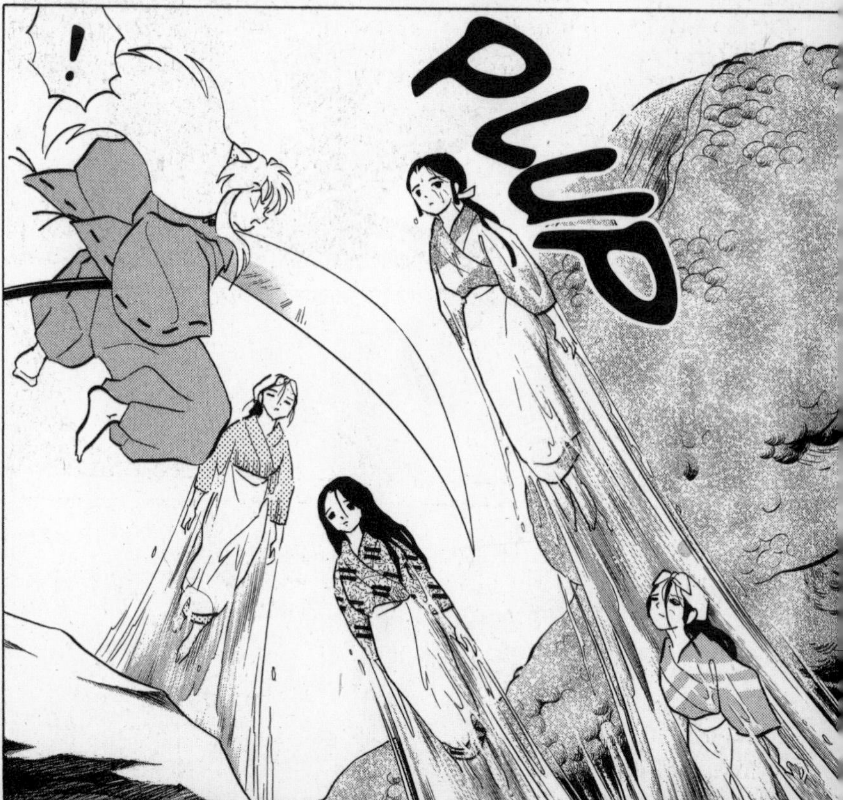
!
PLUP

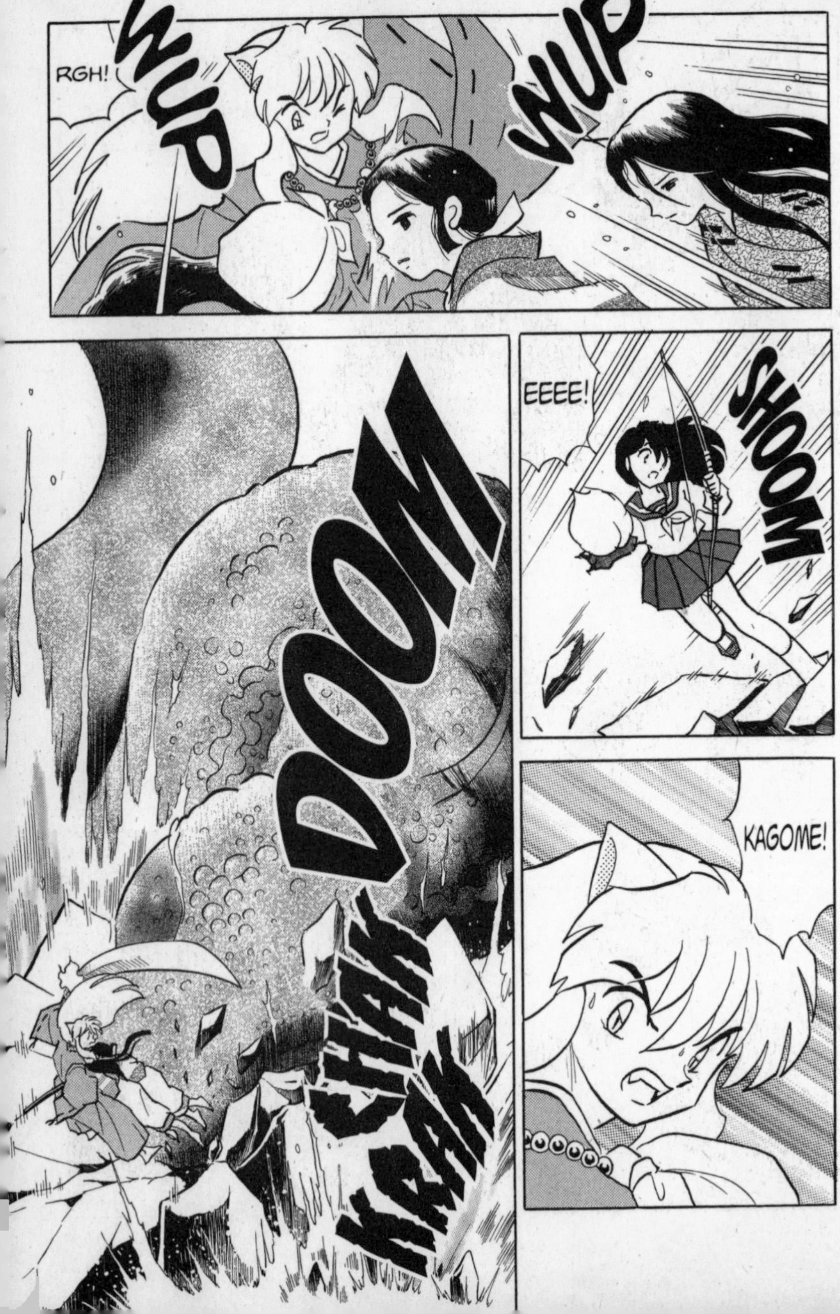
RGH!
WUP
WUP
DOOM
KRAK
CHAK
EEEE!
SHOOM
KAGOME!

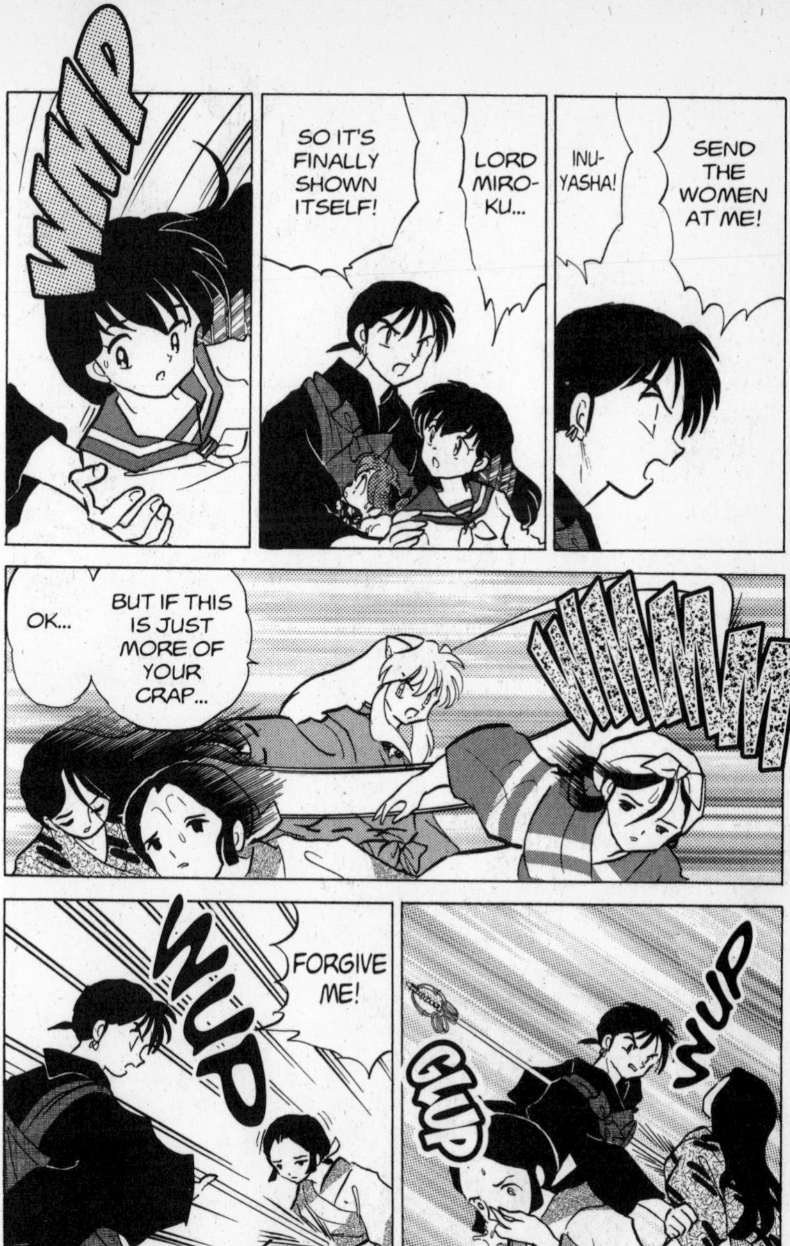
WHHIP
SO IT'S FINALLY SHOWN ITSELF!
LORD MIRO-KU...
INU-YASHA!
SEND THE WOMEN AT ME!
OK...
BUT IF THIS IS JUST MORE OF YOUR CRAP...
WMMMMM
WUP
FORGIVE ME!
GLUP
WUP

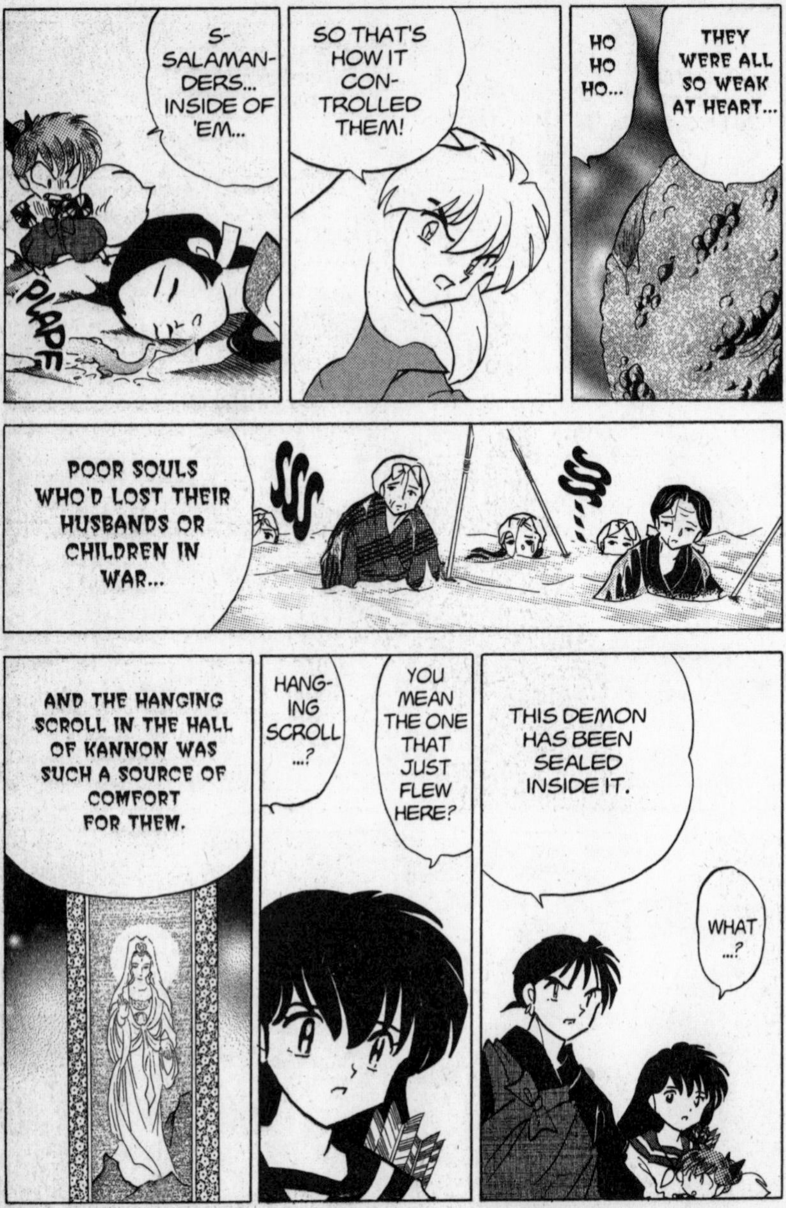
S-SALAMANDERS... INSIDE OF 'EM...
PLAPF
SO THAT'S HOW IT CONTROLLED THEM!
HO HO HO...
THEY WERE ALL SO WEAK AT HEART...
POOR SOULS WHO'D LOST THEIR HUSBANDS OR CHILDREN IN WAR...
AND THE HANGING SCROLL IN THE HALL OF KANNON WAS SUCH A SOURCE OF COMFORT FOR THEM.
HANGING SCROLL ...?
YOU MEAN THE ONE THAT JUST FLEW HERE?
THIS DEMON HAS BEEN SEALED INSIDE IT.
WHAT ...?

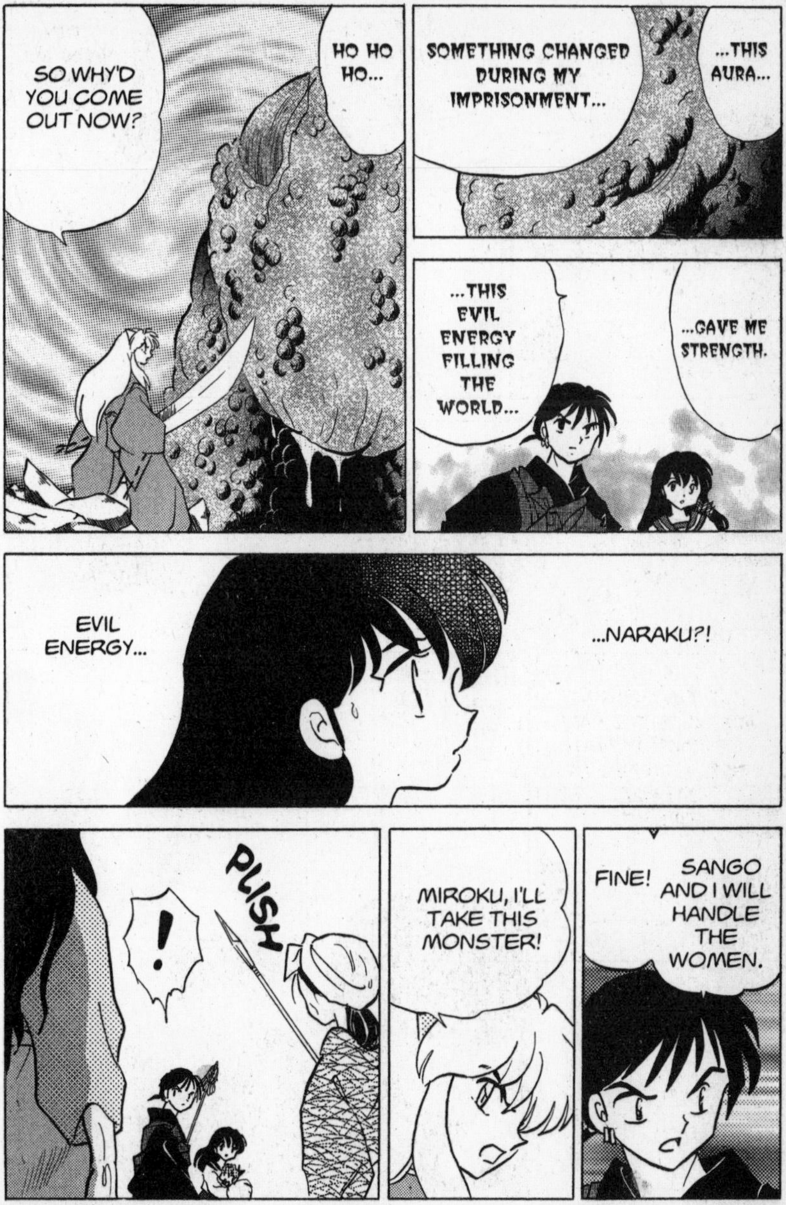
SO WHY'D YOU COME OUT NOW?
HO HO HO...
SOMETHING CHANGED DURING MY IMPRISONMENT...
...THIS AURA...
...THIS EVIL ENERGY FILLING THE WORLD...
...GAVE ME STRENGTH.
EVIL ENERGY...
...NARAKU?!
!
PLISH
MIROKU, I'LL TAKE THIS MONSTER!
FINE!
SANGO AND I WILL HANDLE THE WOMEN.

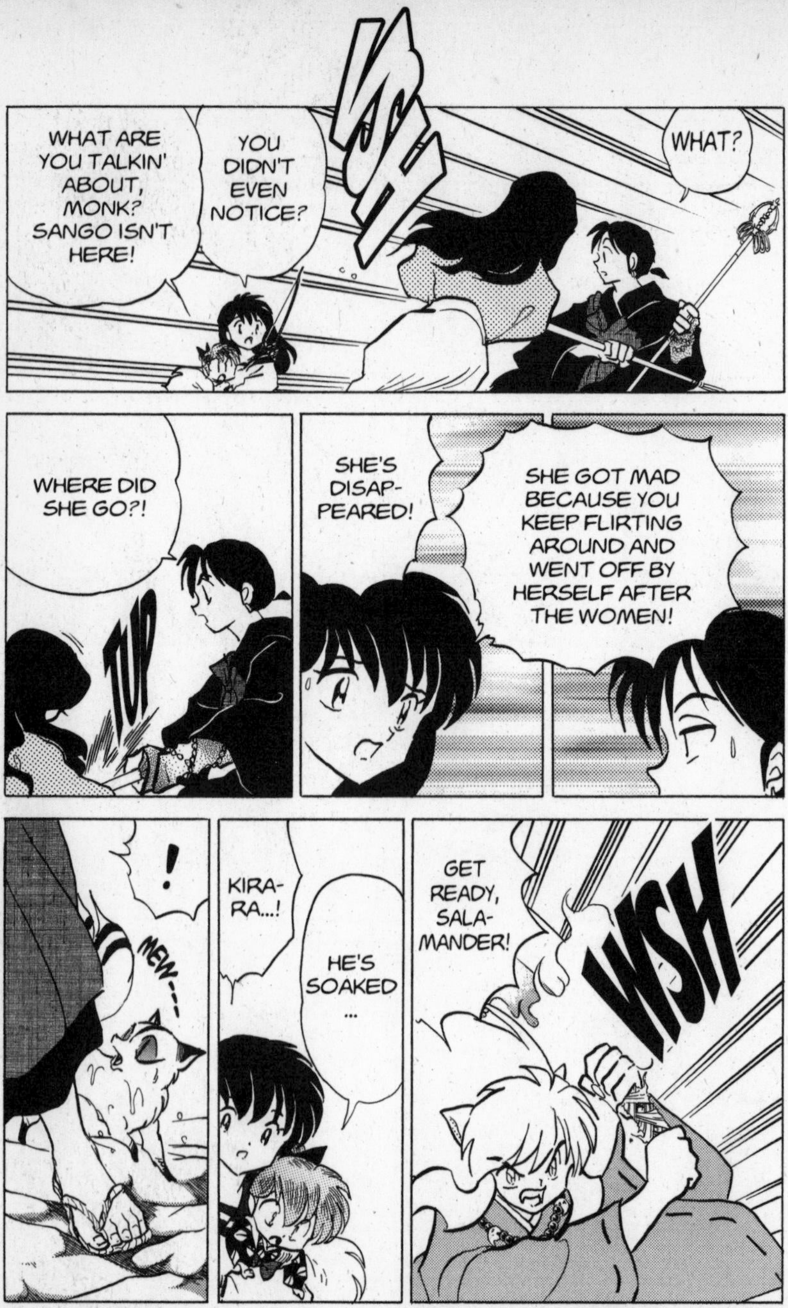
WHAT ARE YOU TALKIN' ABOUT, MONK? SANGO ISN'T HERE!
YOU DIDN'T EVEN NOTICE?
VSH
WHAT?
WHERE DID SHE GO?!
TUP
SHE'S DISAP-PEARED!
SHE GOT MAD BECAUSE YOU KEEP FLIRTING AROUND AND WENT OFF BY HERSELF AFTER THE WOMEN!
!
MEW...
KIRA-RA...!
HE'S SOAKED ...
GET READY, SALA-MANDER!
WSH

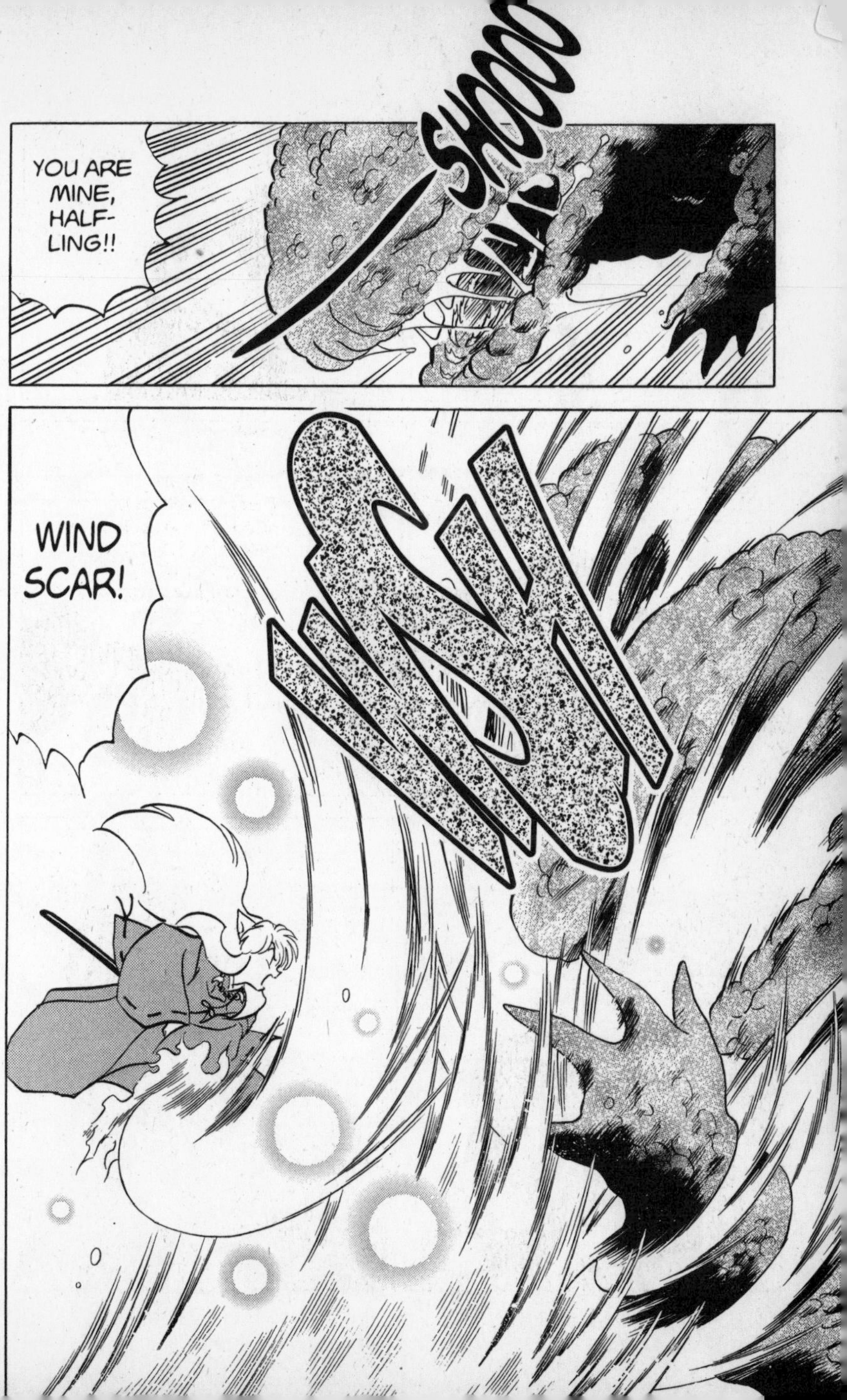
SHOOOO
YOU ARE MINE, HALF-LING!!
WIND SCAR!

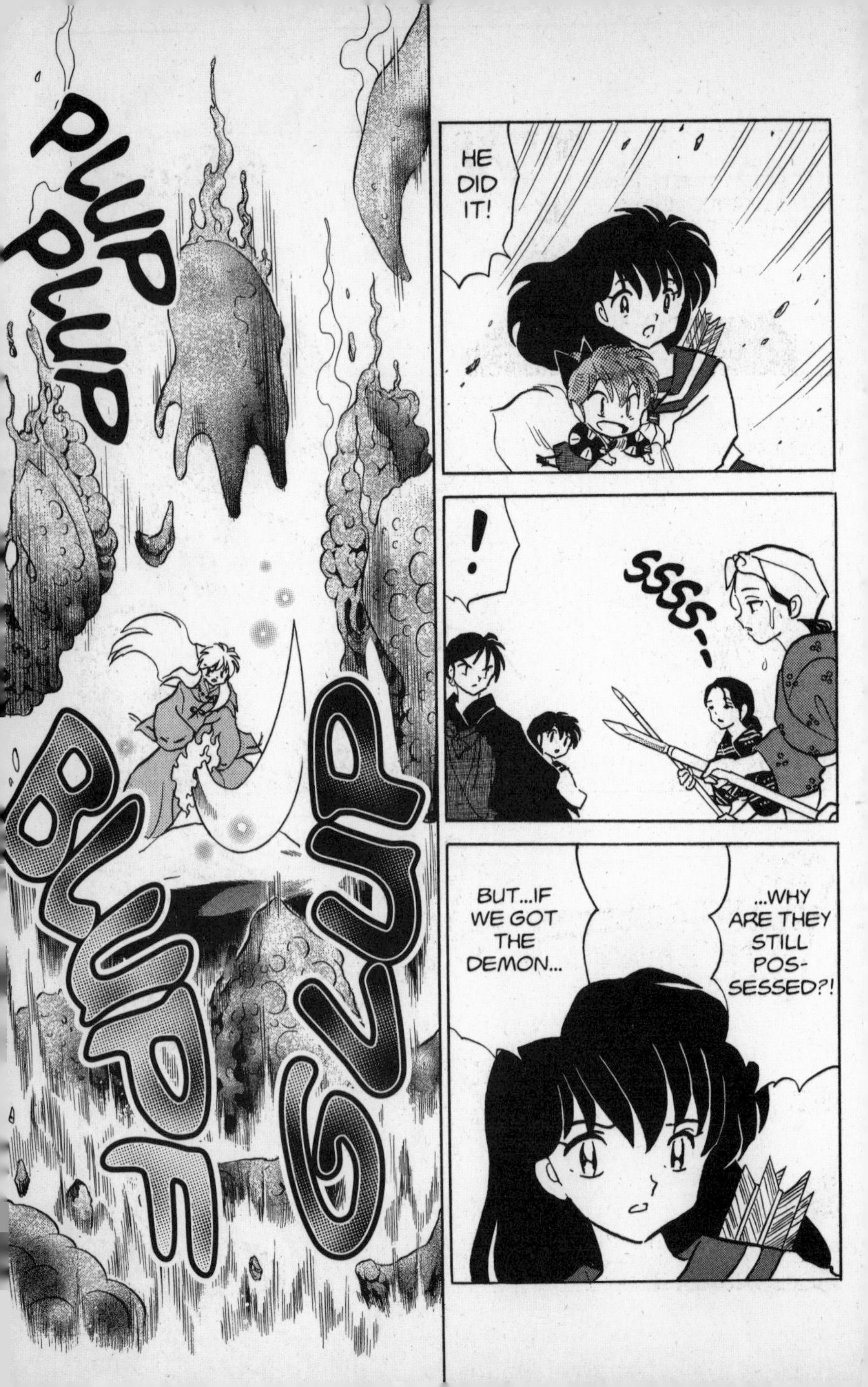
PLUP PLUP
BLUPF
GLUP
HE DID IT!
!
SSSS...
BUT...IF WE GOT THE DEMON...
...WHY ARE THEY STILL POS-SESSED?!

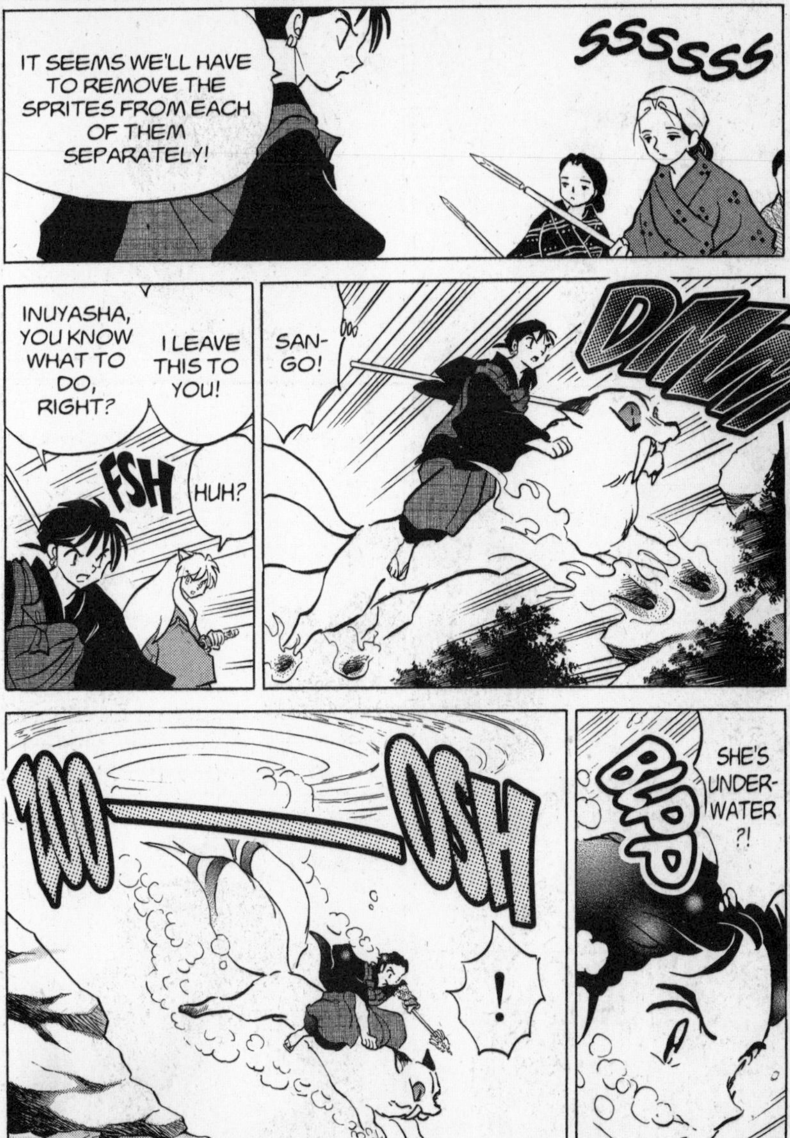
IT SEEMS WE'LL HAVE TO REMOVE THE SPRITES FROM EACH OF THEM SEPARATELY!
SSSSSS
INUYASHA, YOU KNOW WHAT TO DO, RIGHT?
I LEAVE THIS TO YOU!
FSH
HUH?
SAN-GO!
DMM
TOO—OSH
!
BLPP
SHE'S UNDER-WATER ?!

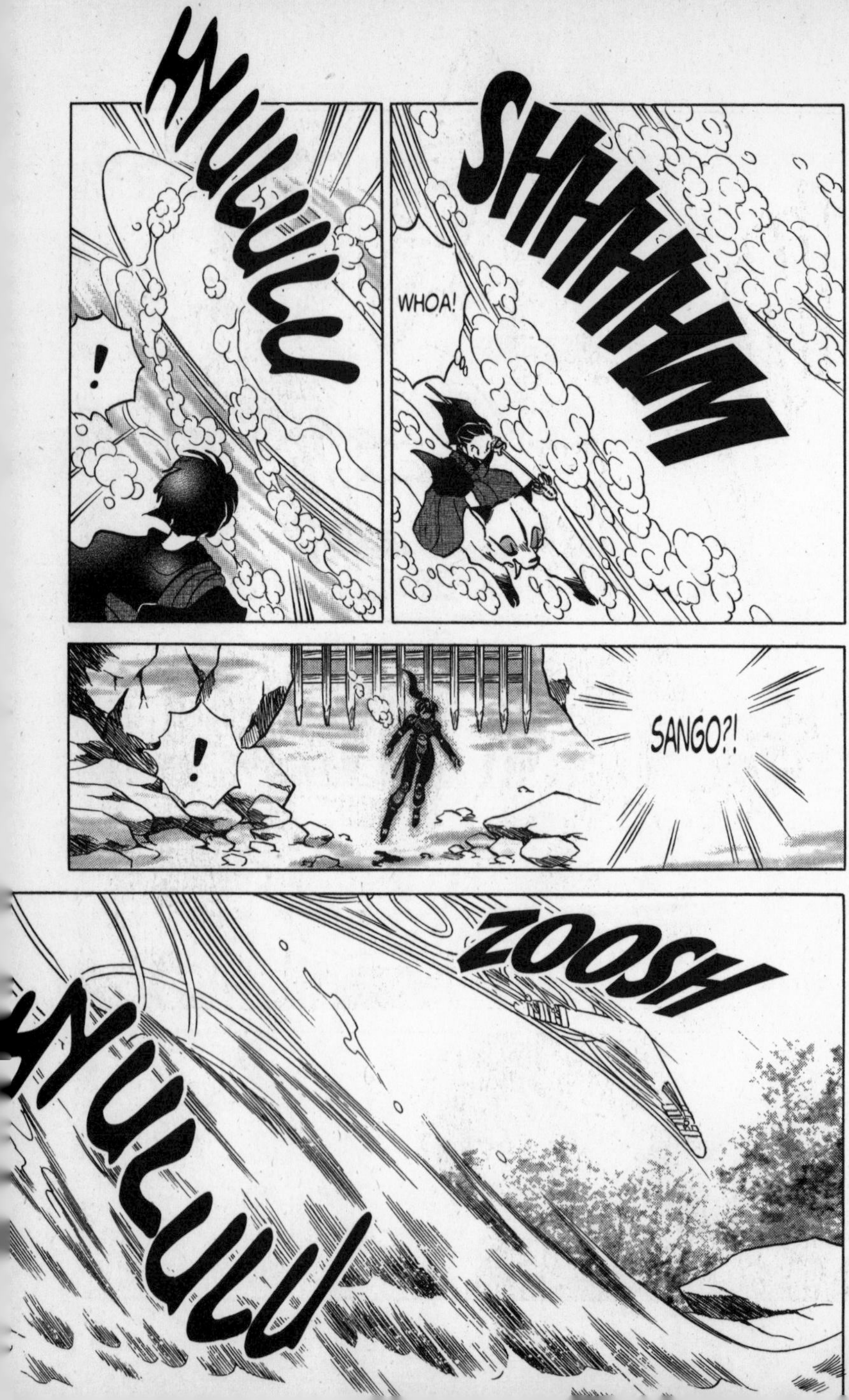
HYUUUUU
!
SHHHHM
WHOA!
!
SANGO?!
HYUUUUU
ZOOSH

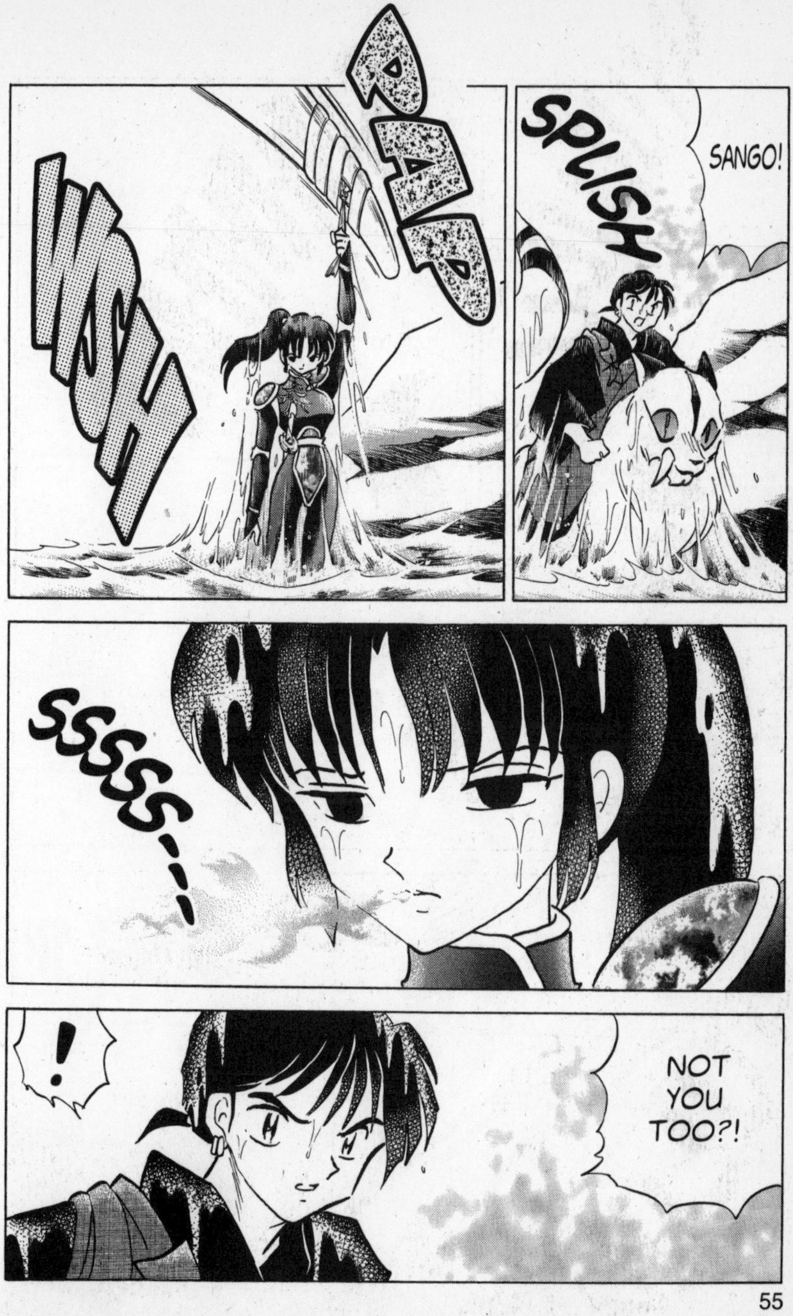
WSH
PAAP
SPLISH
SANGO!
SSSSS...
!
NOT YOU TOO?!

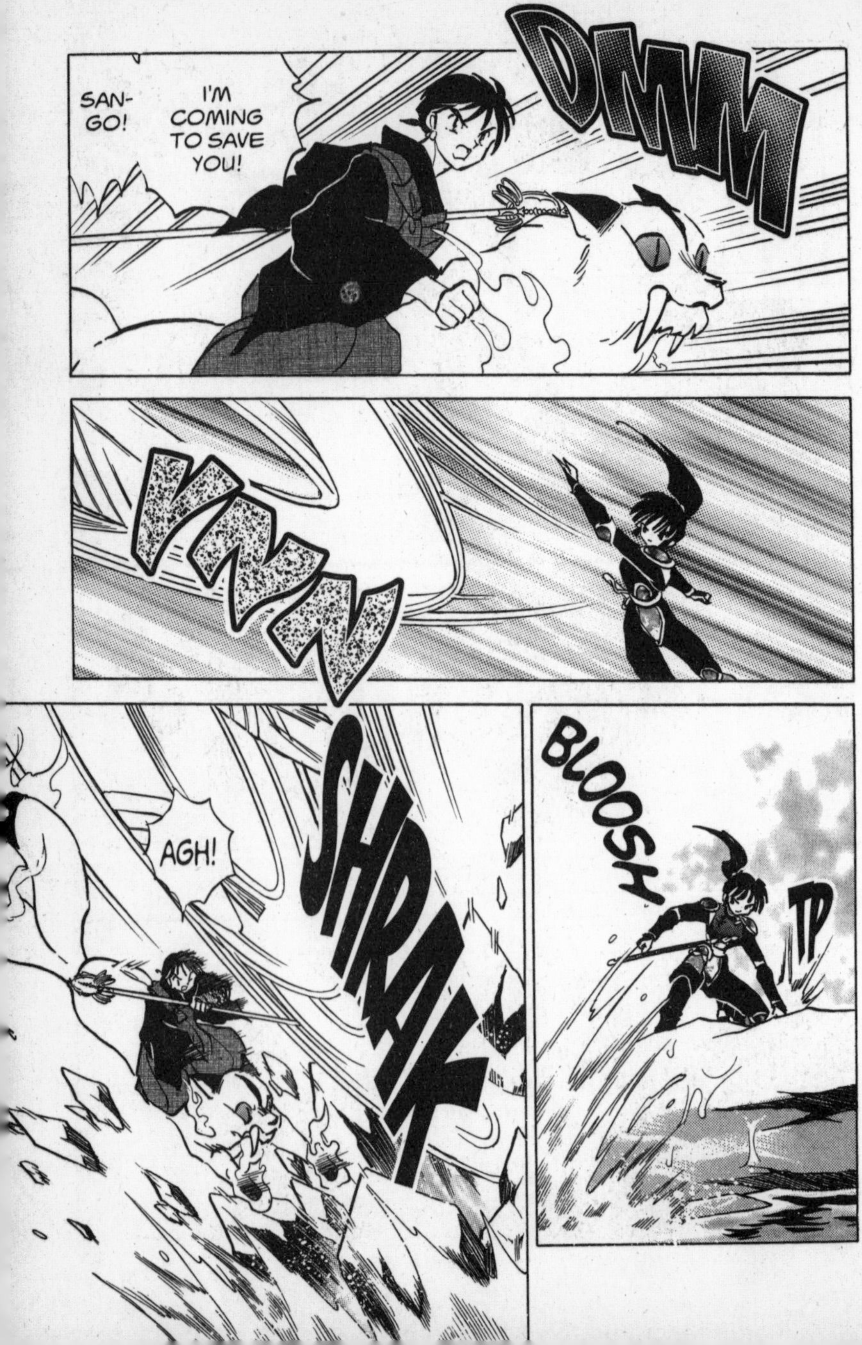
SAN-GO!
I'M COMING TO SAVE YOU!
DMM
VMMM
AGH!
SHRAK
BLOOSH
TP

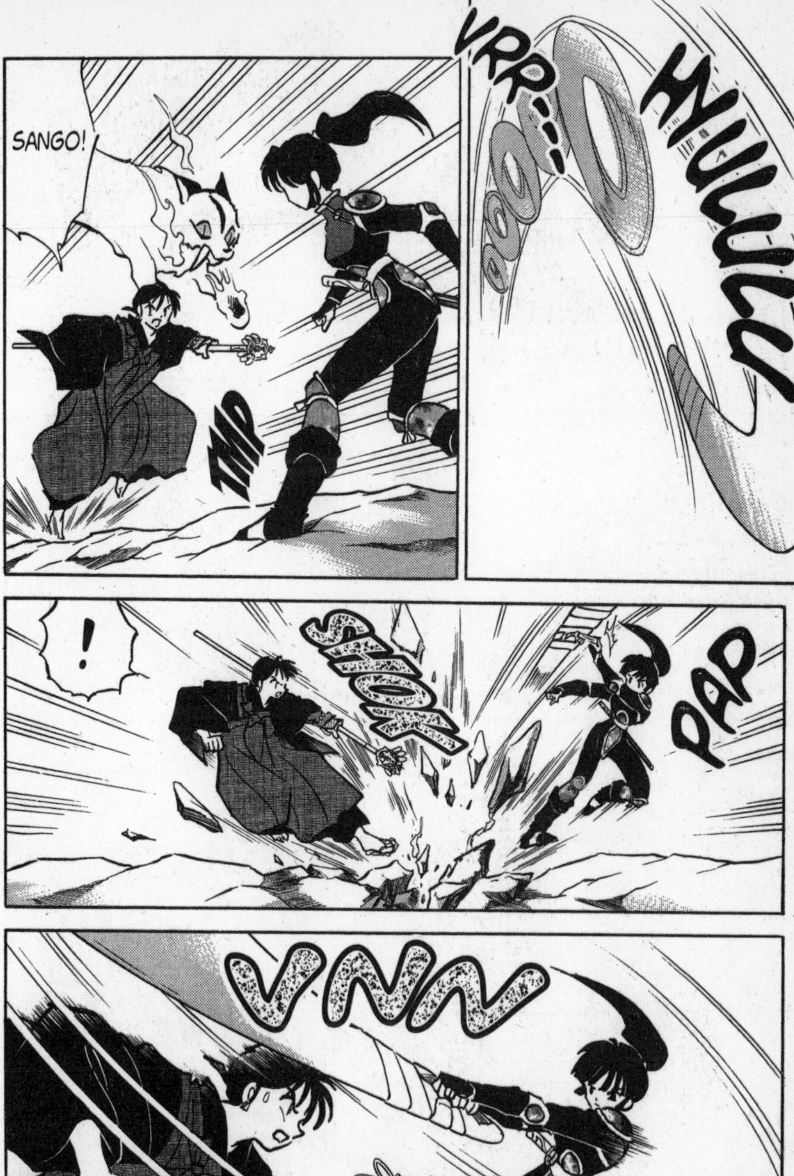
SANGO!
TMP
VRR...
HYUUUU
!
SHOK
PAP
VNN

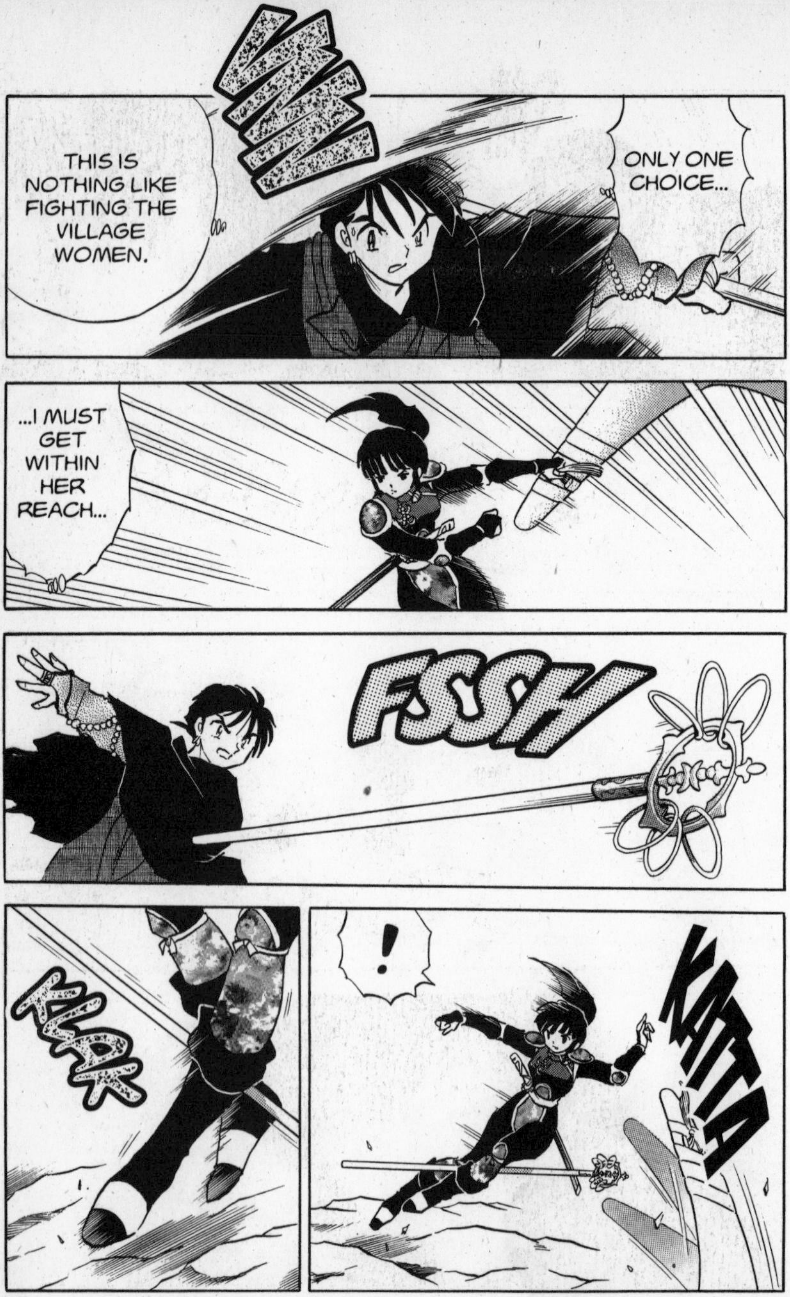
THIS IS NOTHING LIKE FIGHTING THE VILLAGE WOMEN.
ONLY ONE CHOICE...
...I MUST GET WITHIN HER REACH...
FSSH
KLAK
!
KATTA

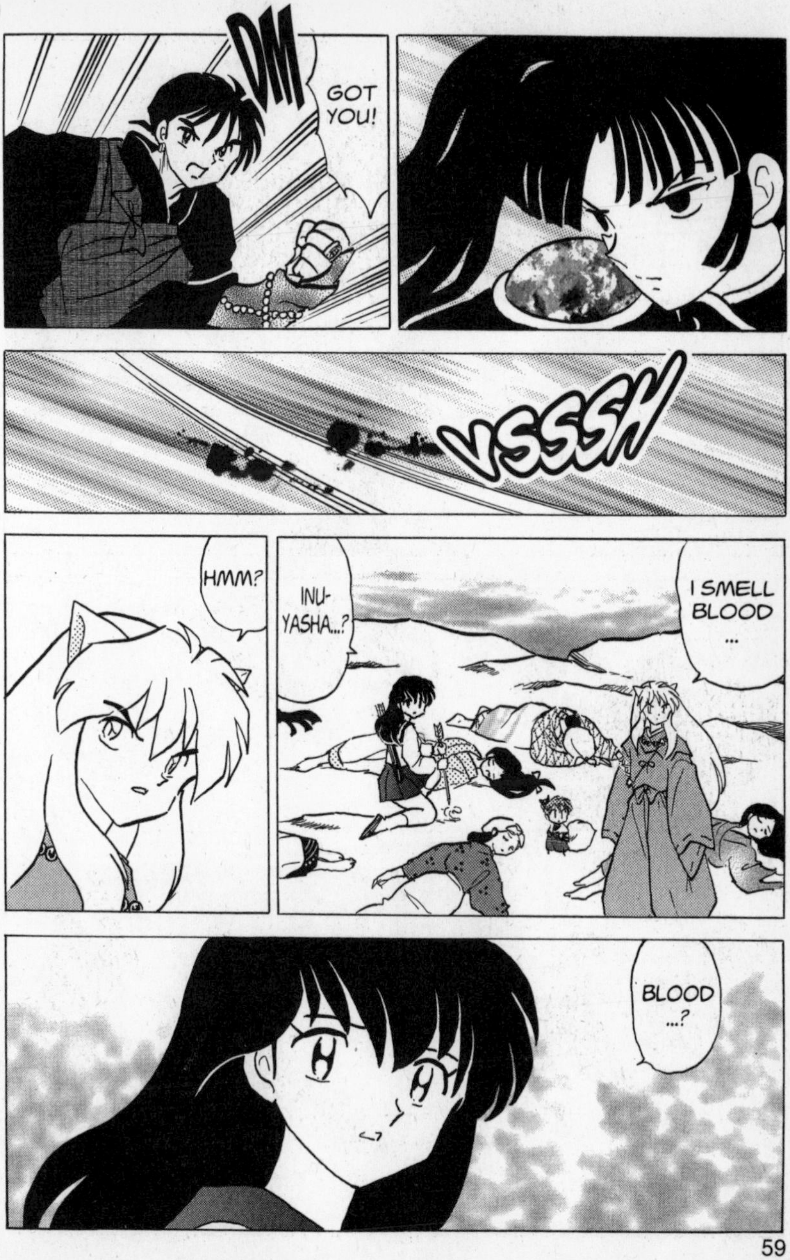
DM
GOT YOU!
VSSSH
HMM?
INU-YASHA...?
I SMELL BLOOD ...
BLOOD ...?

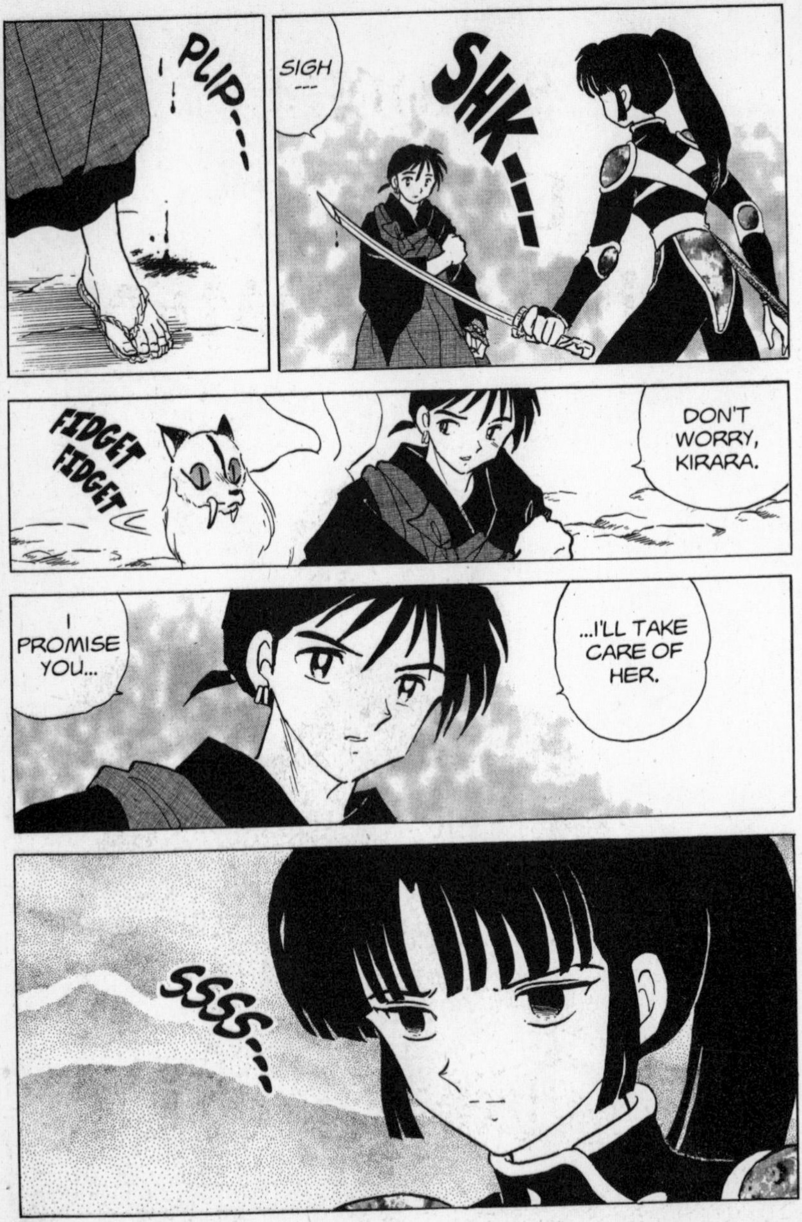
PLIP...
SIGH ---
SHK...
FIDGET FIDGET
DON'T WORRY, KIRARA.
I PROMISE YOU...
...I'LL TAKE CARE OF HER.
SSSS...

SCROLL 4
UNIQUE AMONG WOMEN

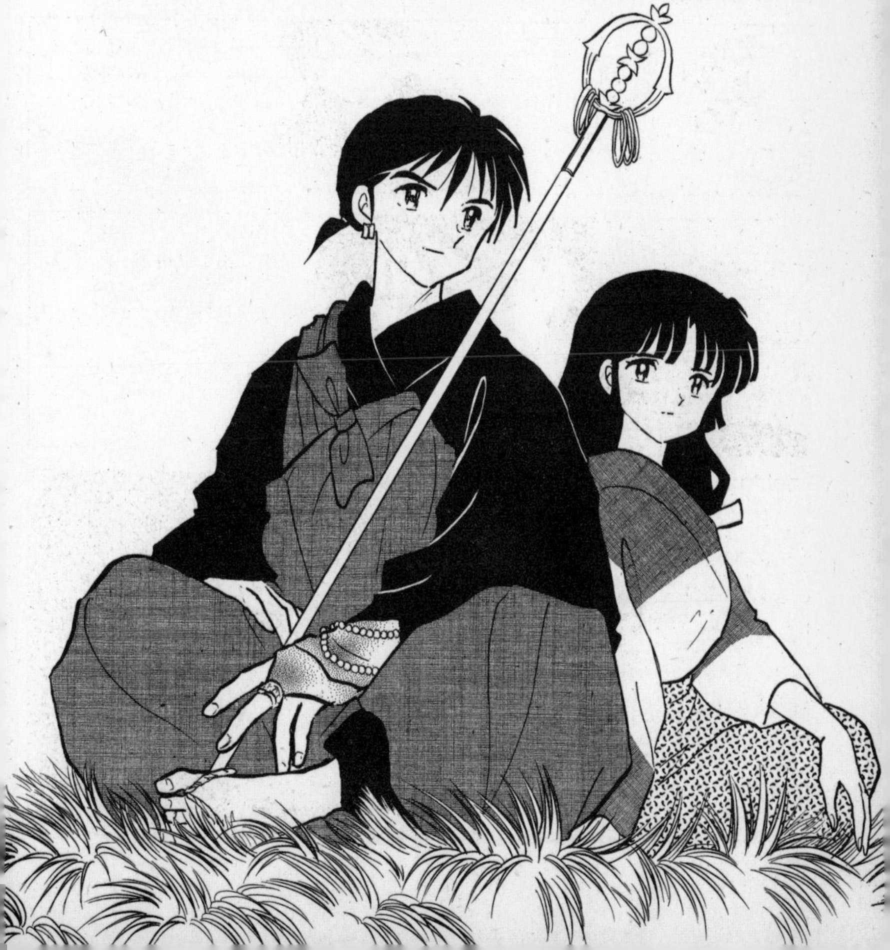

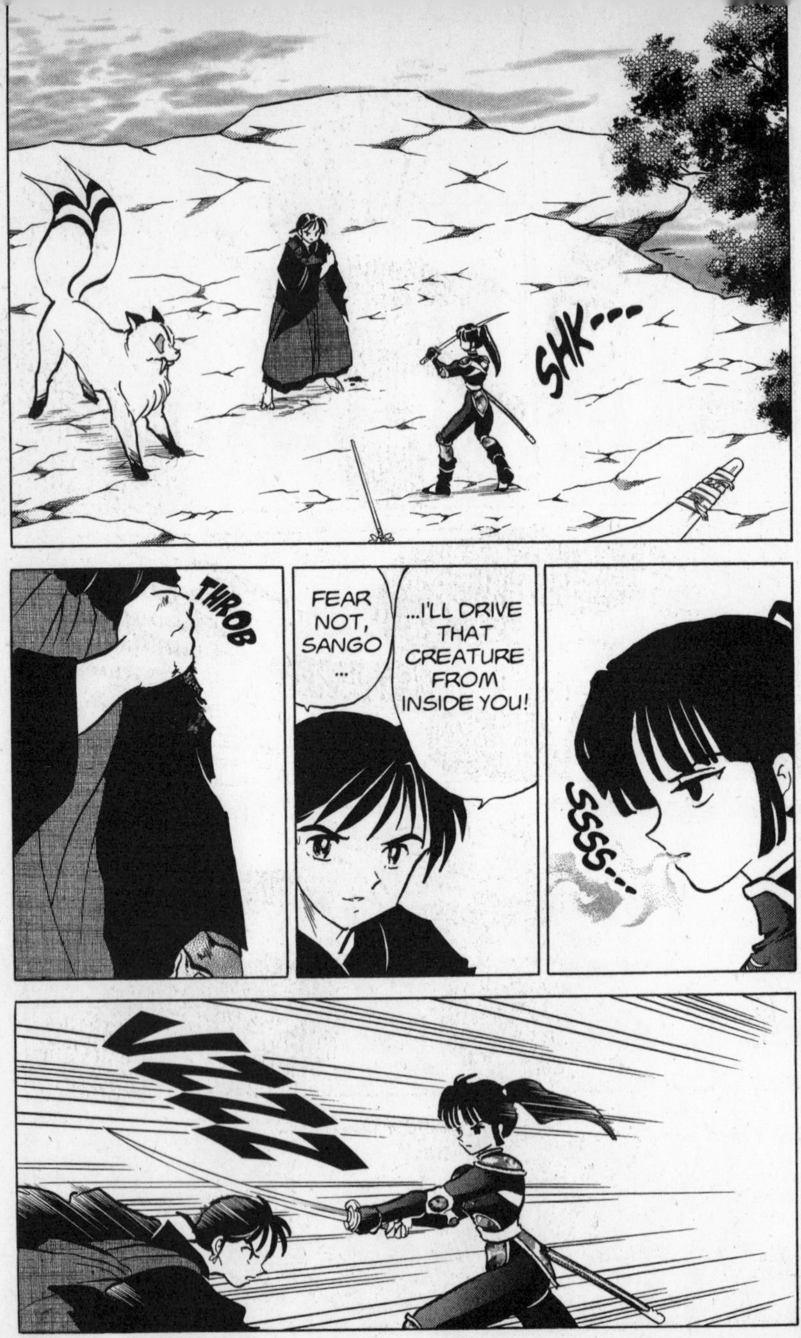
SHK...
THROB
FEAR NOT, SANGO...
...I'LL DRIVE THAT CREATURE FROM INSIDE YOU!
SSSS...
VZZZ

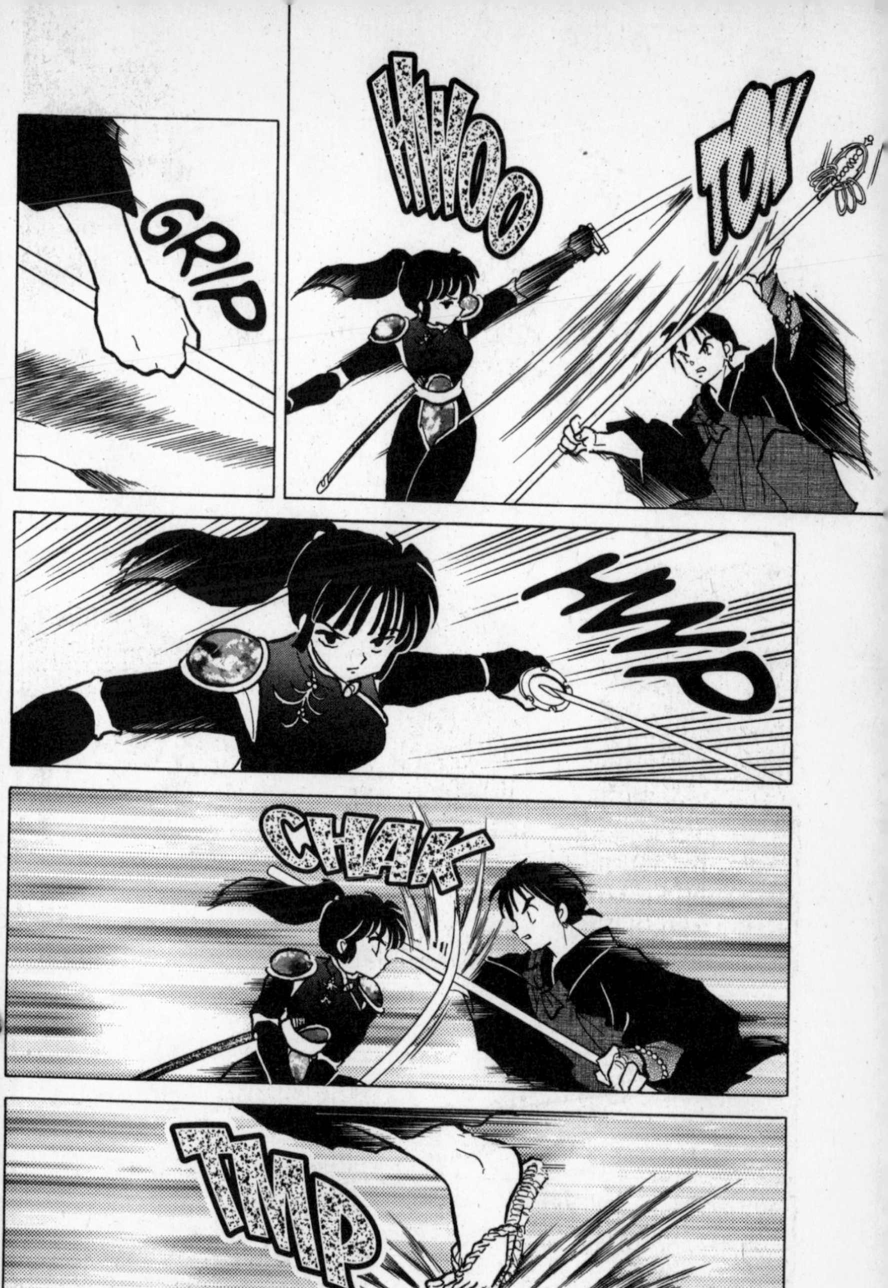
GRIP
HWOO
TOK
HMP
CHAK
TMP

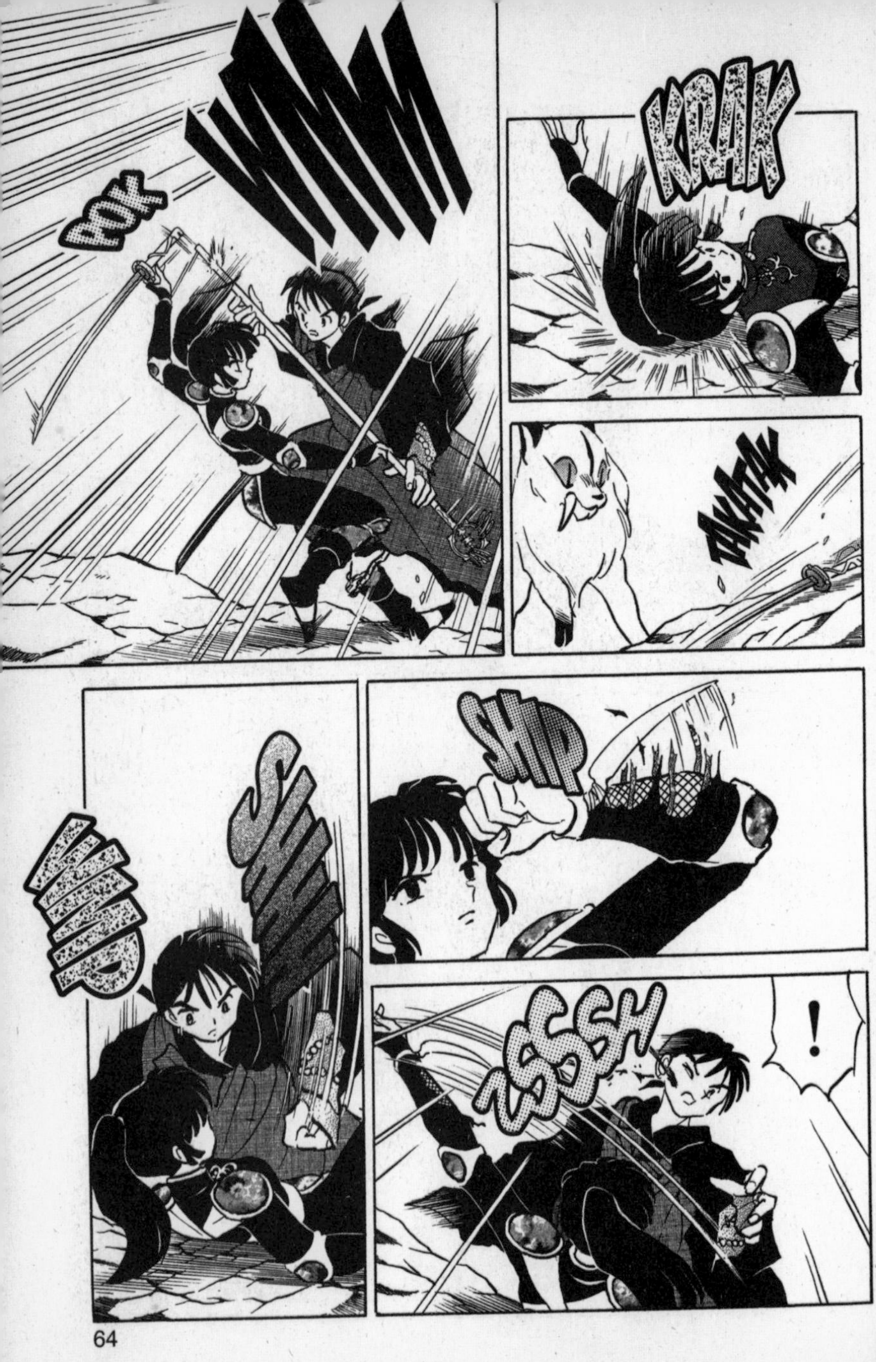
POK
WMMM
KRAK
TAKATAK
SHHHH
SHIP
ZSSSH
!

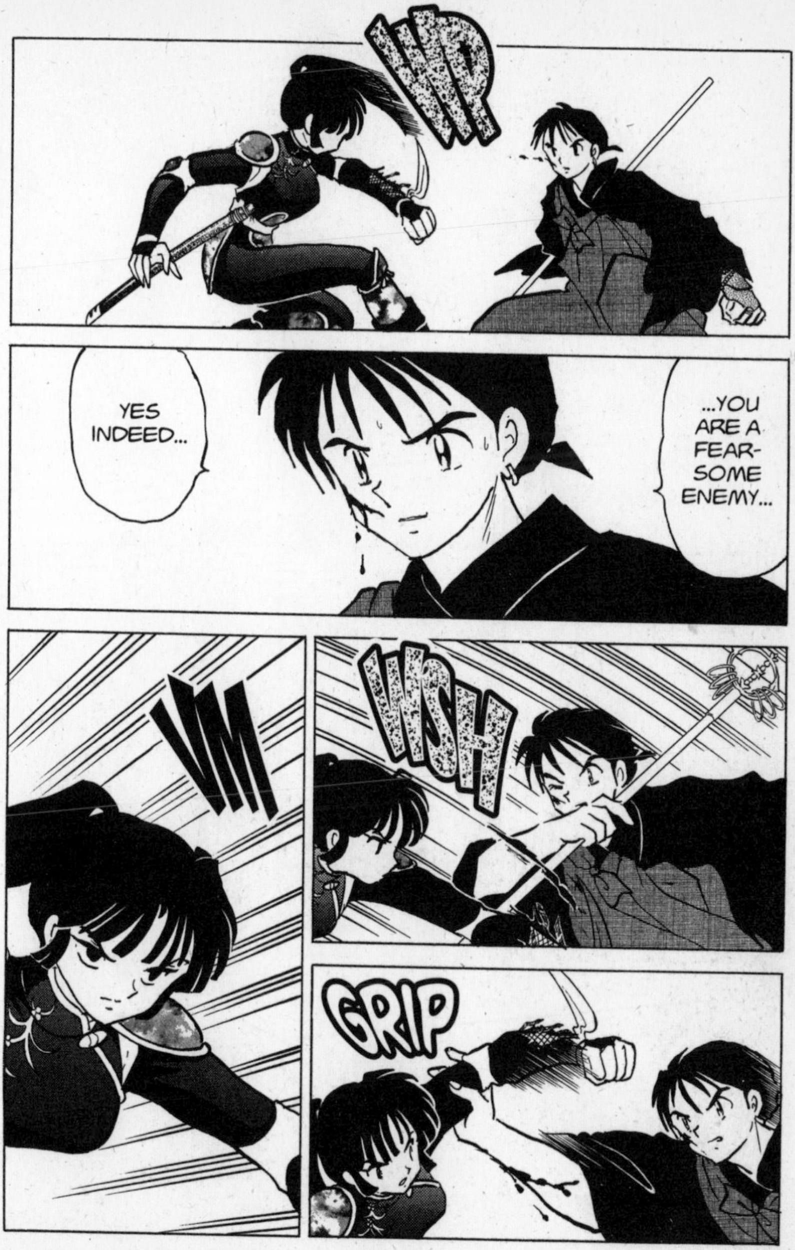
WIP
YES INDEED...
...YOU ARE A FEAR-SOME ENEMY...
VM
WSH
GRIP

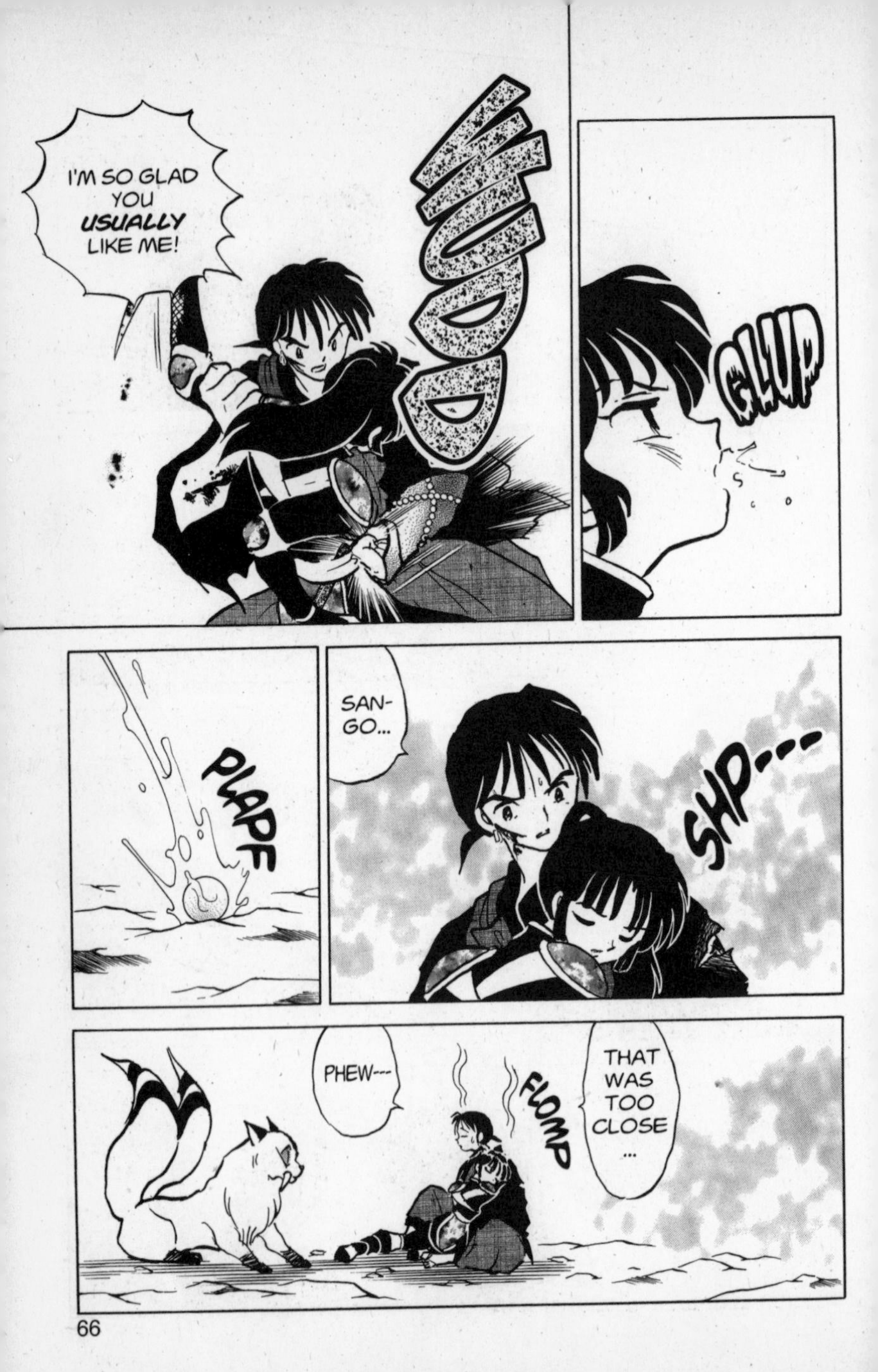
I'M SO GLAD YOU USUALLY LIKE ME!
WHUDD
GLUP
PLAPF
SAN-GO...
SHP---
PHEW---
FLOMP
THAT WAS TOO CLOSE ...

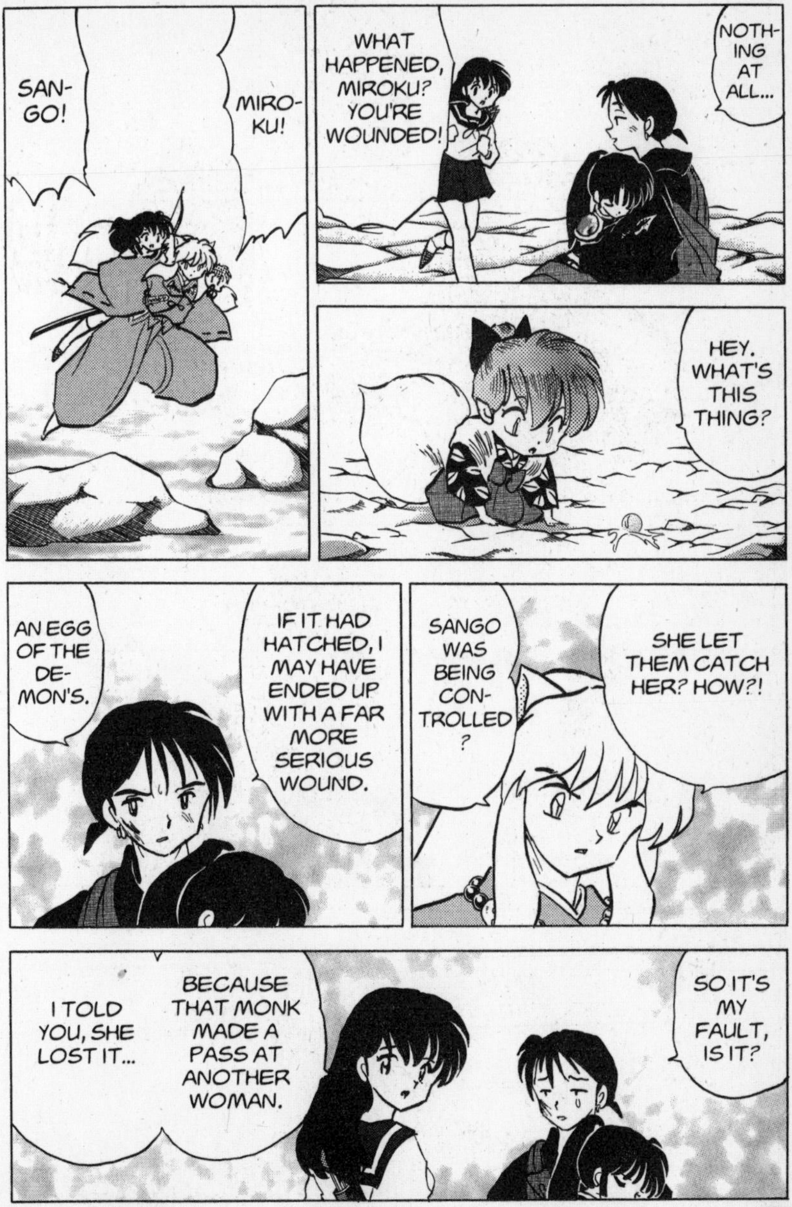
SAN-GO!
MIRO-KU!
WHAT HAPPENED, MIROKU? YOU'RE WOUNDED!
NOTH-ING AT ALL...
HEY. WHAT'S THIS THING?
AN EGG OF THE DE-MON'S.
IF IT HAD HATCHED, I MAY HAVE ENDED UP WITH A FAR MORE SERIOUS WOUND.
SANGO WAS BEING CON-TROLLED?
SHE LET THEM CATCH HER? HOW?!
I TOLD YOU, SHE LOST IT...
BECAUSE THAT MONK MADE A PASS AT ANOTHER WOMAN.
SO IT'S MY FAULT, IS IT?

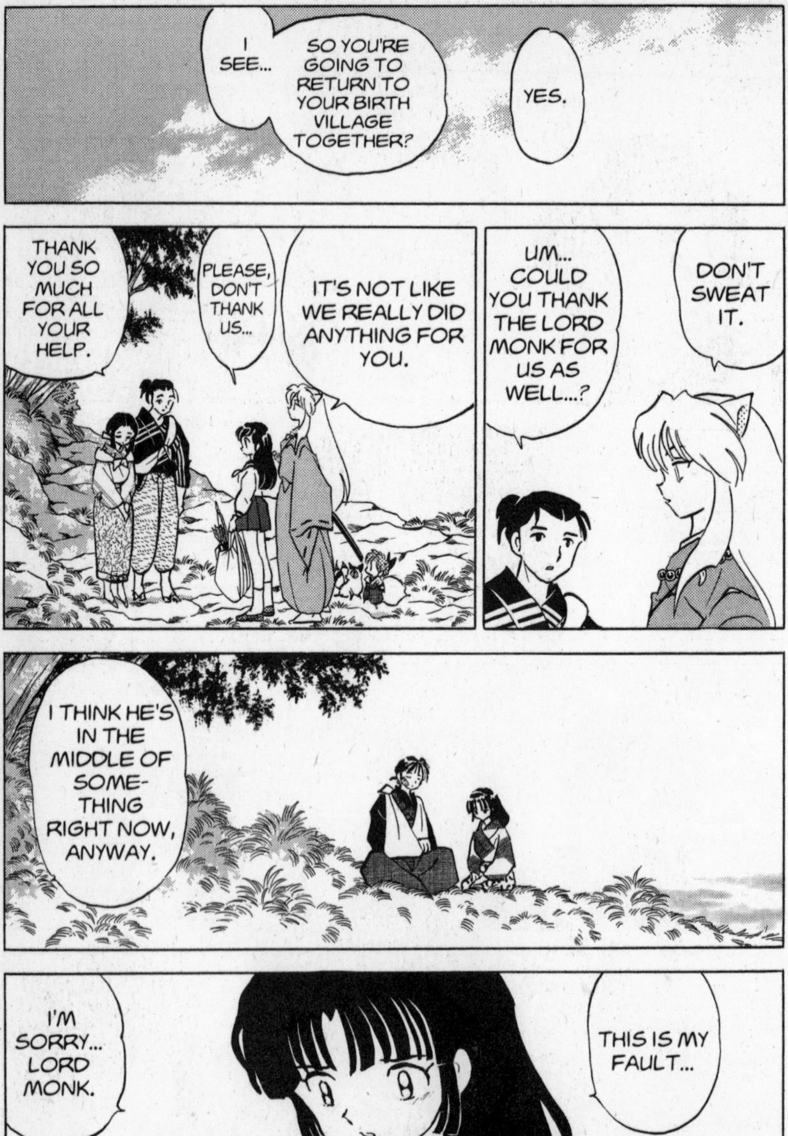
I SEE...
SO YOU'RE GOING TO RETURN TO YOUR BIRTH VILLAGE TOGETHER?
YES.
THANK YOU SO MUCH FOR ALL YOUR HELP.
PLEASE, DON'T THANK US...
IT'S NOT LIKE WE REALLY DID ANYTHING FOR YOU.
UM... COULD YOU THANK THE LORD MONK FOR US AS WELL...?
DON'T SWEAT IT.
I THINK HE'S IN THE MIDDLE OF SOME-THING RIGHT NOW, ANYWAY.
I'M SORRY... LORD MONK.
THIS IS MY FAULT...

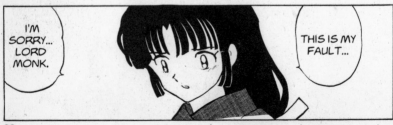

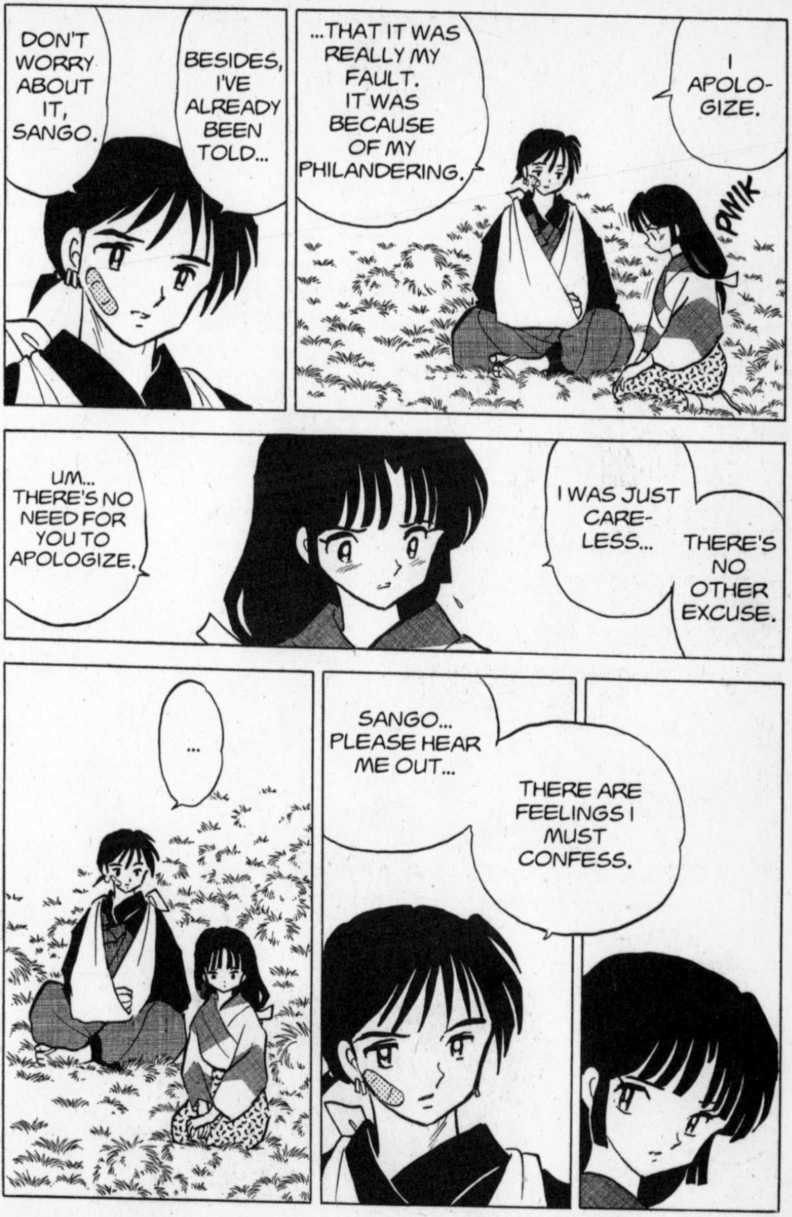
DON'T WORRY ABOUT IT, SANGO.
BESIDES, I'VE ALREADY BEEN TOLD...
...THAT IT WAS REALLY MY FAULT. IT WAS BECAUSE OF MY PHILANDERING.
I APOLOGIZE.
PWIK
UM... THERE'S NO NEED FOR YOU TO APOLOGIZE.
I WAS JUST CARELESS...
THERE'S NO OTHER EXCUSE.
...
SANGO... PLEASE HEAR ME OUT...
THERE ARE FEELINGS I MUST CONFESS.

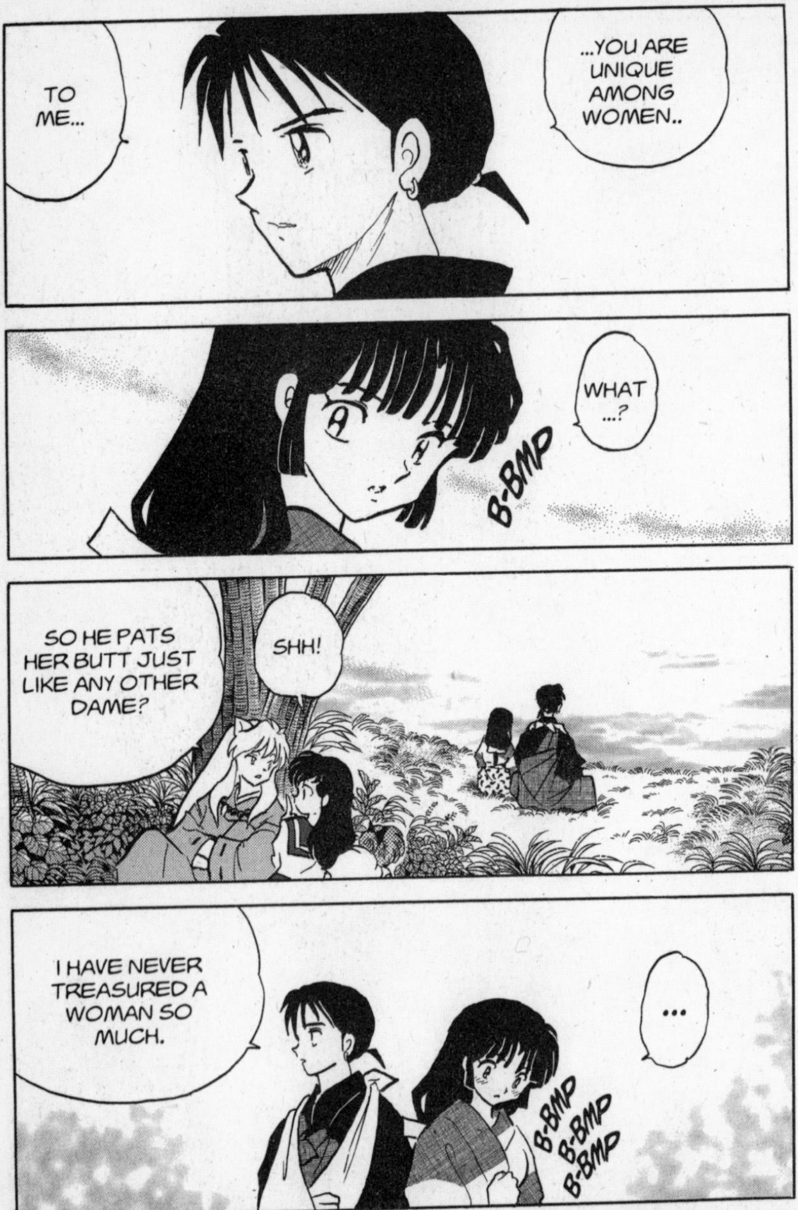
TO ME...
...YOU ARE UNIQUE AMONG WOMEN..
WHAT ...?
B-BMP
SO HE PATS HER BUTT JUST LIKE ANY OTHER DAME?
SHH!
I HAVE NEVER TREASURED A WOMAN SO MUCH.
...
B-BMP
B-BMP
B-BMP

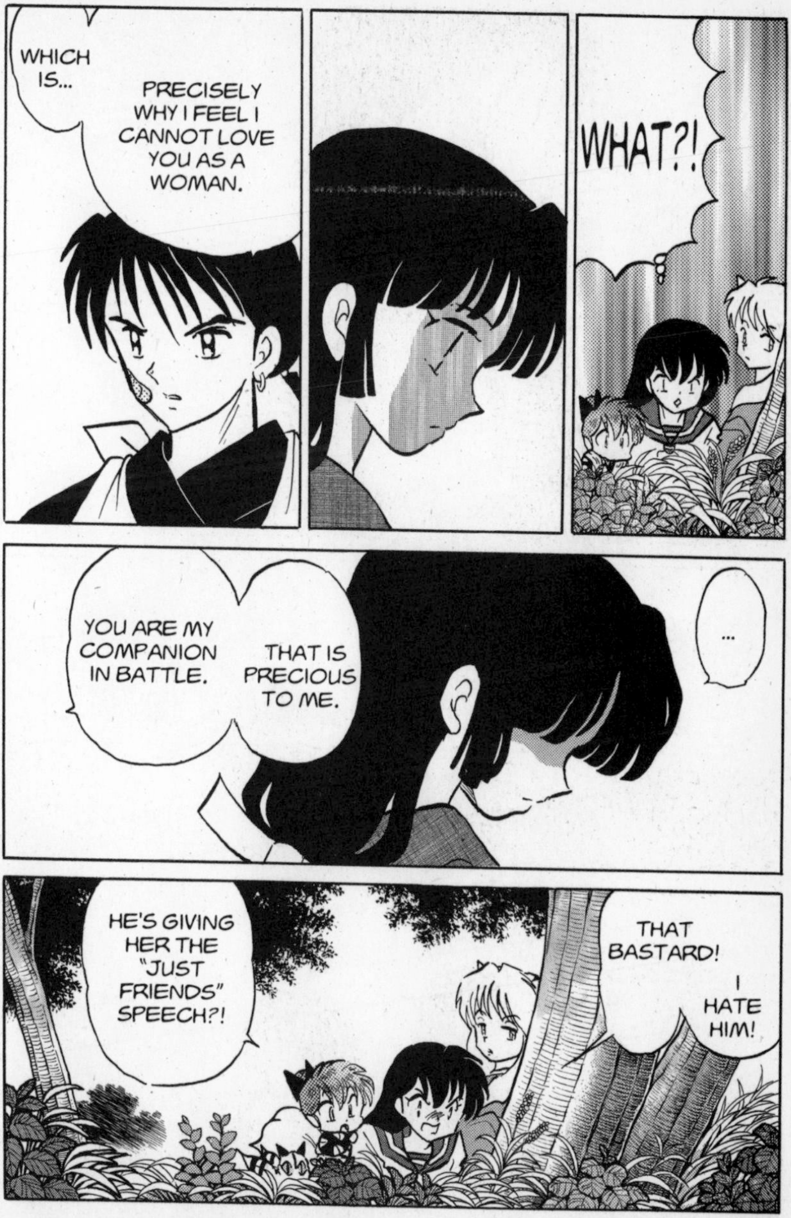
WHICH IS...
PRECISELY WHY I FEEL I CANNOT LOVE YOU AS A WOMAN.
WHAT?!
YOU ARE MY COMPANION IN BATTLE.
THAT IS PRECIOUS TO ME.
...
HE'S GIVING HER THE "JUST FRIENDS" SPEECH?!
THAT BASTARD!
I HATE HIM!

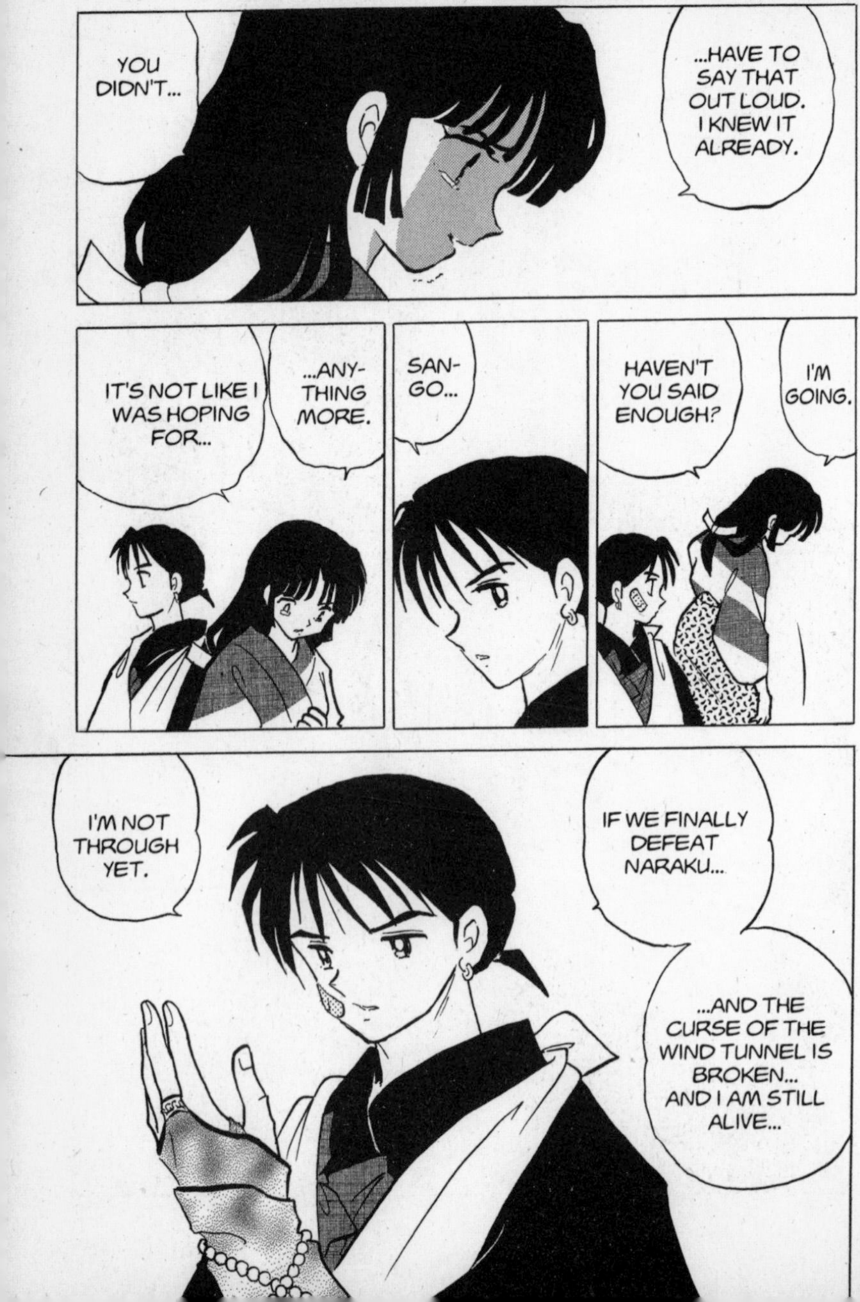
YOU DIDN'T...
...HAVE TO SAY THAT OUT LOUD. I KNEW IT ALREADY.
IT'S NOT LIKE I WAS HOPING FOR...
...ANY-THING MORE.
SAN-GO...
HAVEN'T YOU SAID ENOUGH?
I'M GOING.
I'M NOT THROUGH YET.
IF WE FINALLY DEFEAT NARAKU...
...AND THE CURSE OF THE WIND TUNNEL IS BROKEN... AND I AM STILL ALIVE...

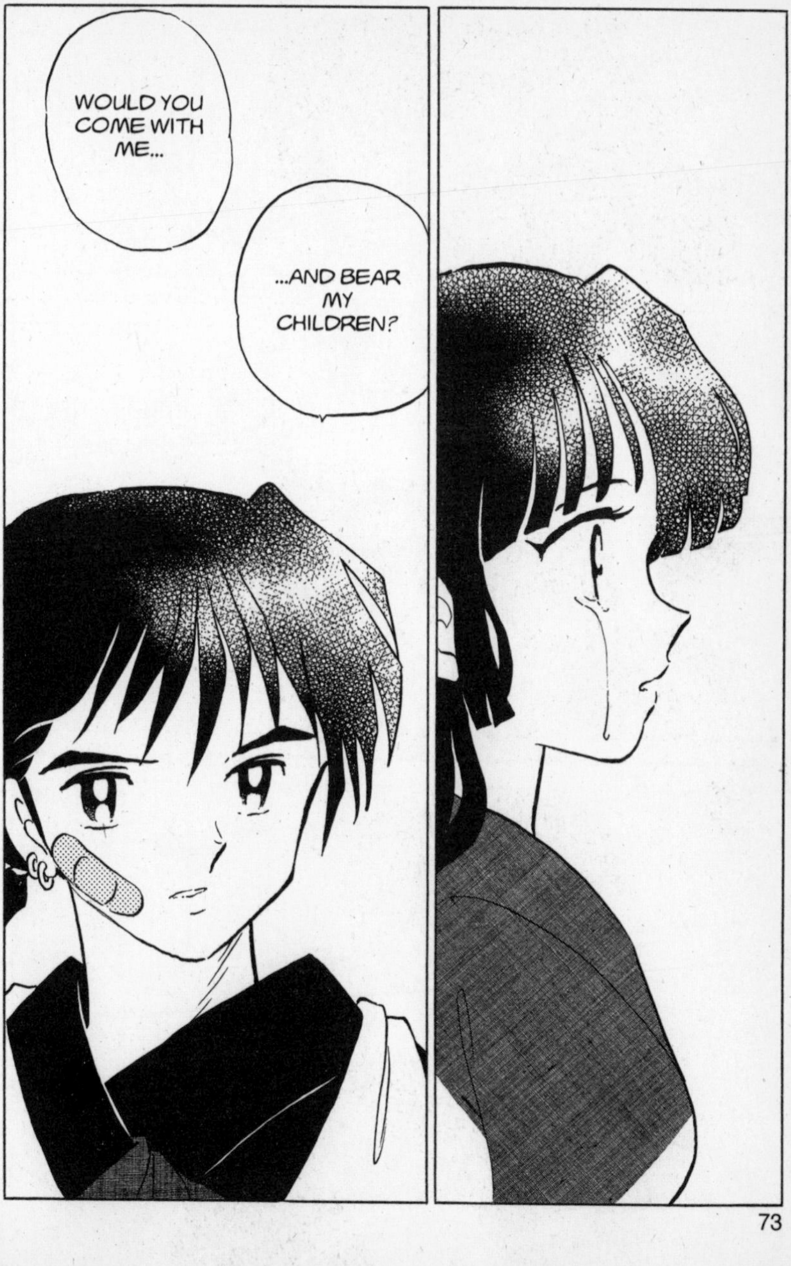
WOULD YOU COME WITH ME...
...AND BEAR MY CHILDREN?

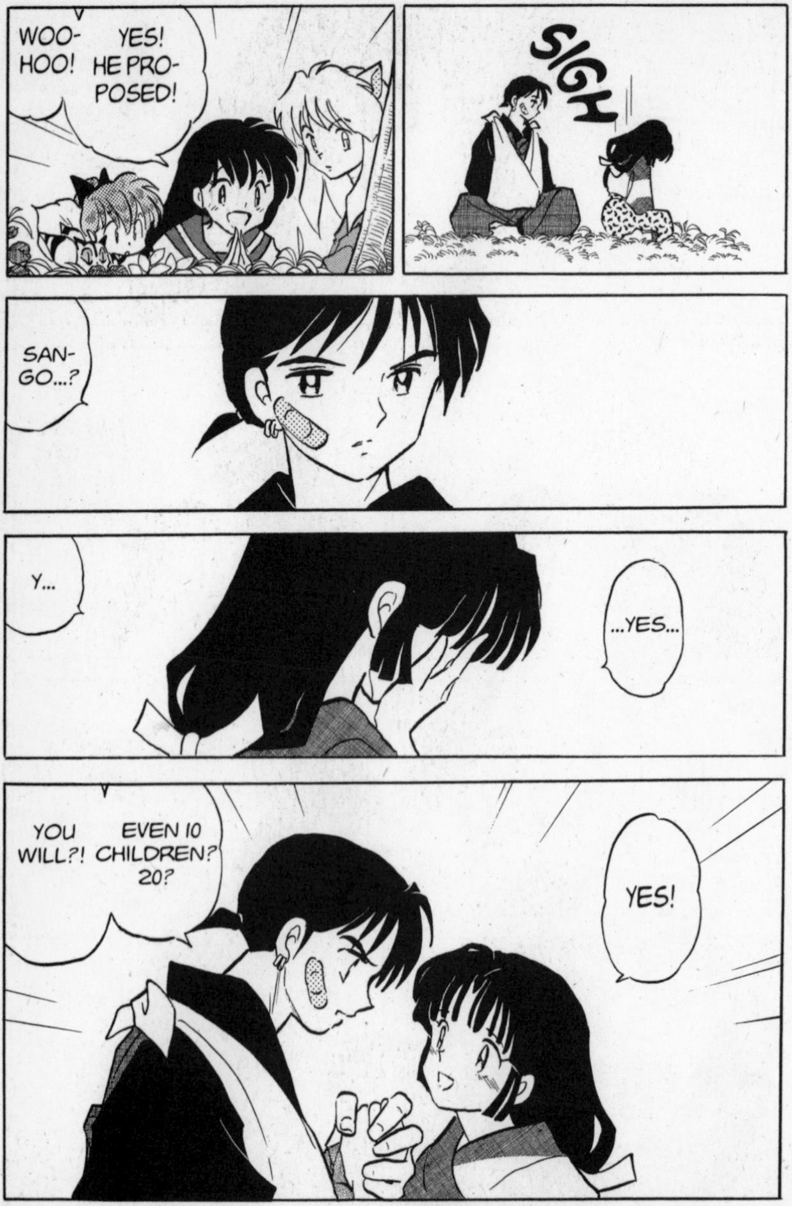
WOO-HOO!
YES! HE PRO-POSED!
SIGH
SAN-GO...?
Y...
...YES...
YOU WILL?!
EVEN 10 CHILDREN? 20?
YES!

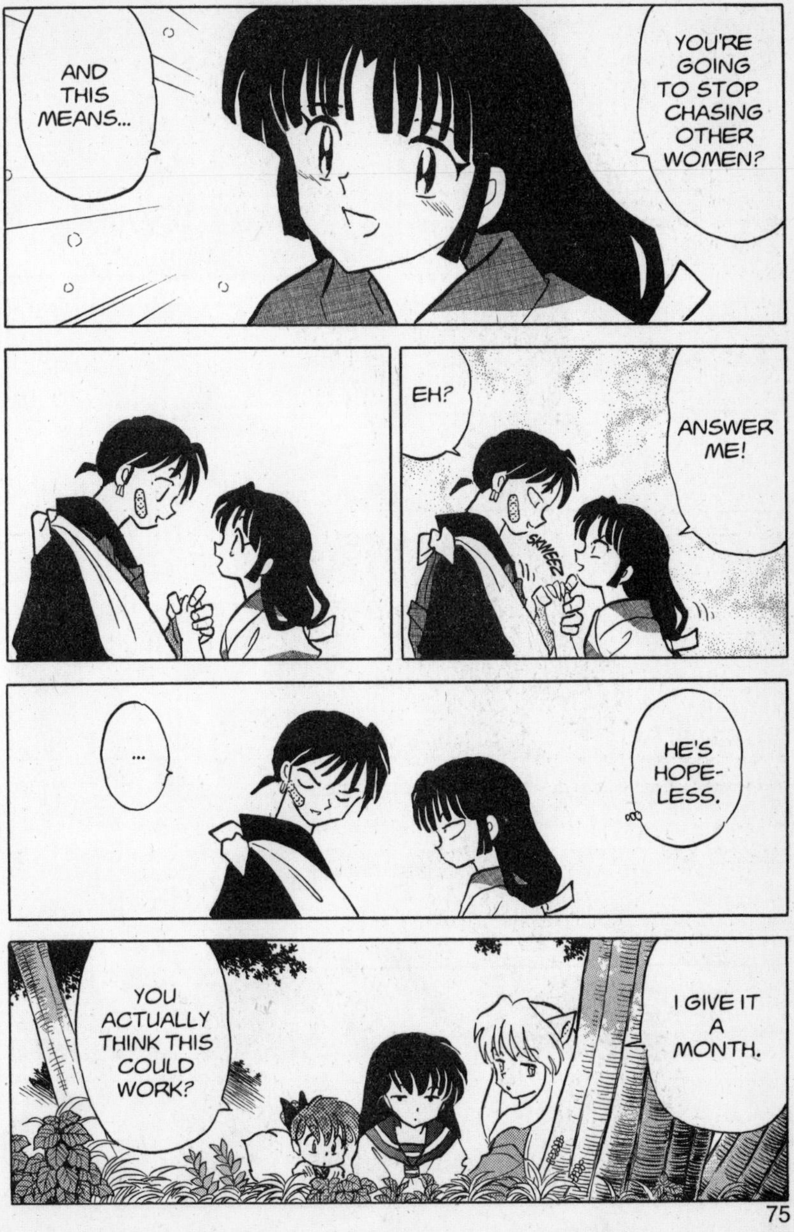
AND THIS MEANS...
YOU'RE GOING TO STOP CHASING OTHER WOMEN?
EH?
ANSWER ME!
SKWEEZ
...
HE'S HOPE-LESS.
YOU ACTUALLY THINK THIS COULD WORK?
I GIVE IT A MONTH.

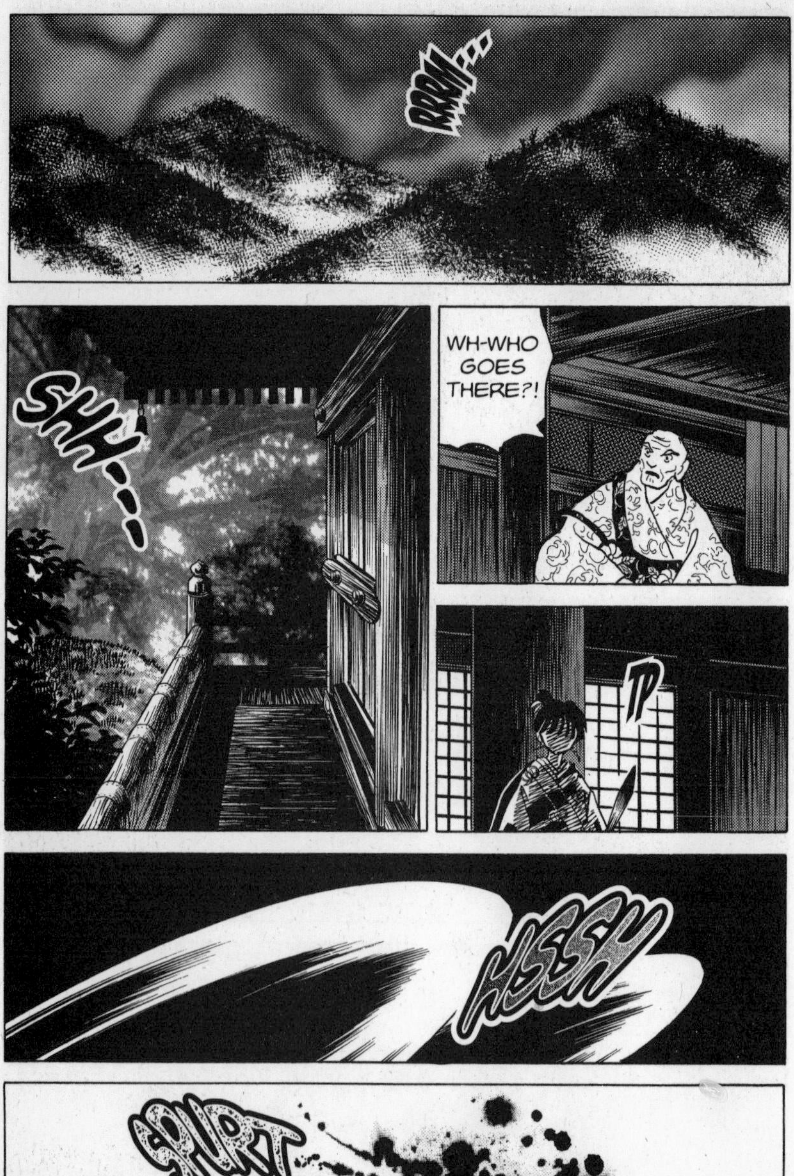
RRRM...
SHH...
WH-WHO GOES THERE?!
TP
WSSH
SPURT

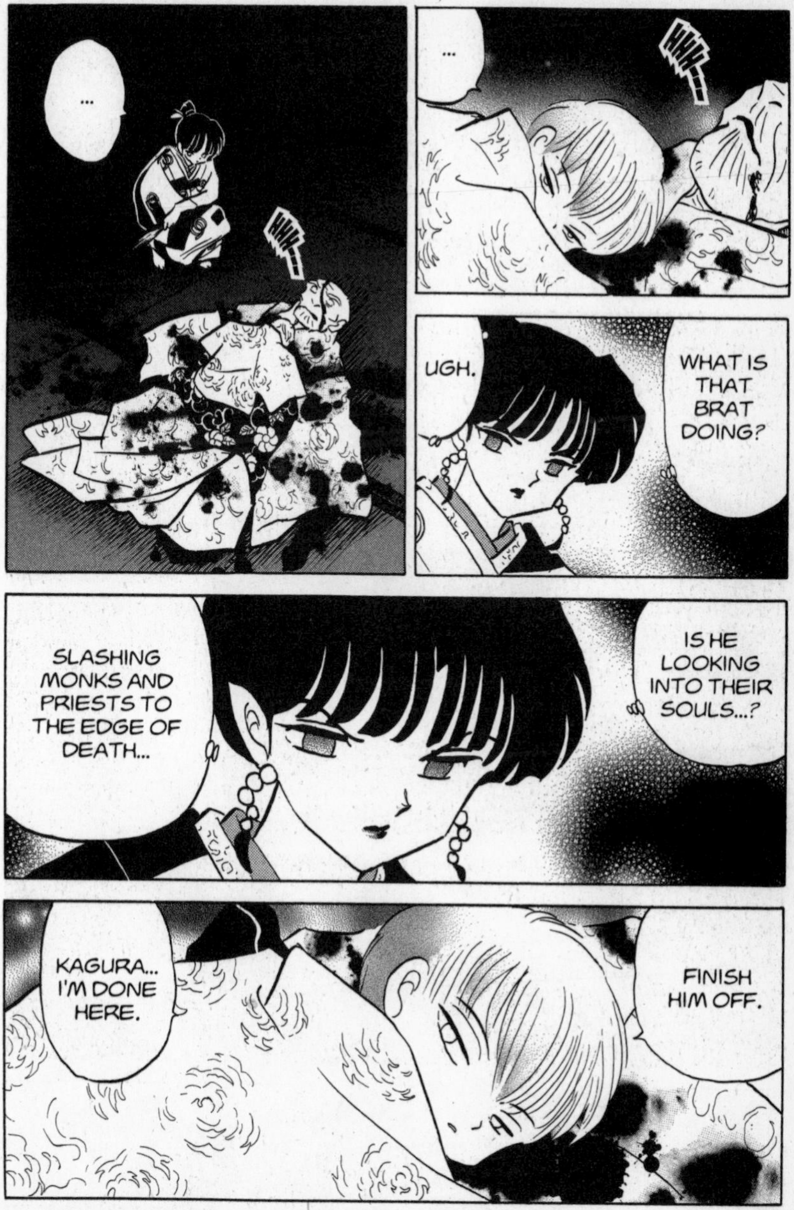
...
WHAT IS THAT BRAT DOING?
UGH.
...
IS HE LOOKING INTO THEIR SOULS...?
SLASHING MONKS AND PRIESTS TO THE EDGE OF DEATH...
FINISH HIM OFF.
KAGURA... I'M DONE HERE.

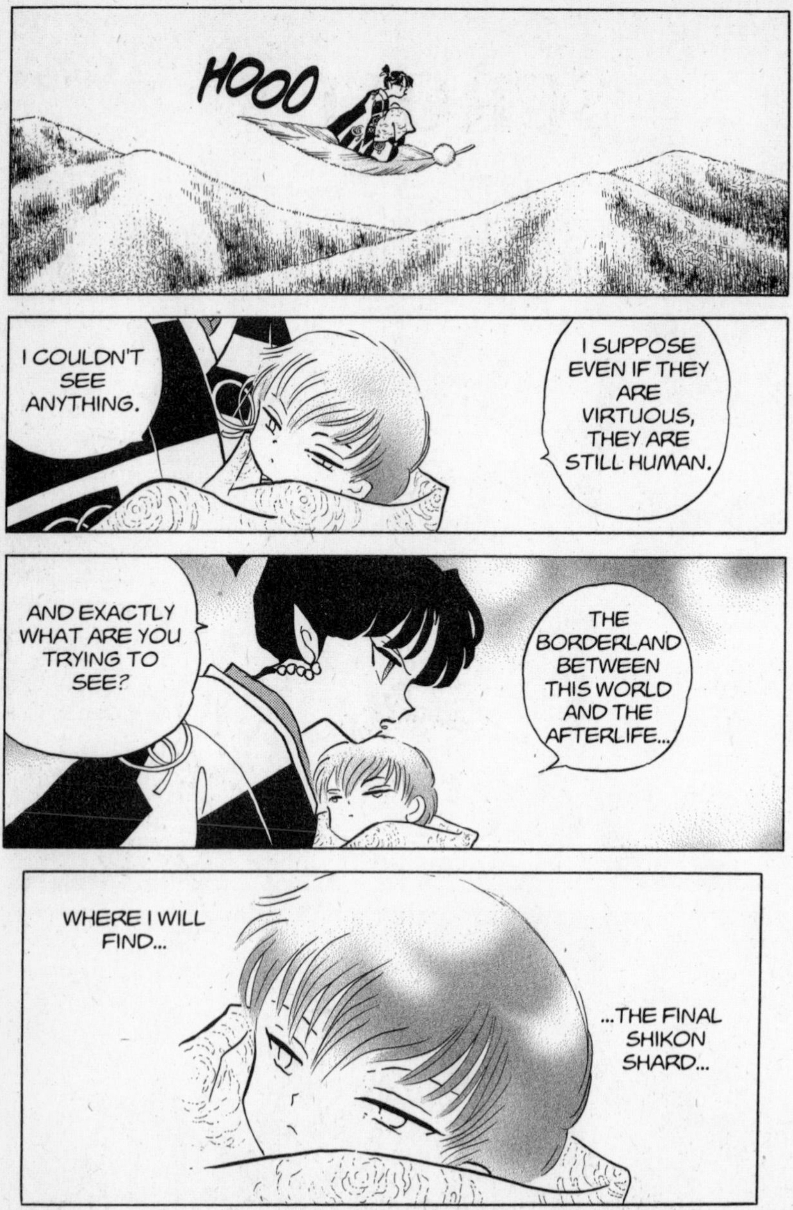
HOOO
I COULDN'T SEE ANYTHING.
I SUPPOSE EVEN IF THEY ARE VIRTUOUS, THEY ARE STILL HUMAN.
AND EXACTLY WHAT ARE YOU TRYING TO SEE?
THE BORDERLAND BETWEEN THIS WORLD AND THE AFTERLIFE...
WHERE I WILL FIND...
...THE FINAL SHIKON SHARD...

SCROLL 5

SPLIT IN HALF

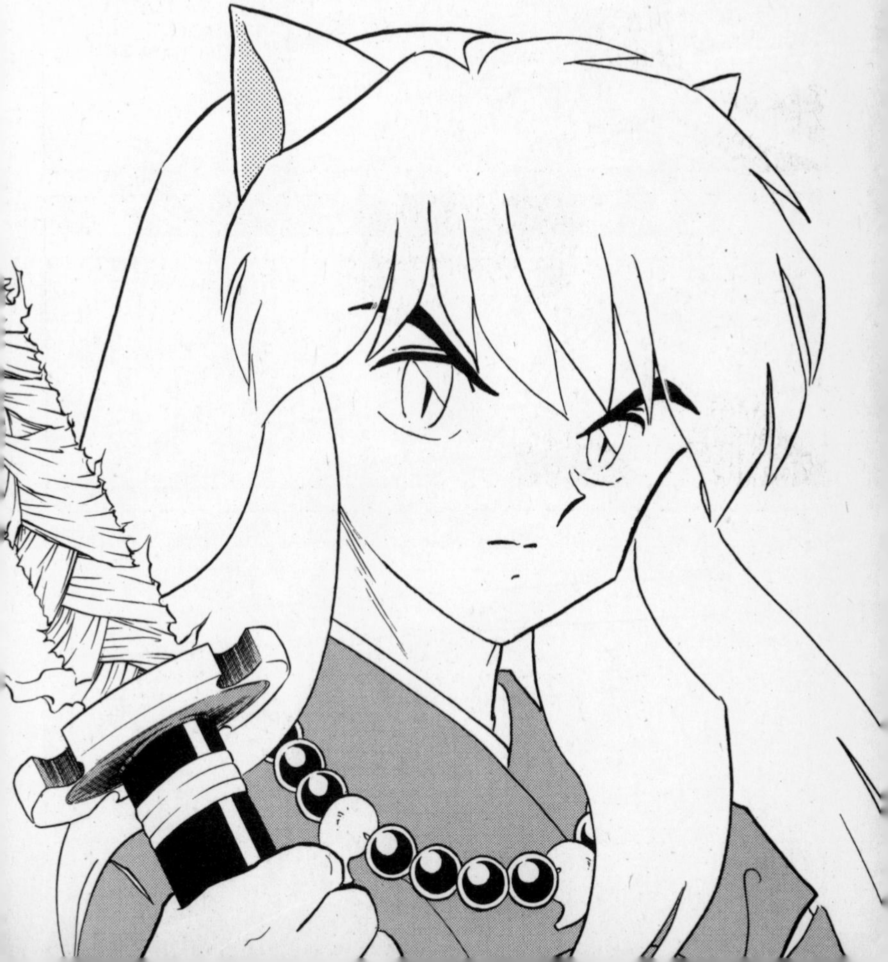

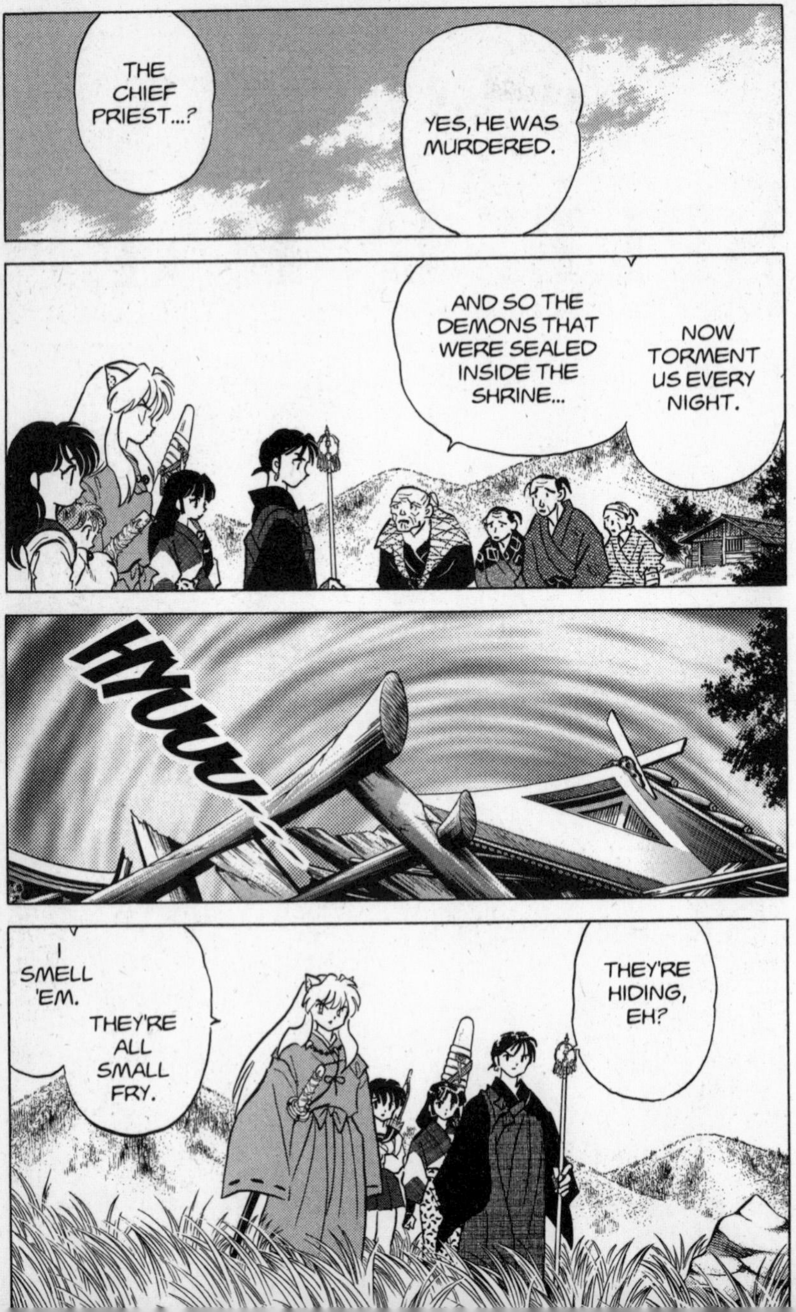
THE CHIEF PRIEST...?
YES, HE WAS MURDERED.
AND SO THE DEMONS THAT WERE SEALED INSIDE THE SHRINE...
NOW TORMENT US EVERY NIGHT.
HYUUU
I SMELL 'EM.
THEY'RE ALL SMALL FRY.
THEY'RE HIDING, EH?

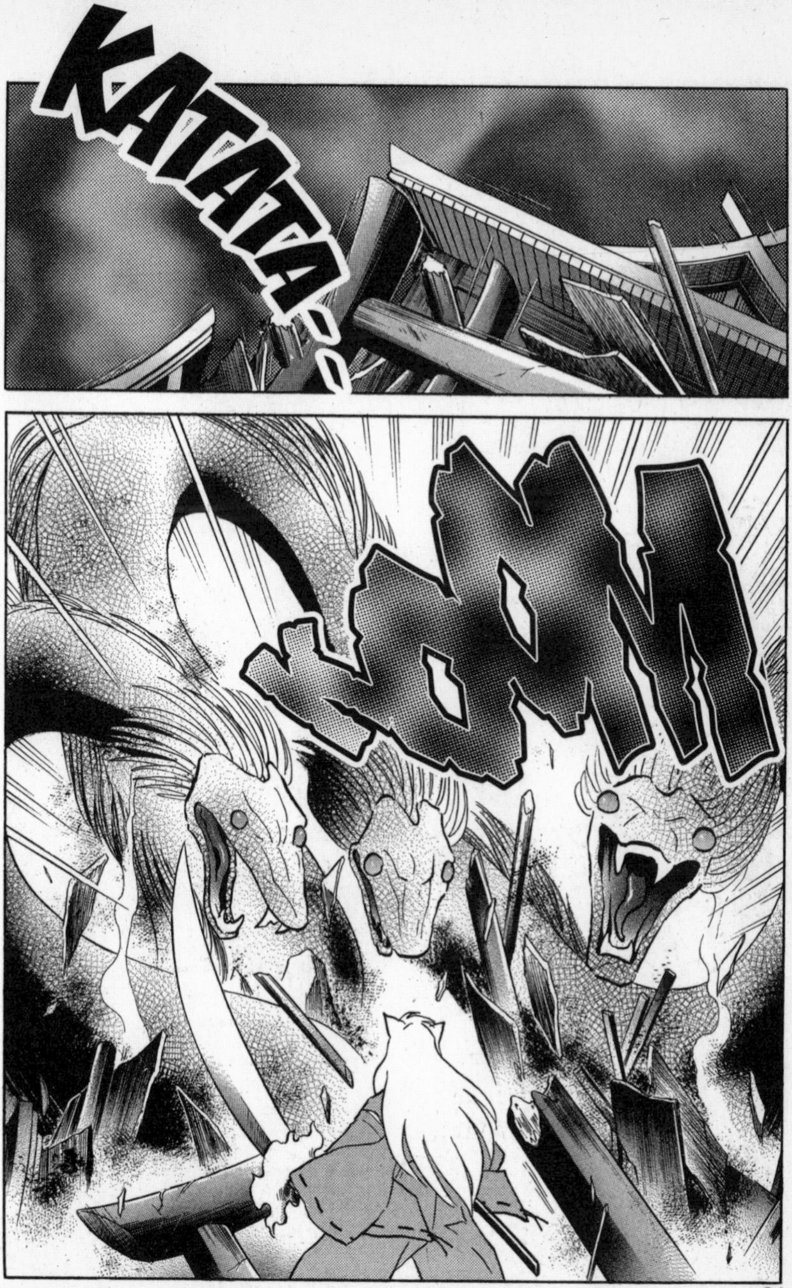
KATATA...

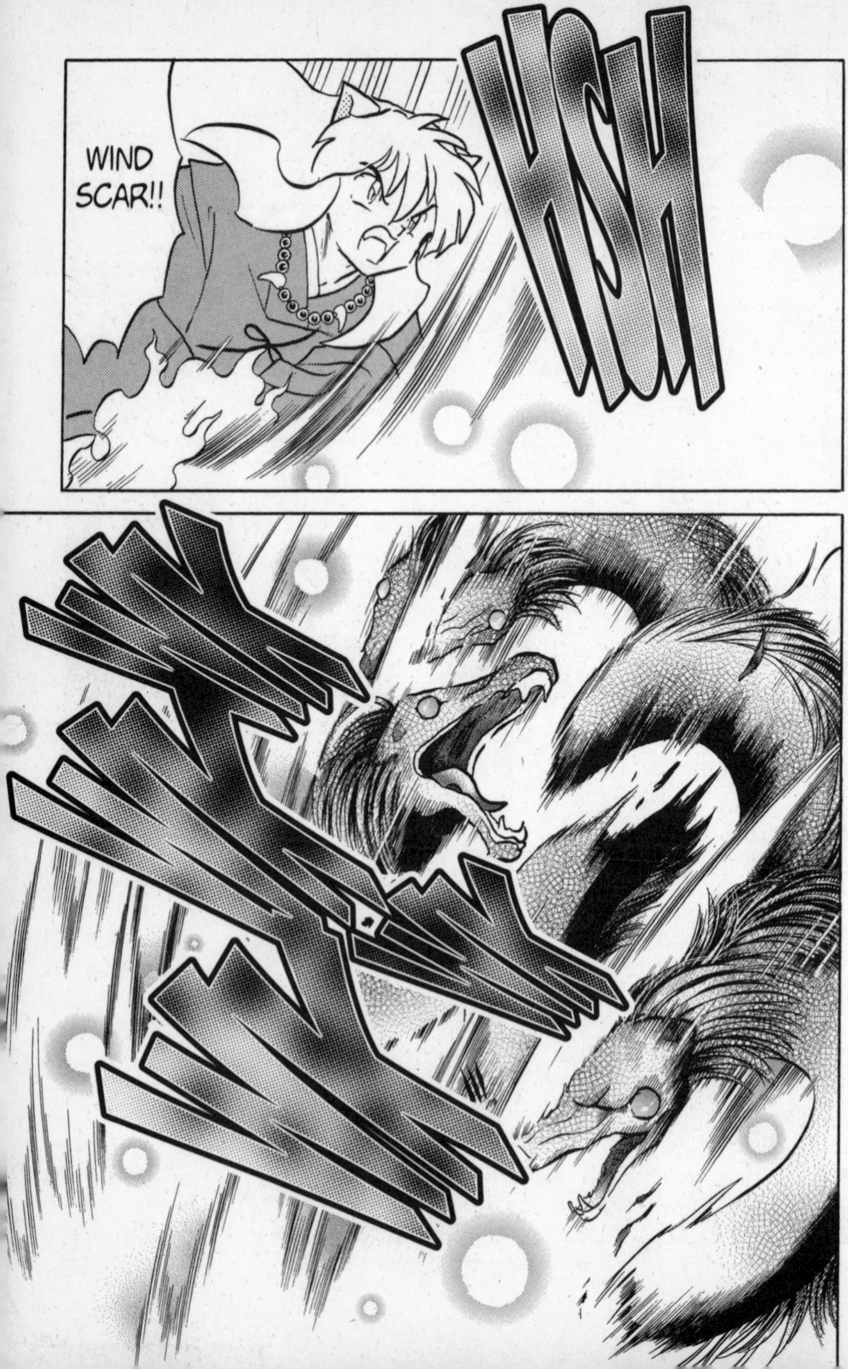
WIND SCAR!!
HSH

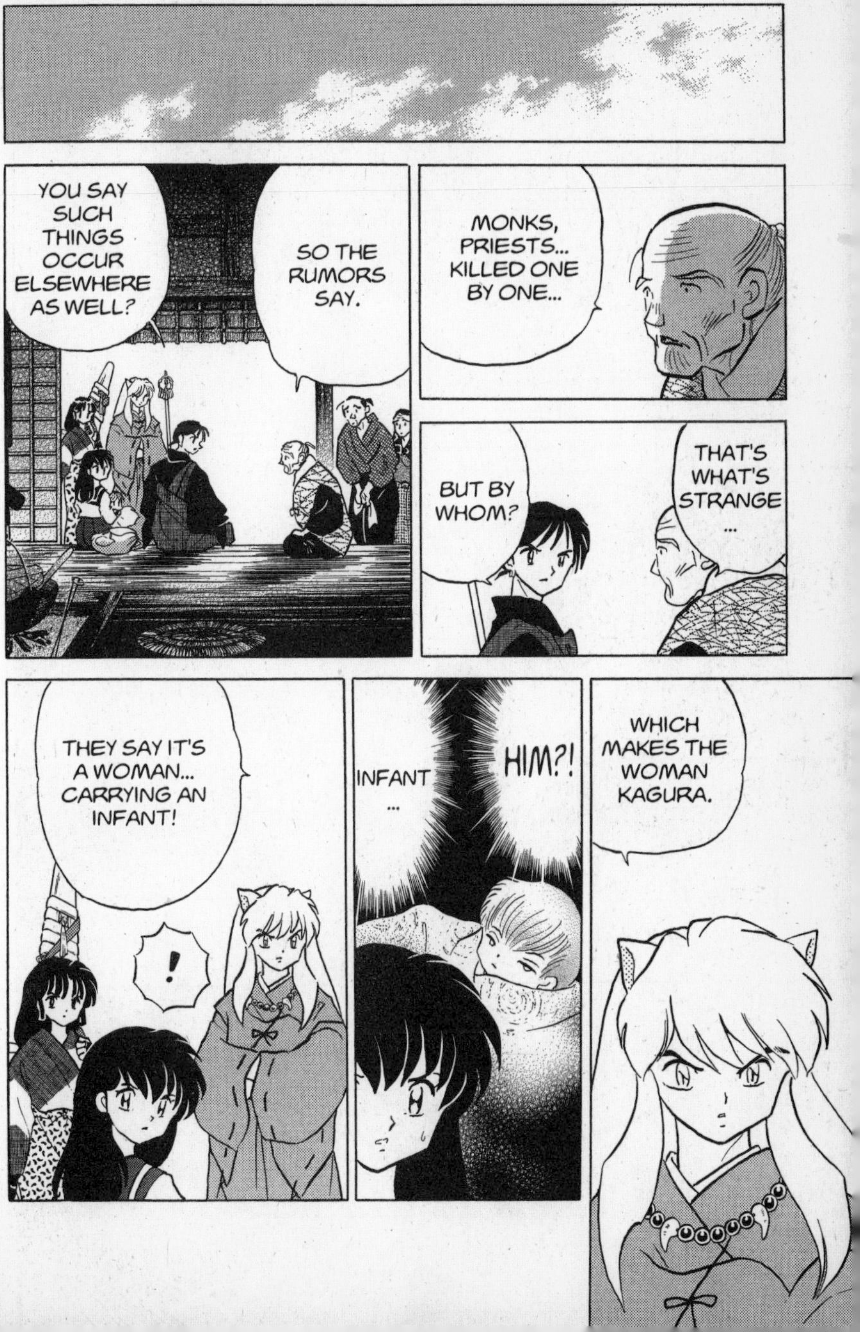
YOU SAY SUCH THINGS OCCUR ELSEWHERE AS WELL?
SO THE RUMORS SAY.
MONKS, PRIESTS... KILLED ONE BY ONE...
BUT BY WHOM?
THAT'S WHAT'S STRANGE ...
THEY SAY IT'S A WOMAN... CARRYING AN INFANT!
!
INFANT ...
HIM?!
WHICH MAKES THE WOMAN KAGURA.

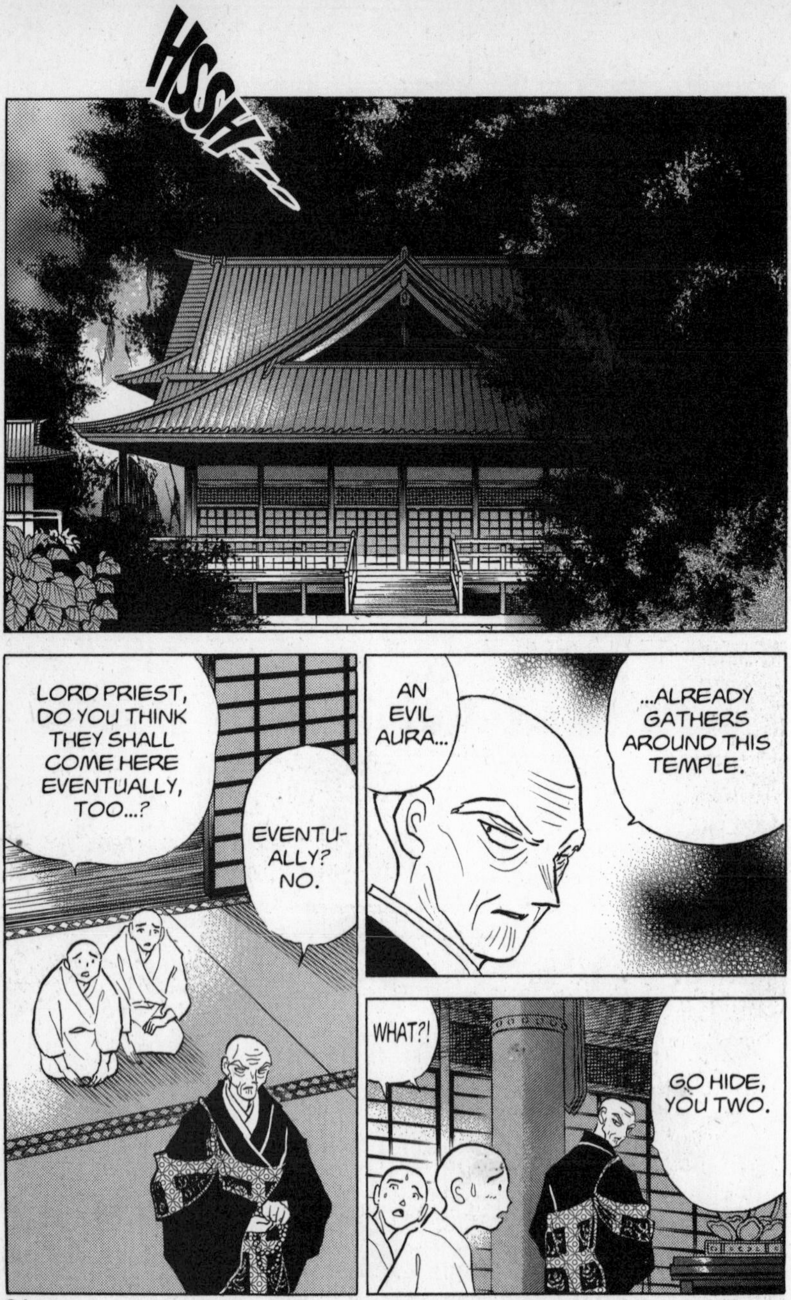
HSSHOO
LORD PRIEST, DO YOU THINK THEY SHALL COME HERE EVENTUALLY, TOO...?
EVENTU-ALLY? NO.
AN EVIL AURA...
...ALREADY GATHERS AROUND THIS TEMPLE.
WHAT?!
GO HIDE, YOU TWO.

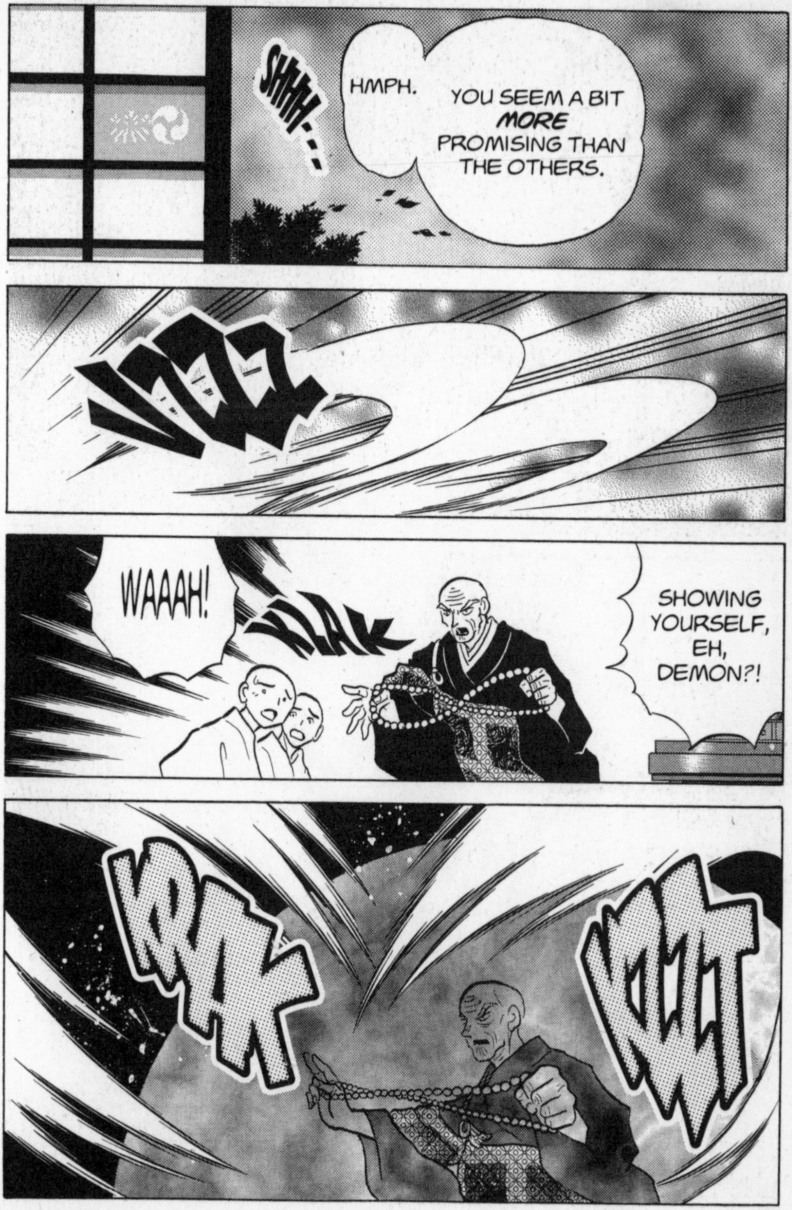

SHHH...
HMPH.
YOU SEEM A BIT **MORE** PROMISING THAN THE OTHERS.
VZZZ
WAAAH!
KLAK
SHOWING YOURSELF, EH, DEMON?!
KRAK
KRZZT

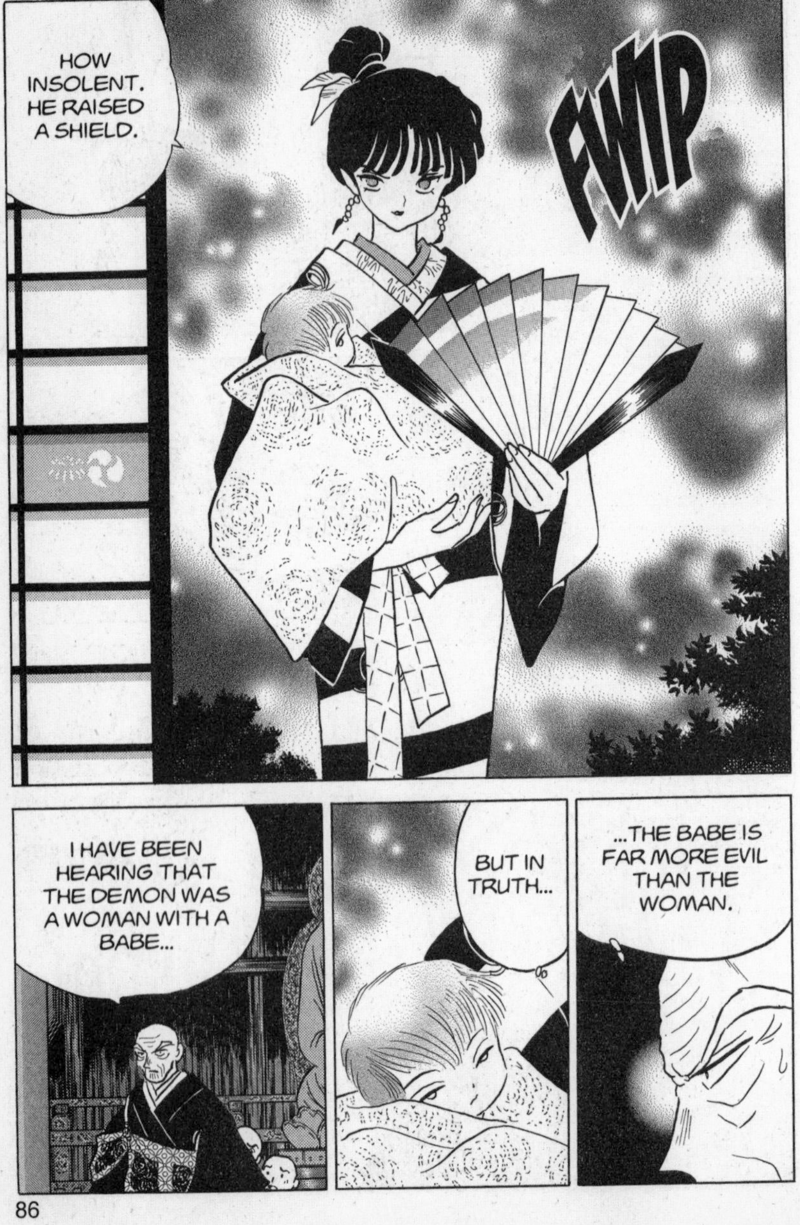
HOW INSOLENT. HE RAISED A SHIELD.
FWIP
I HAVE BEEN HEARING THAT THE DEMON WAS A WOMAN WITH A BABE...
BUT IN TRUTH...
...THE BABE IS FAR MORE EVIL THAN THE WOMAN.

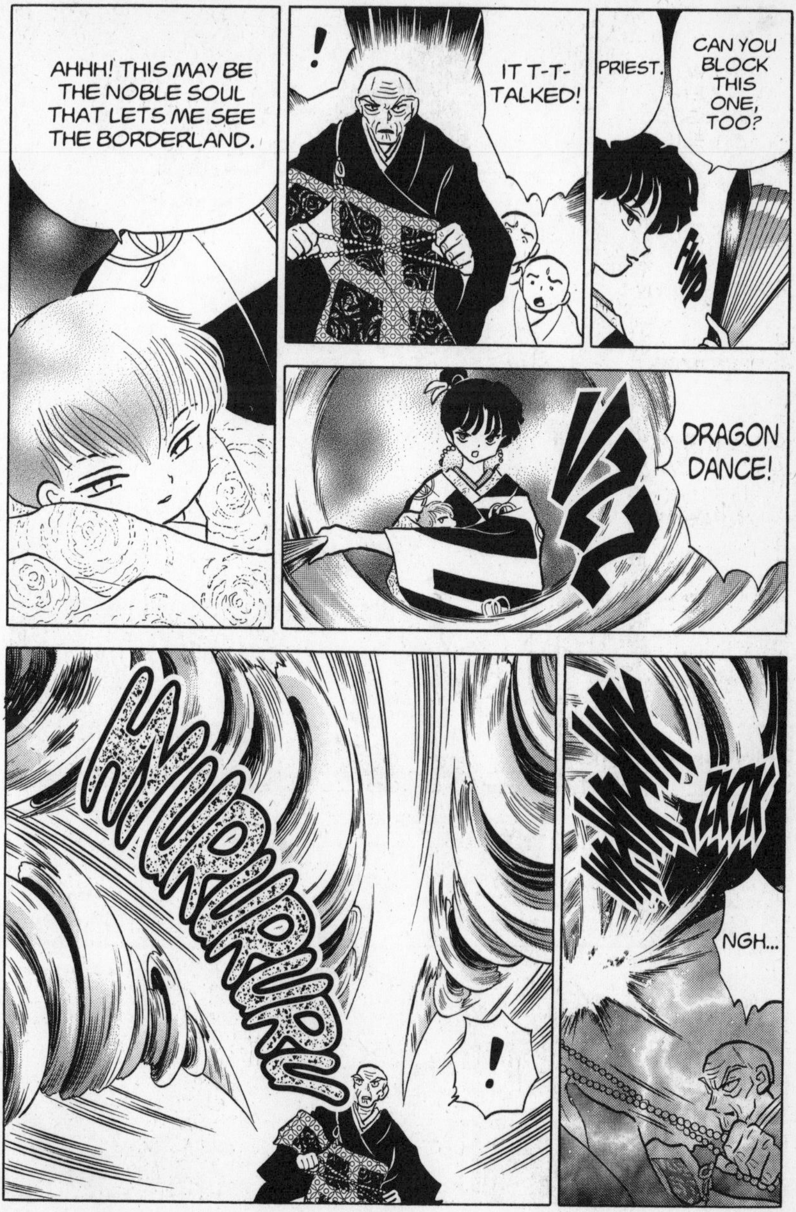
CAN YOU BLOCK THIS ONE, TOO?
PRIEST.
FWIP
IT T-T-TALKED!
!
AHHH! THIS MAY BE THE NOBLE SOUL THAT LETS ME SEE THE BORDERLAND.
DRAGON DANCE!
NGH...
!

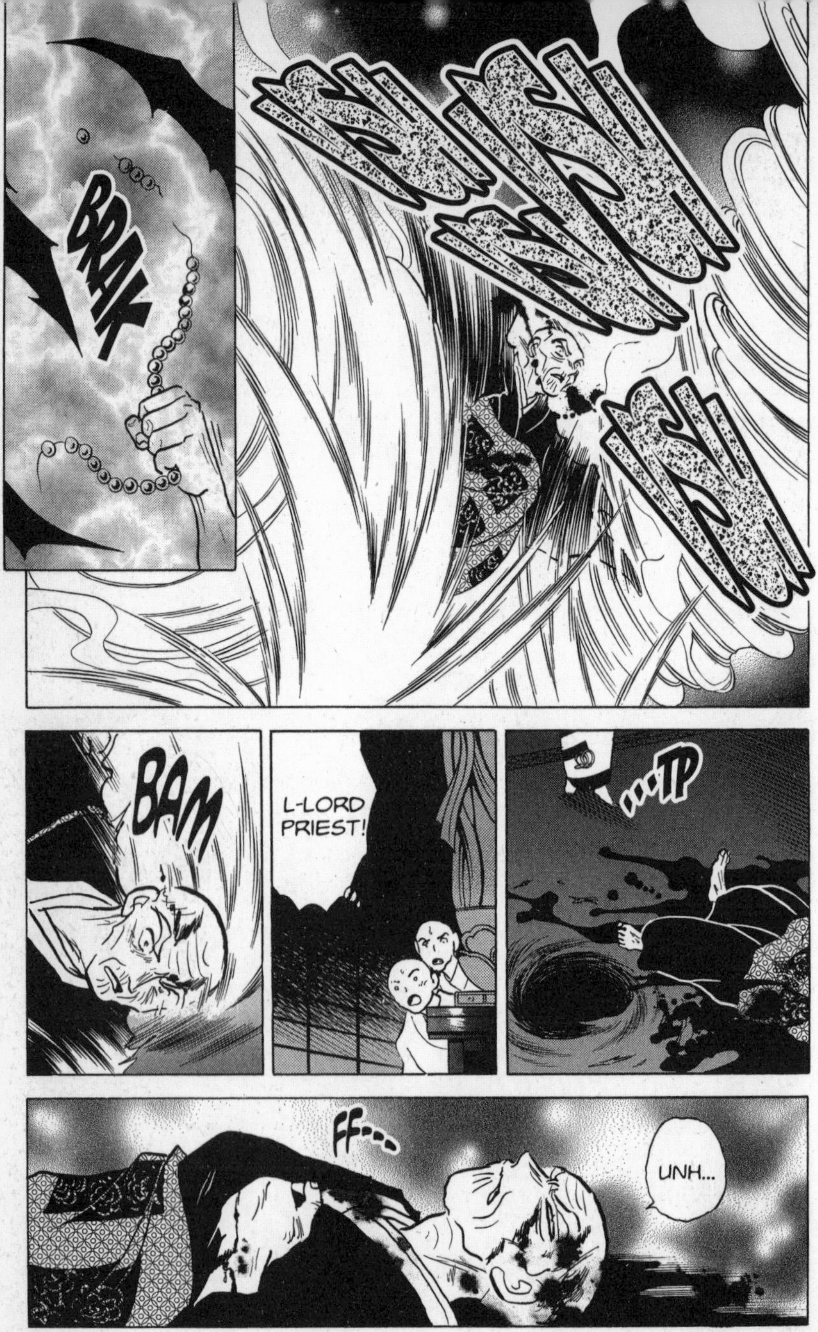
BRAK
BAM
L-LORD PRIEST!
...TP
FF...
UNH...

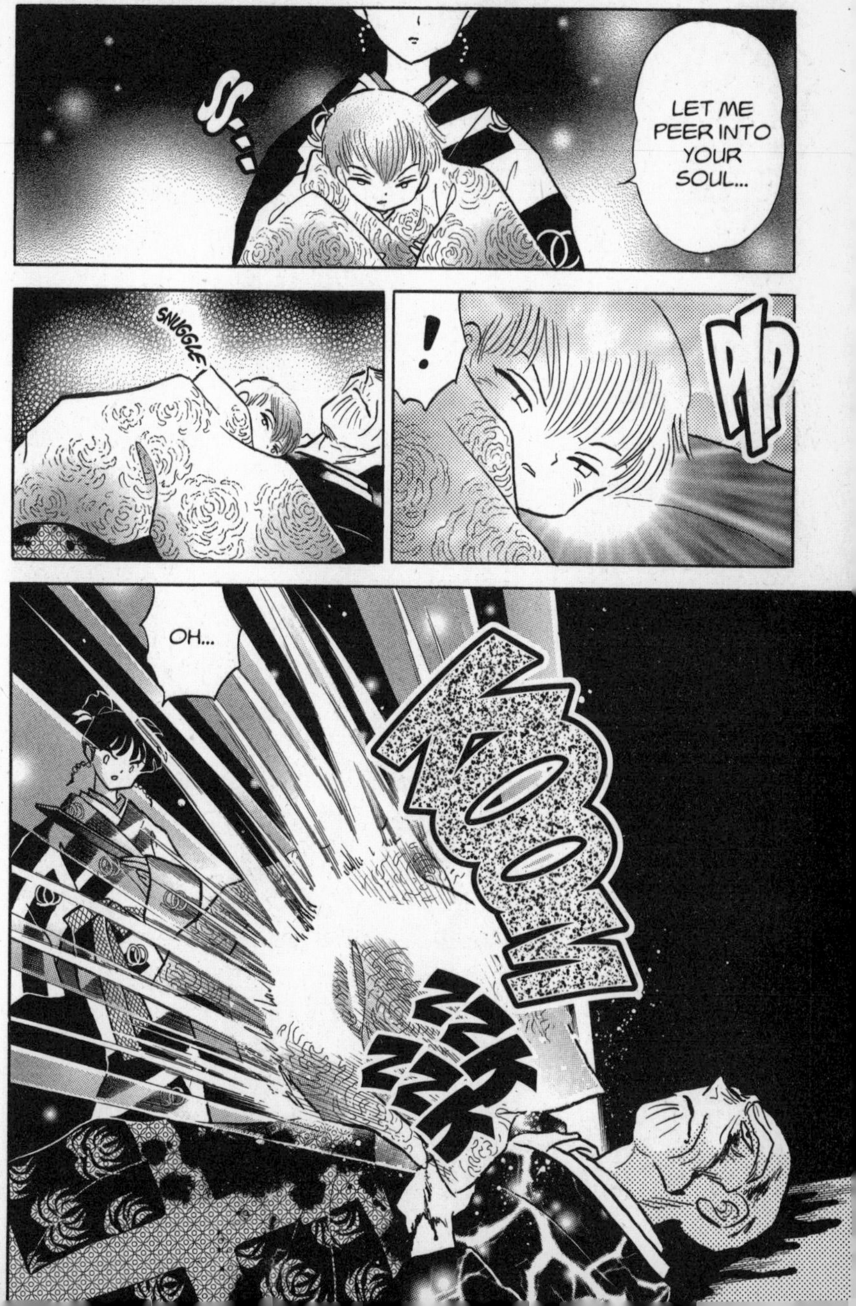

LET ME PEER INTO YOUR SOUL...
SS...
SNUGGLE
!
PIP
OH...
VOOM!!
ZZZ
ZZZ

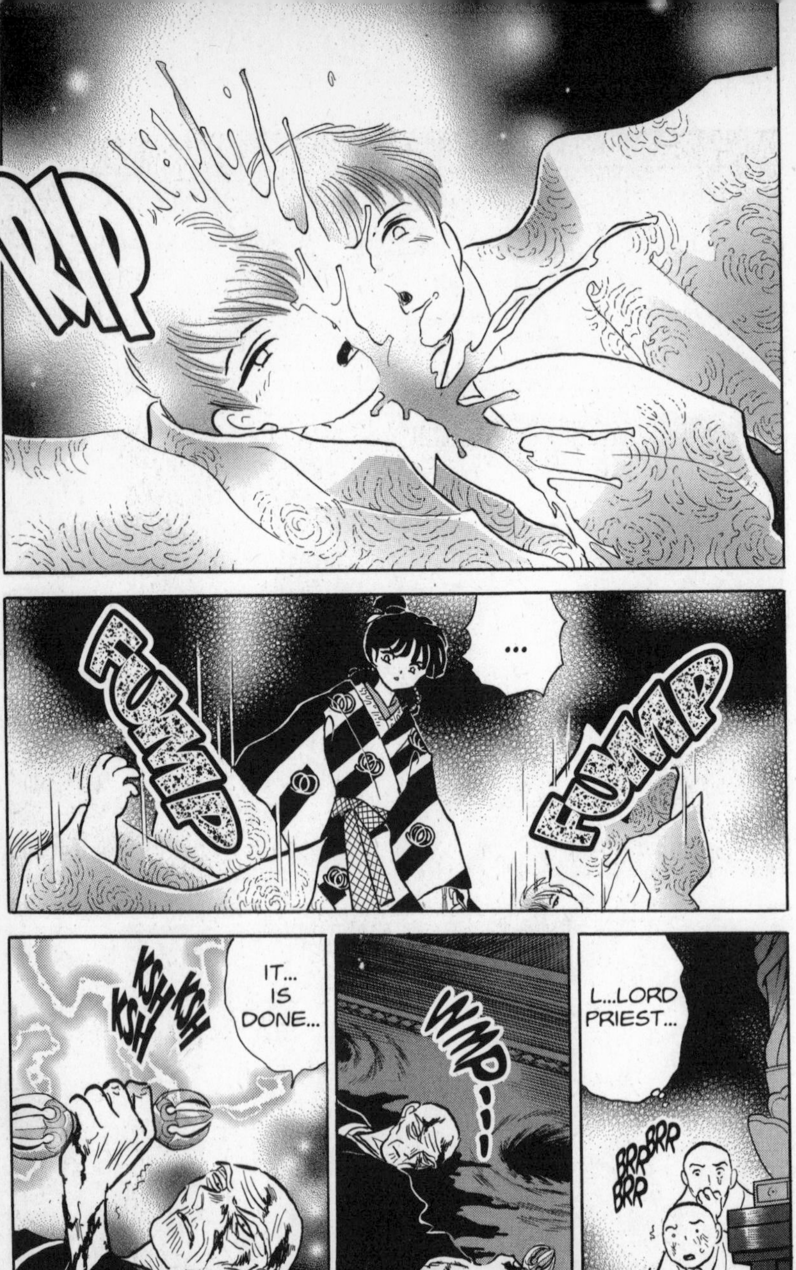
RIP
FUMP
...
FUMP
KSH KSH KSH
IT... IS DONE...
WMP...
L...LORD PRIEST...
BRR BRR BRR

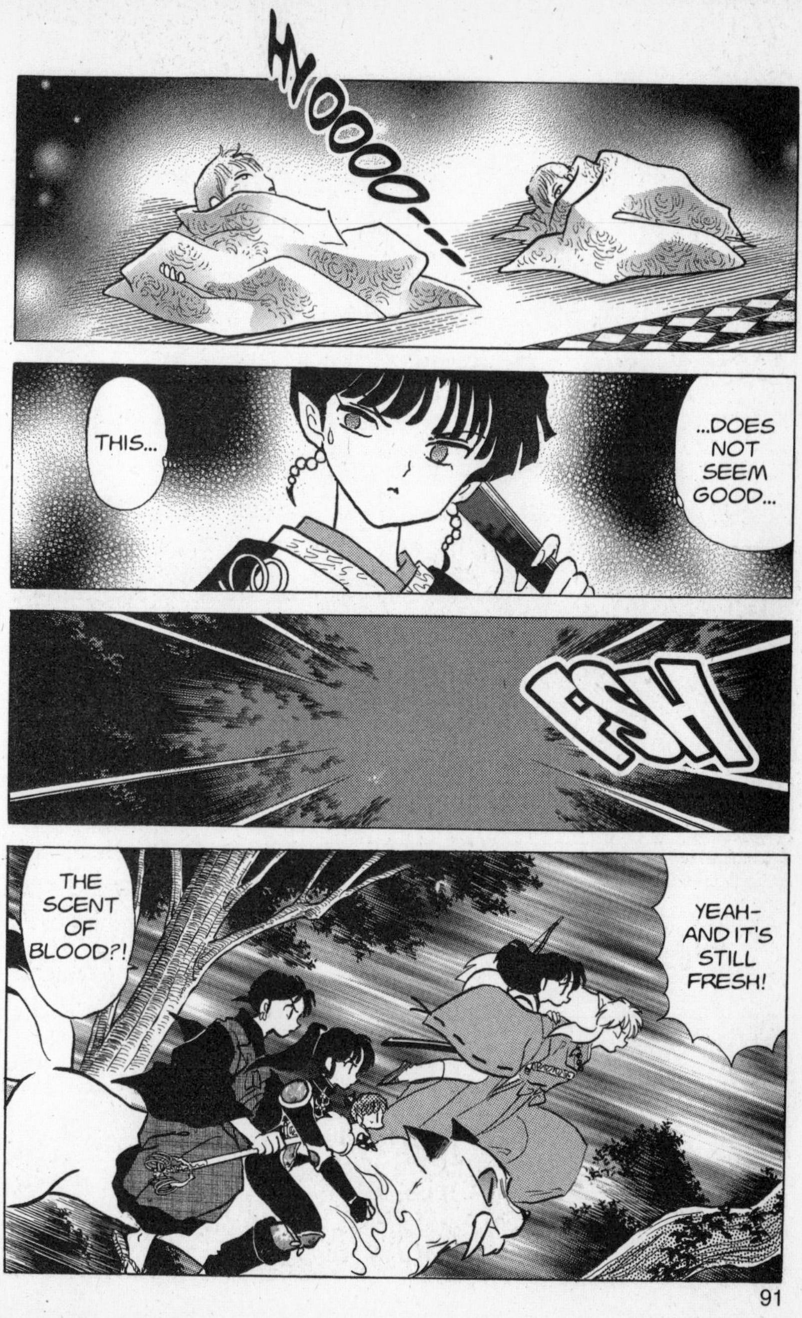
HYOOOO...!!
THIS...
...DOES NOT SEEM GOOD...
FSH
THE SCENT OF BLOOD?!
YEAH- AND IT'S STILL FRESH!

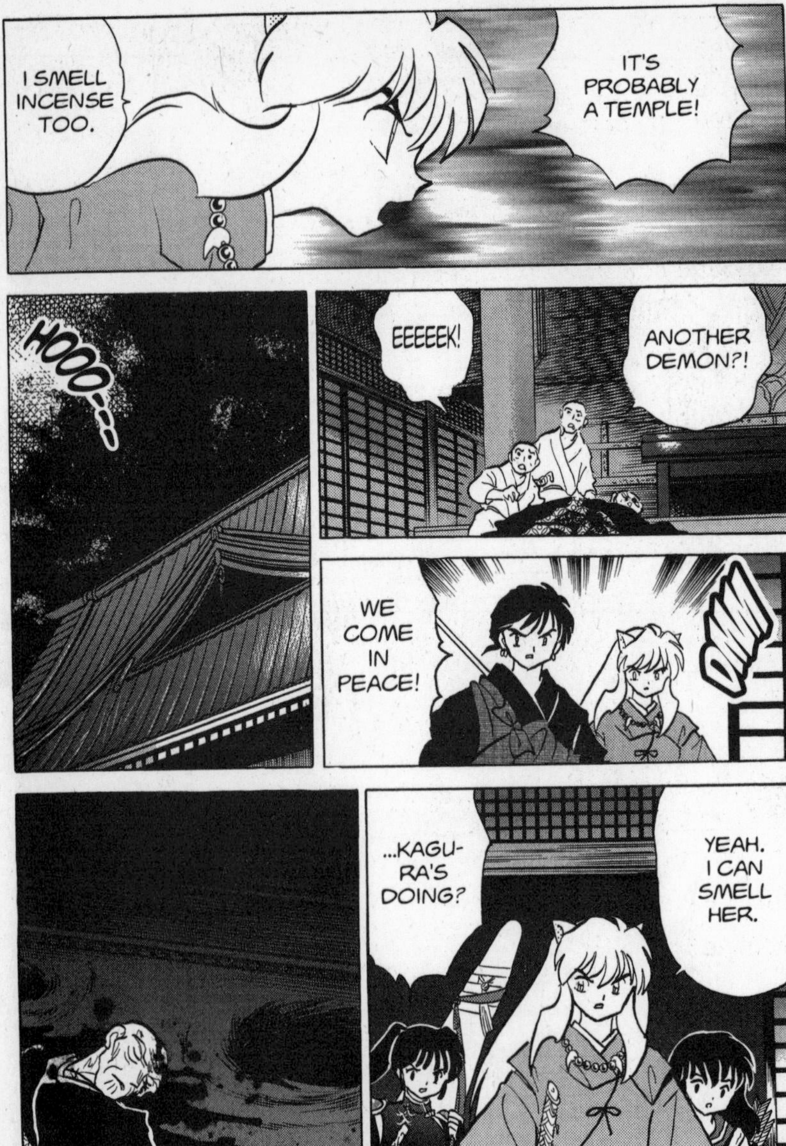
I SMELL INCENSE TOO.
IT'S PROBABLY A TEMPLE!
HOOO...
EEEEEK!
ANOTHER DEMON?!
WE COME IN PEACE!
...KAGU-RA'S DOING?
YEAH. I CAN SMELL HER.

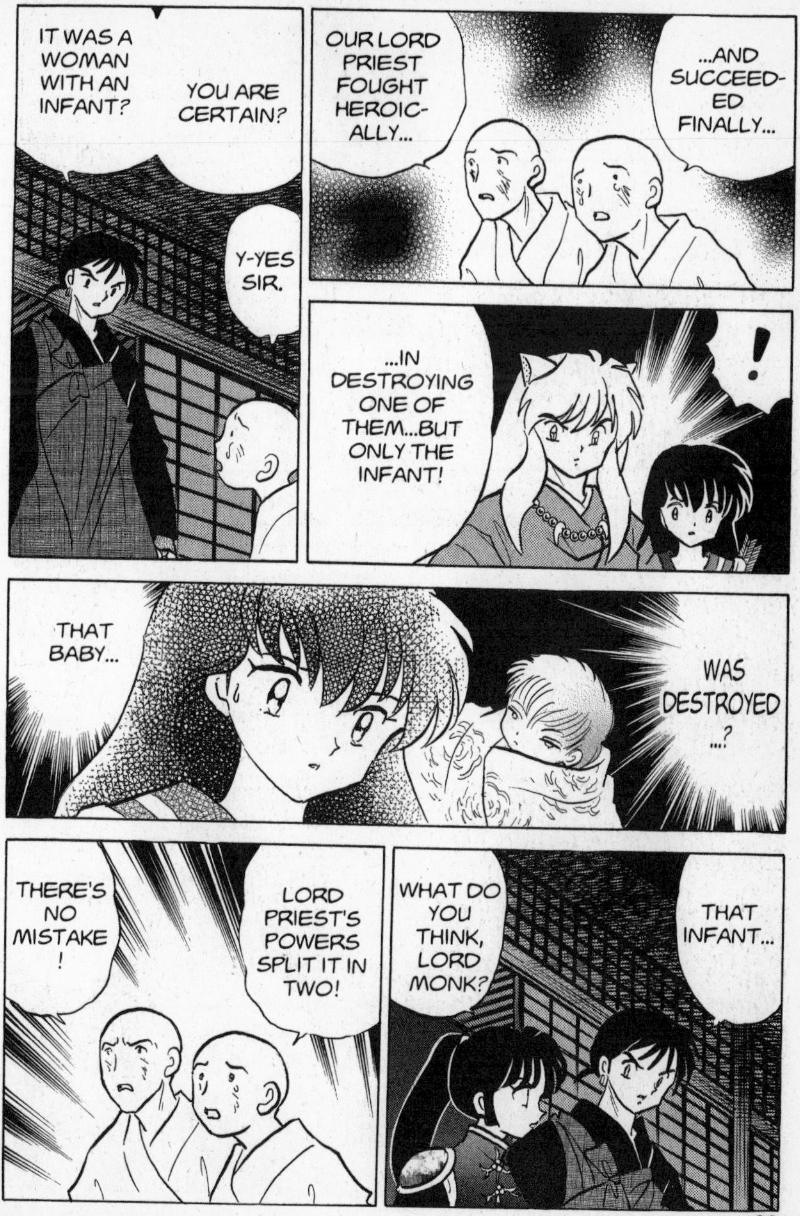
IT WAS A WOMAN WITH AN INFANT?
YOU ARE CERTAIN?
Y-YES SIR.
OUR LORD PRIEST FOUGHT HEROIC-ALLY...
...AND SUCCEED-ED FINALLY...
...IN DESTROYING ONE OF THEM...BUT ONLY THE INFANT!
!
THAT BABY...
WAS DESTROYED ...?
THERE'S NO MISTAKE !
LORD PRIEST'S POWERS SPLIT IT IN TWO!
WHAT DO YOU THINK, LORD MONK?
THAT INFANT...

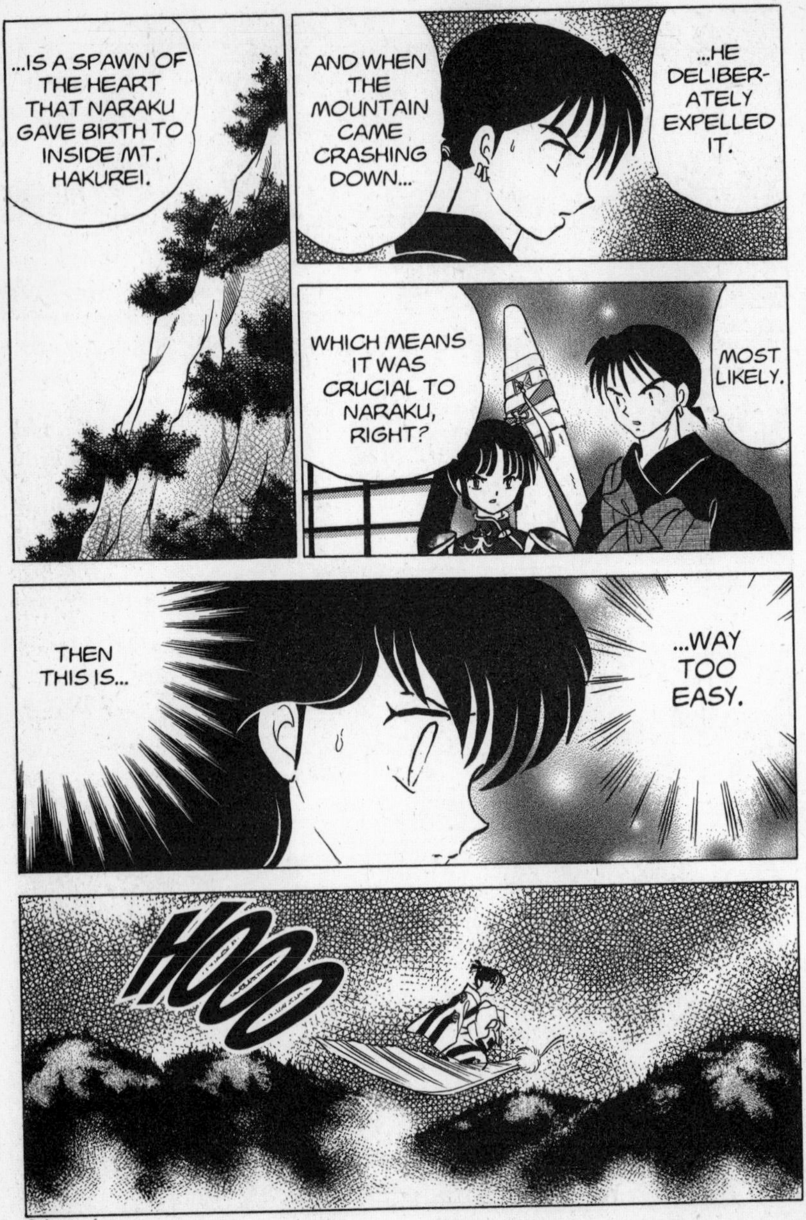
...IS A SPAWN OF THE HEART THAT NARAKU GAVE BIRTH TO INSIDE MT. HAKUREI.
AND WHEN THE MOUNTAIN CAME CRASHING DOWN...
...HE DELIBER-ATELY EXPELLED IT.
WHICH MEANS IT WAS CRUCIAL TO NARAKU, RIGHT?
MOST LIKELY.
THEN THIS IS...
...WAY TOO EASY.
HOOO

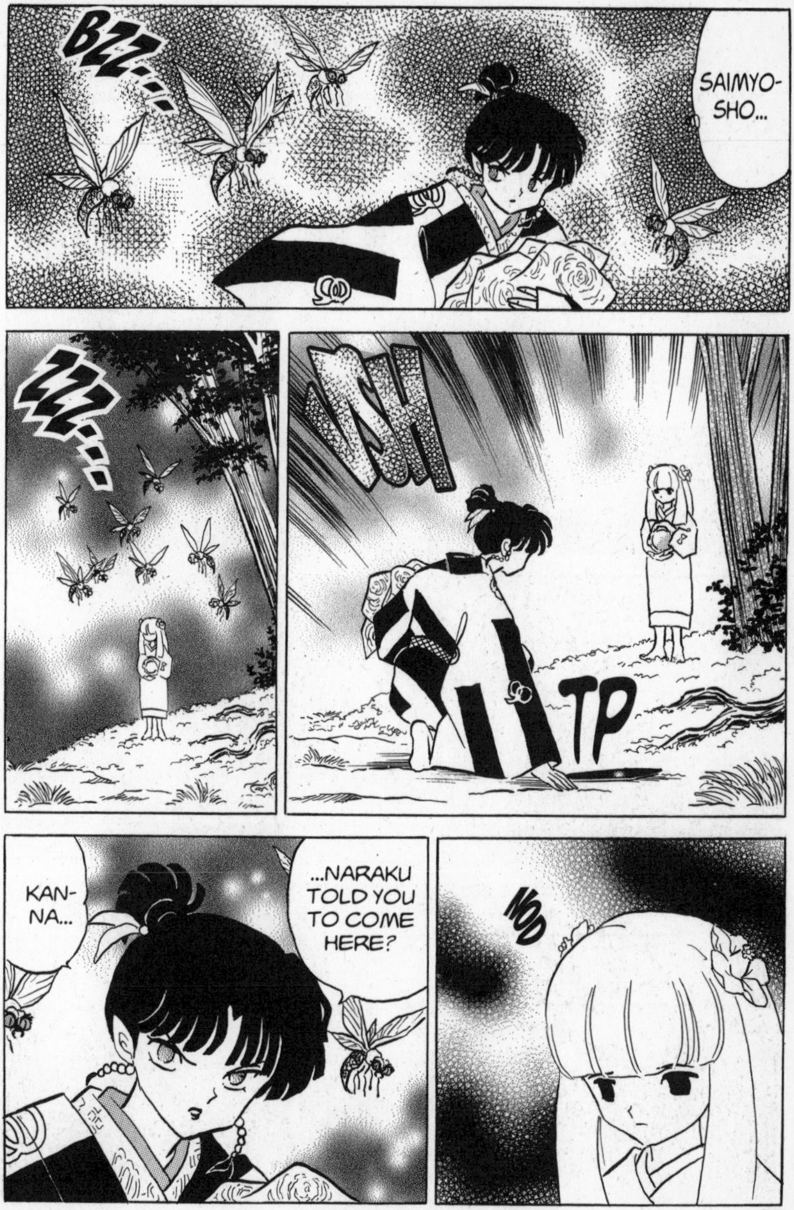
BZZ...
SAIMYO-SHO...
ZZZ...
WSH
TP
KAN-NA...
...NARAKU TOLD YOU TO COME HERE?
NOD

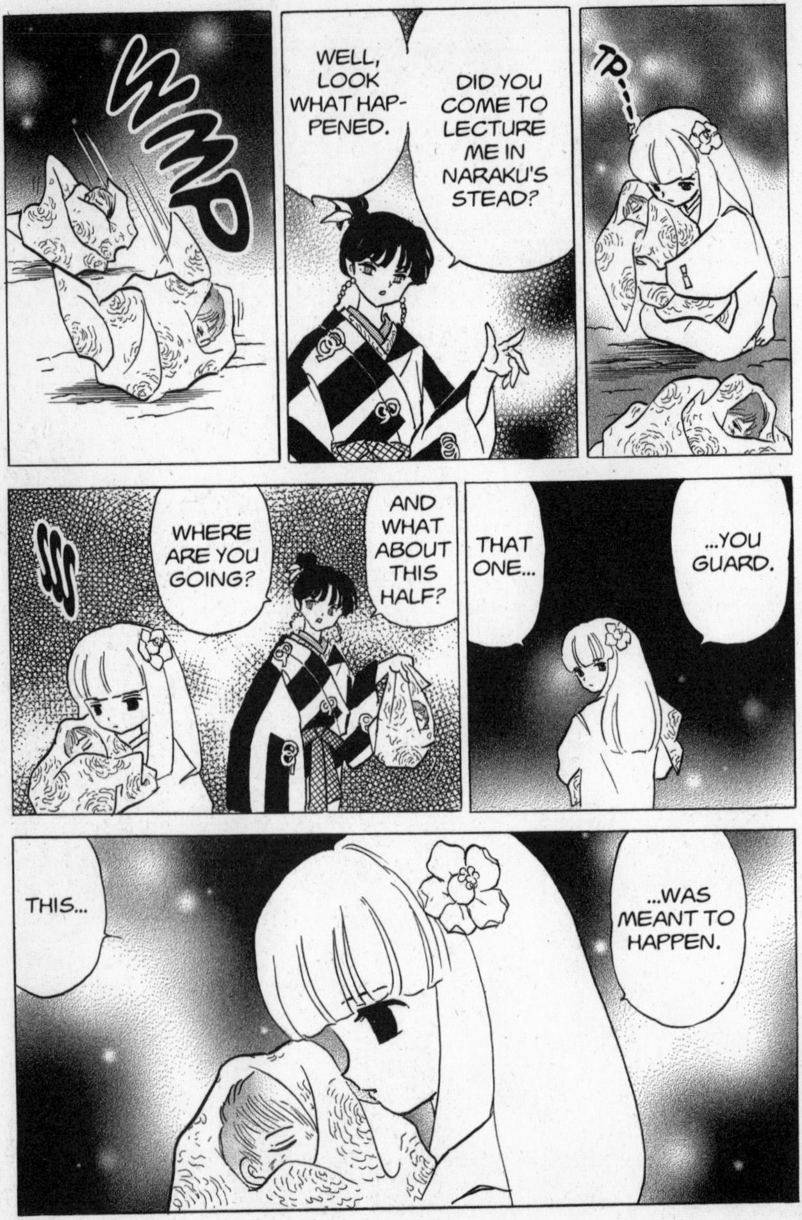
WMP
WELL, LOOK WHAT HAP-PENED.
DID YOU COME TO LECTURE ME IN NARAKU'S STEAD?
TP...
SSS
WHERE ARE YOU GOING?
AND WHAT ABOUT THIS HALF?
THAT ONE...
...YOU GUARD.
THIS...
...WAS MEANT TO HAPPEN.

SCROLL 6
THE BLAZING HOOF

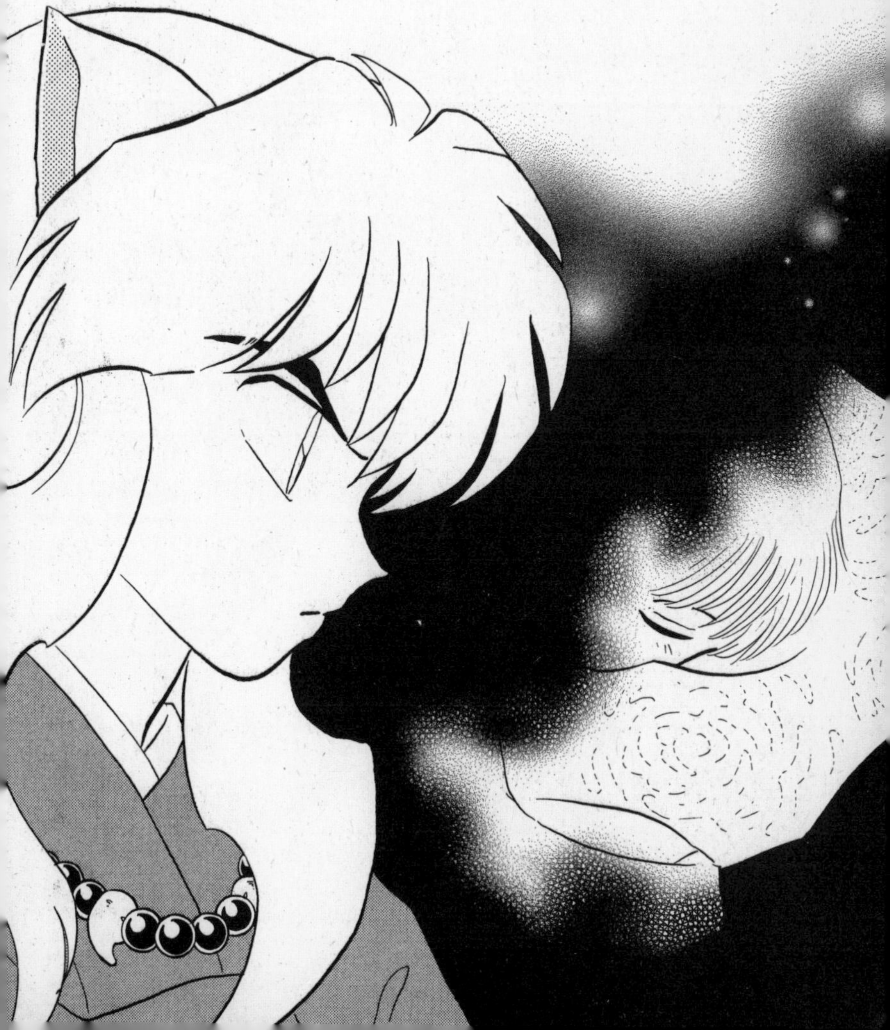

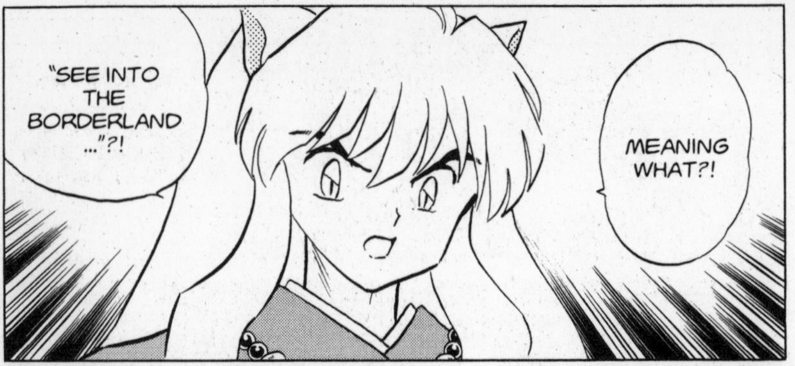
"SEE INTO THE BORDERLAND ..."?!
MEANING WHAT?!

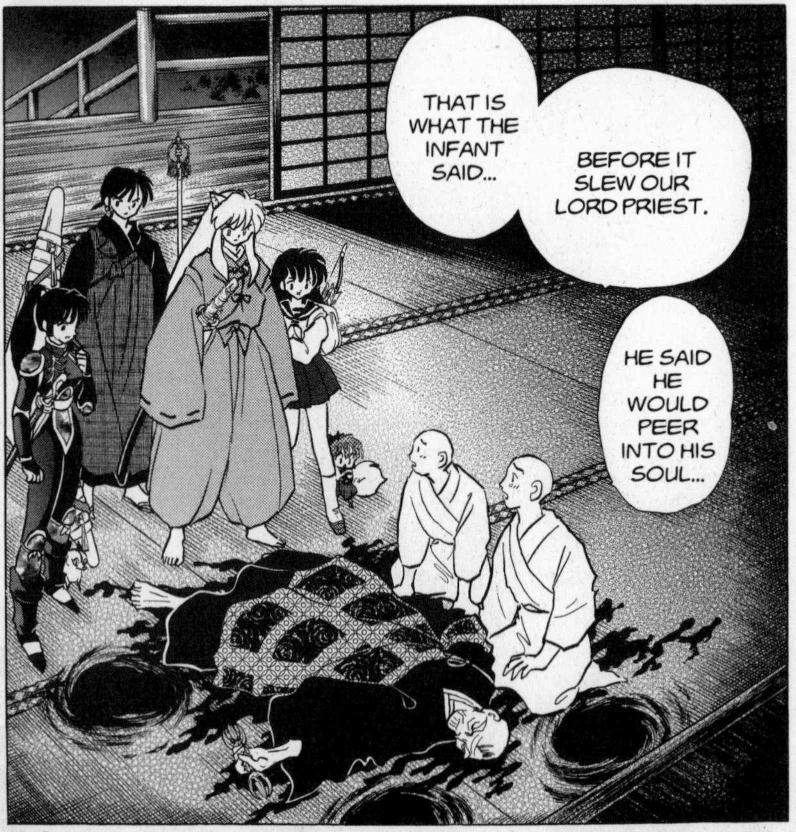
THAT IS WHAT THE INFANT SAID...
BEFORE IT SLEW OUR LORD PRIEST.
HE SAID HE WOULD PEER INTO HIS SOUL...

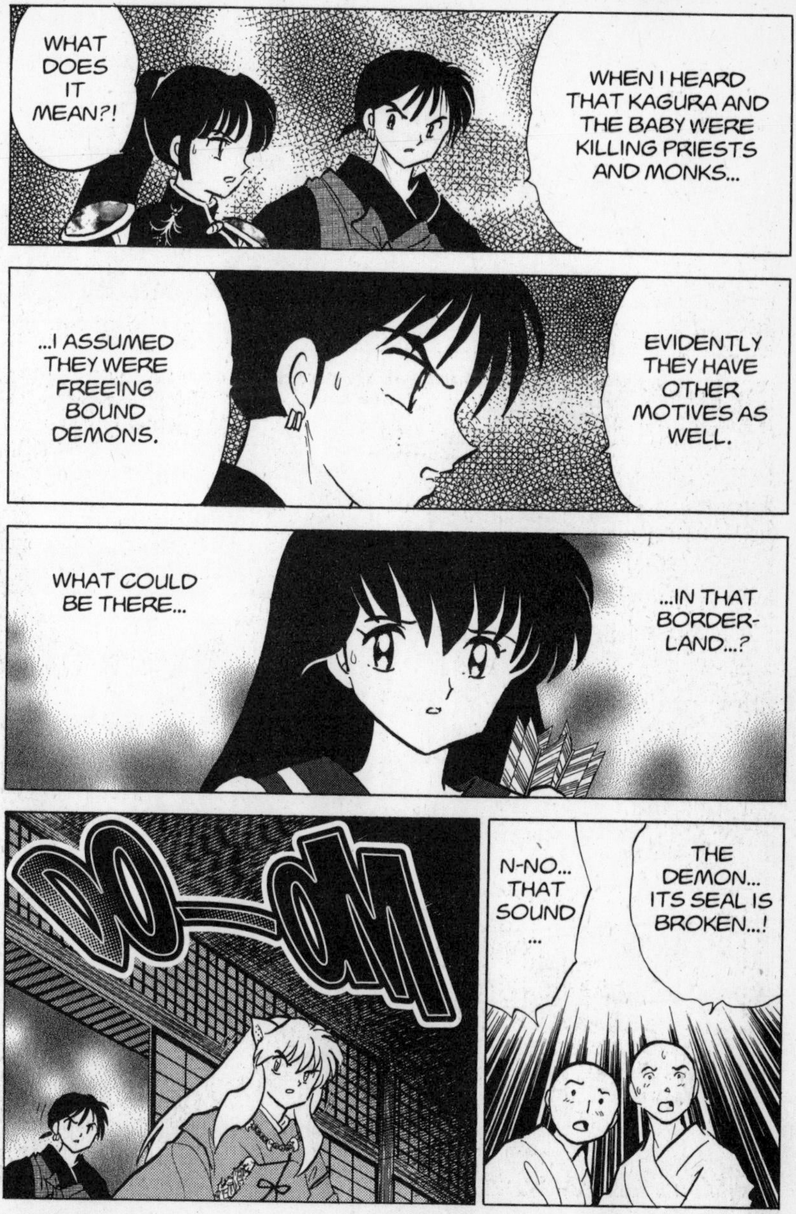
WHAT DOES IT MEAN?!
WHEN I HEARD THAT KAGURA AND THE BABY WERE KILLING PRIESTS AND MONKS...
...I ASSUMED THEY WERE FREEING BOUND DEMONS.
EVIDENTLY THEY HAVE OTHER MOTIVES AS WELL.
WHAT COULD BE THERE...
...IN THAT BORDER-LAND...?
DO-OM
N-NO... THAT SOUND...
THE DEMON... ITS SEAL IS BROKEN...!

IN THE MOUNTAIN BEHIND US?!

Y-YES!

A HORSE-DEMON CALLED *ENTEI* THAT OUR LORD PRIEST BARELY MANAGED TO TRAP WITH A MAGIC SEAL!

A HORSE-DEMON?

YES.

TMP TMP

HE IS SAID TO HAVE BELONGED TO A MAN-EATING OGRE BEFORE HE WAS SEALED AWAY.

DOOM

KKKK KKKK KKKK KKKK

DHAK

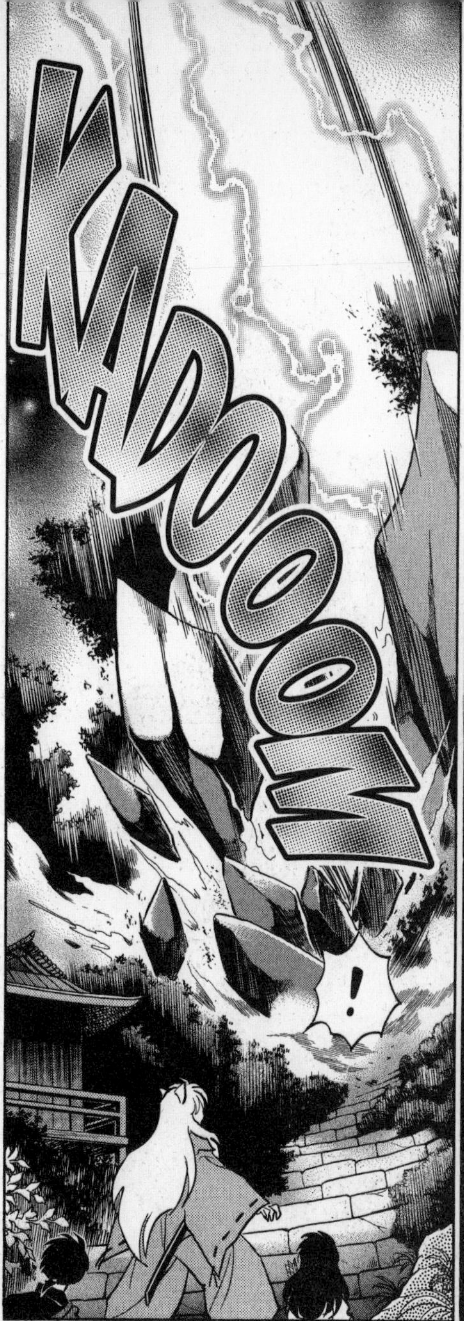
KADOOOM
!
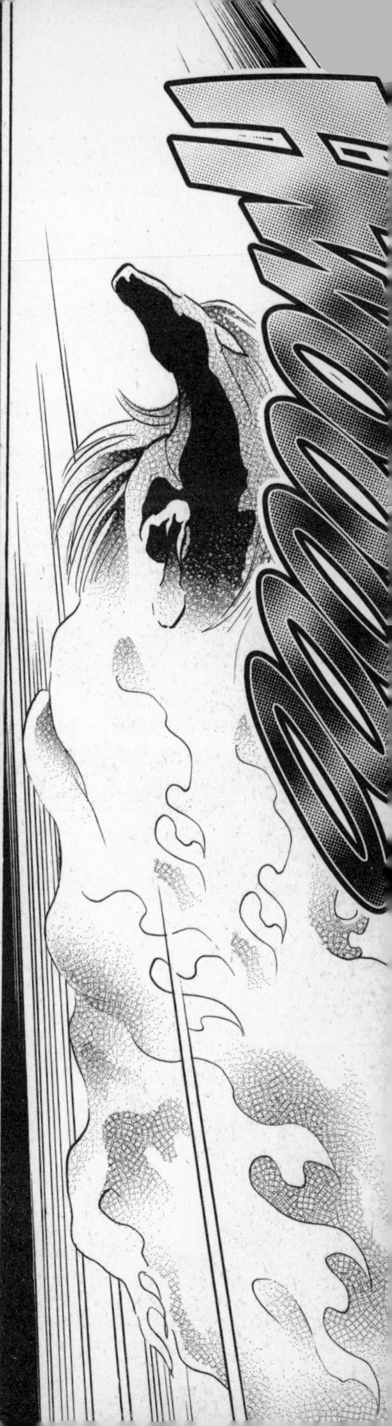

LOOK OUT!

MIASMA!

HSSSH

WHP

...HOOO

WRRR...

RUNNING AWAY...?

AFTER HIM!

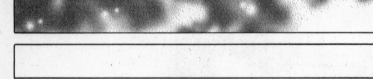

HSH---

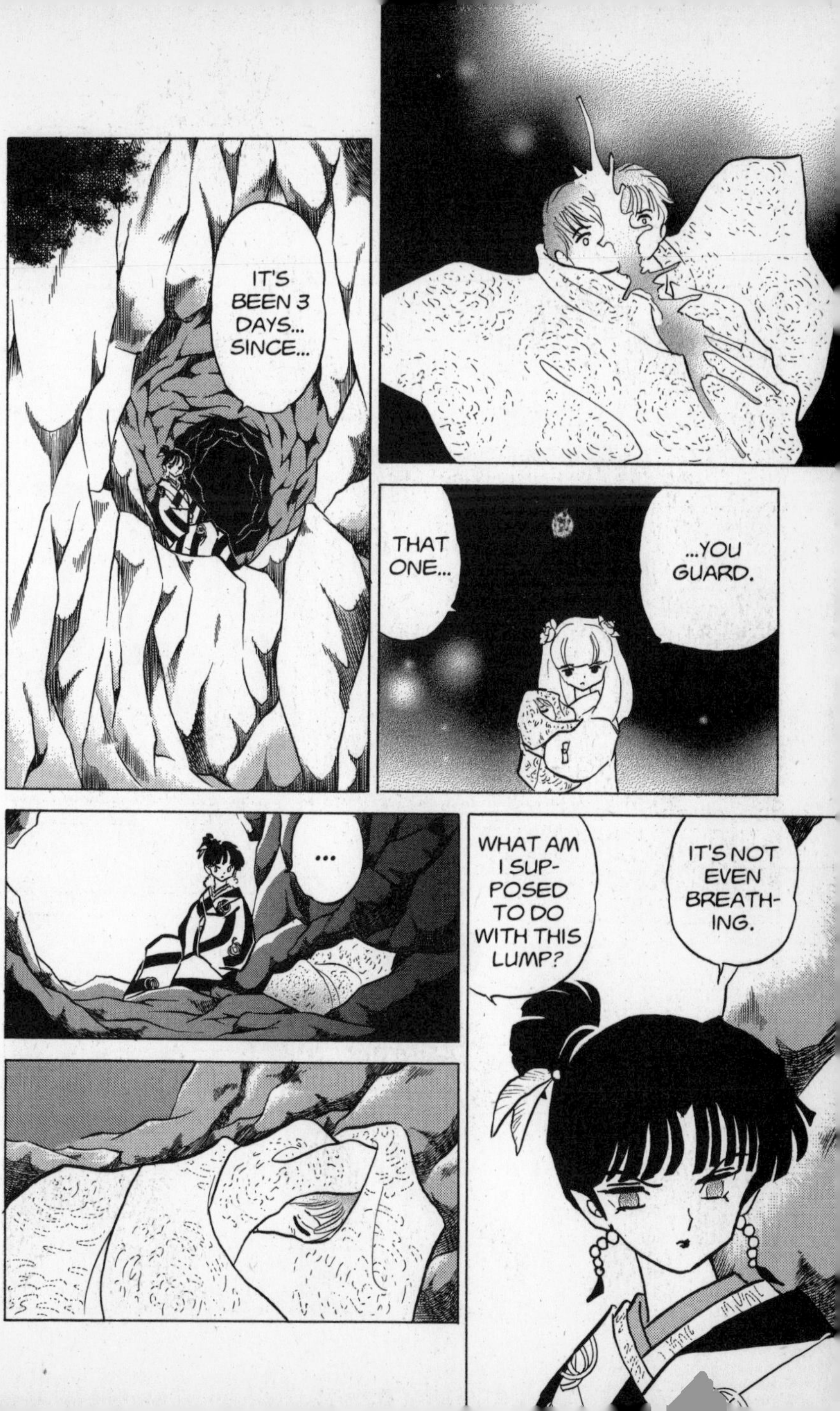
IT'S BEEN 3 DAYS... SINCE...
THAT ONE...
...YOU GUARD.
...
WHAT AM I SUP-POSED TO DO WITH THIS LUMP?
IT'S NOT EVEN BREATH-ING.

SO.

COMING TO LIFE, EH?

TP

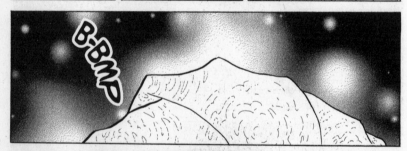

B-BMP

...

HE'S ALIVE...

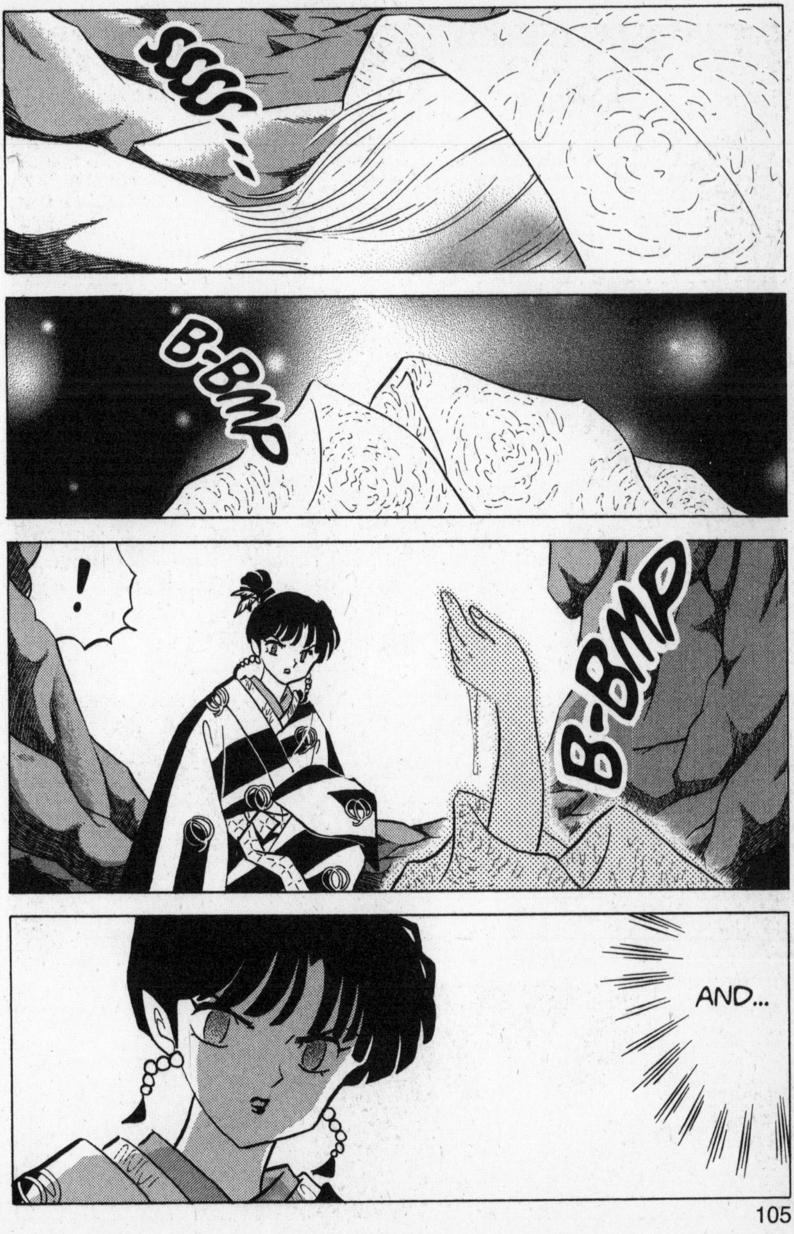
SSSS...
B-BMP
!
B-BMP
AND...

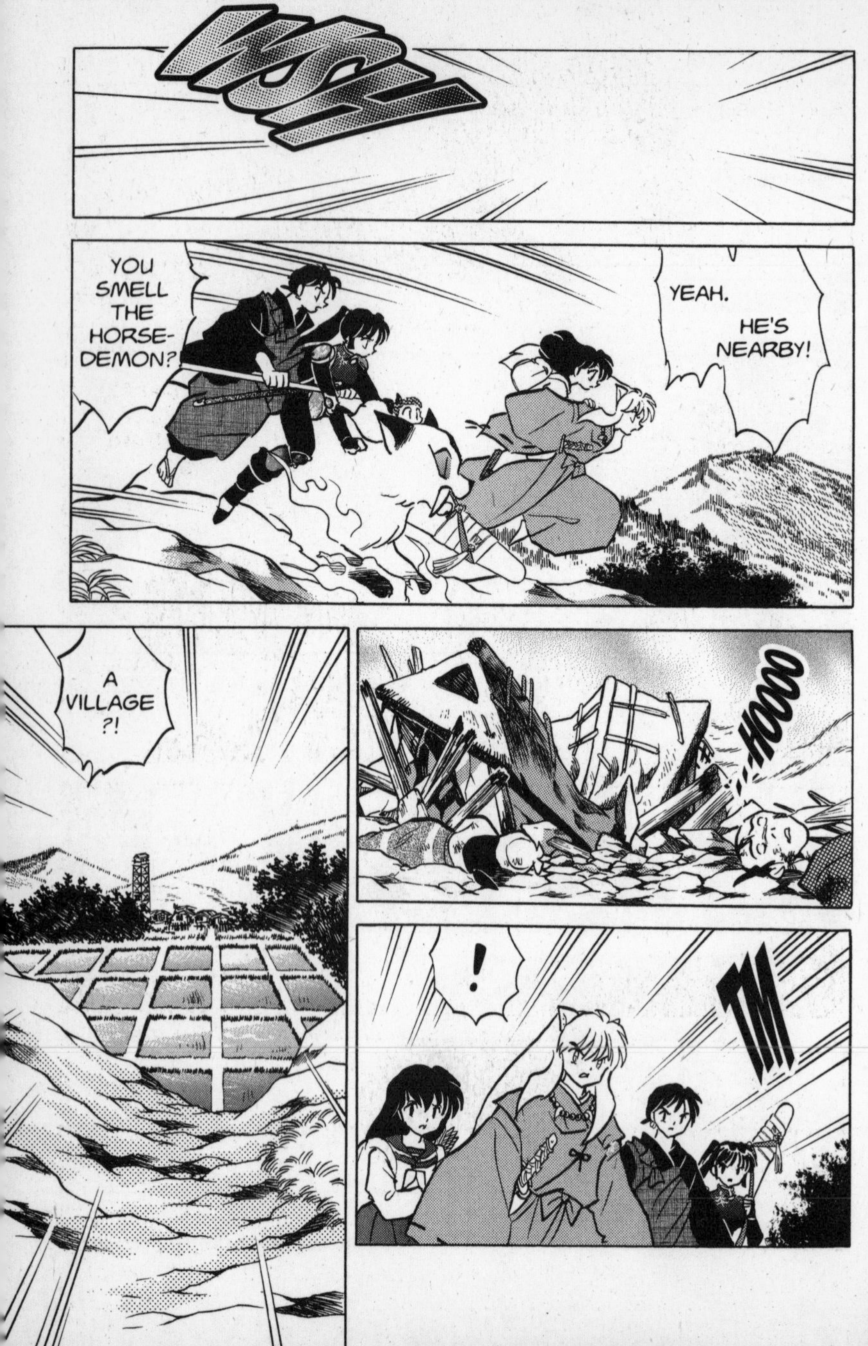
WSH
YOU SMELL THE HORSE-DEMON?
YEAH.
HE'S NEARBY!
A VILLAGE?!
HOOOO
!
TM

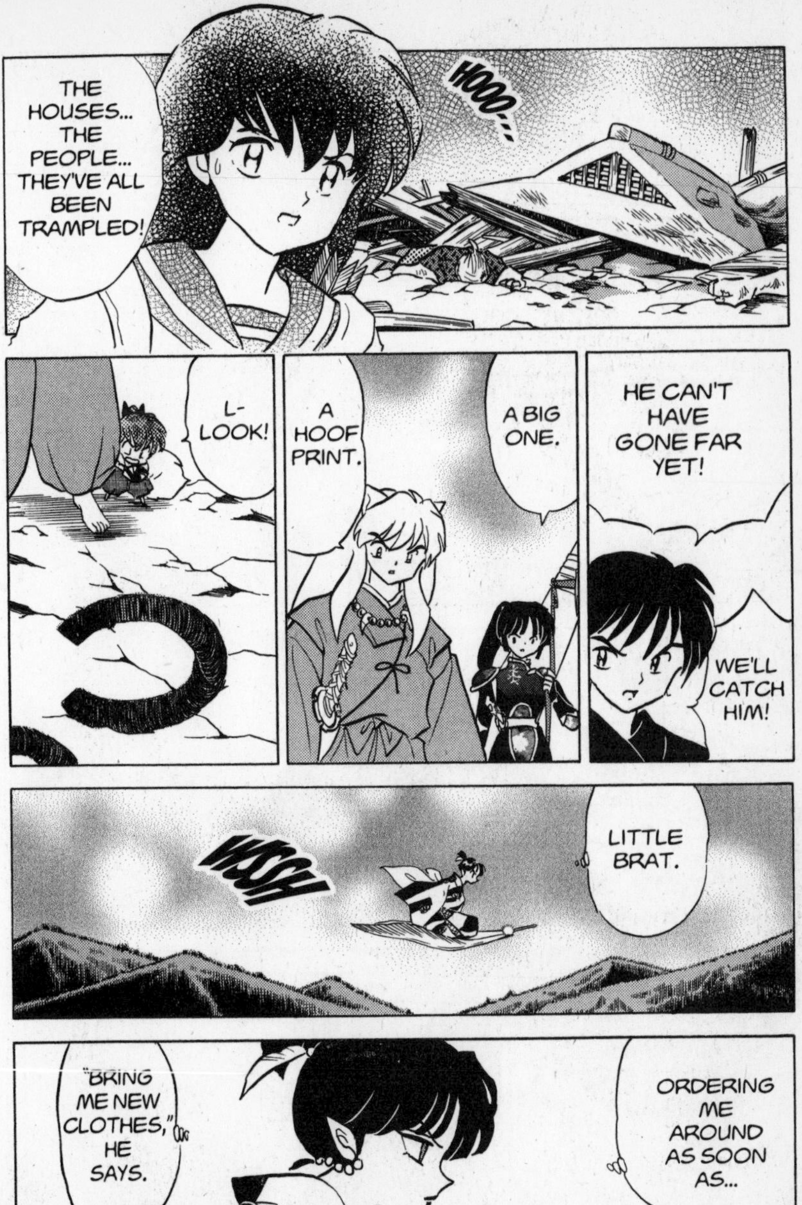
THE HOUSES... THE PEOPLE... THEY'VE ALL BEEN TRAMPLED!
HOOO...
L-LOOK!
A HOOF PRINT.
A BIG ONE.
HE CAN'T HAVE GONE FAR YET!
WE'LL CATCH HIM!
WSSH
LITTLE BRAT.
"BRING ME NEW CLOTHES," HE SAYS.
ORDERING ME AROUND AS SOON AS...

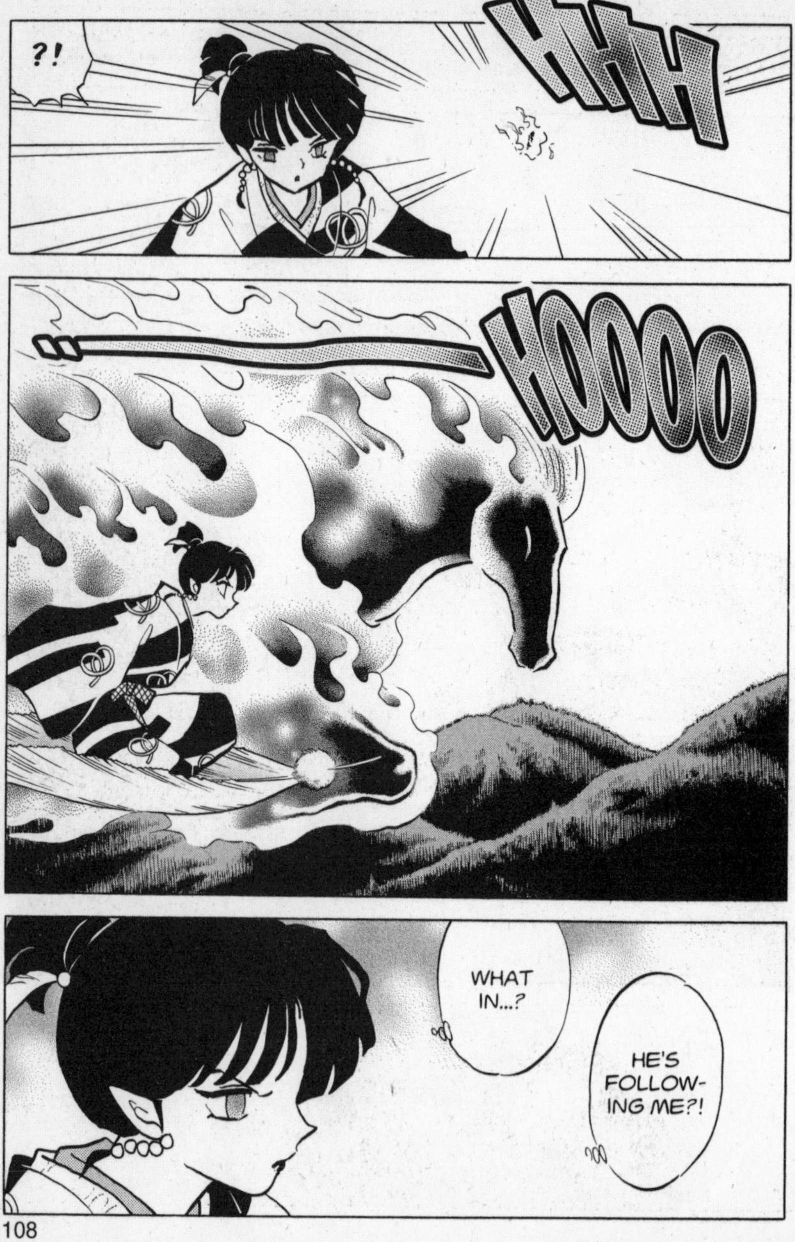
?!
HHHH
HOOOO
WHAT IN...?
HE'S FOLLOWING ME?!

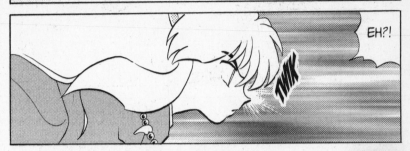

EH?!

TWTK

INU-YASHA...?

KAGURA'S SCENT!

!

BE CAREFUL, EVERYONE!

I SENSE A DEMONIC AURA...

...AND IT'S COMING FAST!

RRRRR

KRAK

!

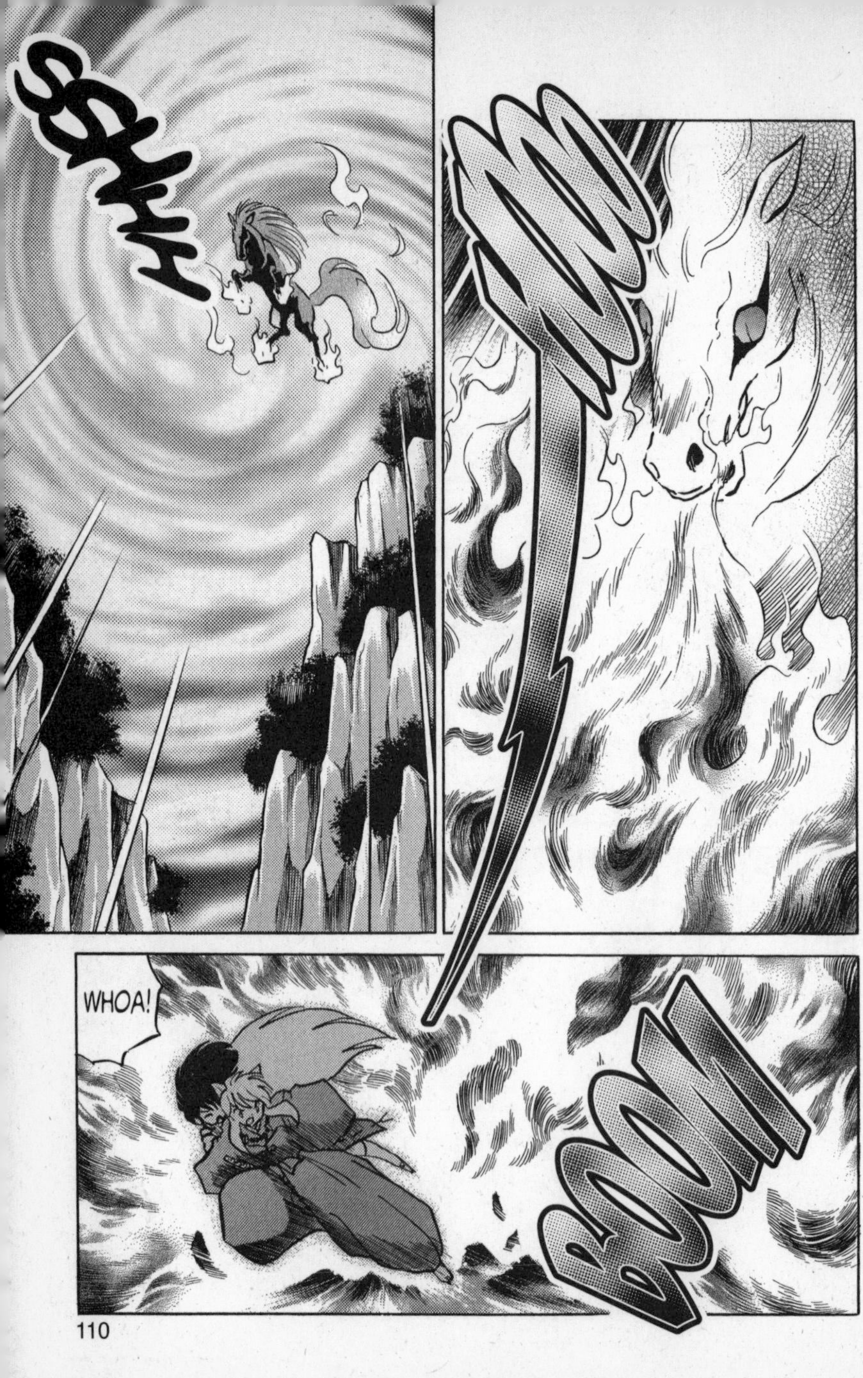
SSHHH
WHOA!
BOOM

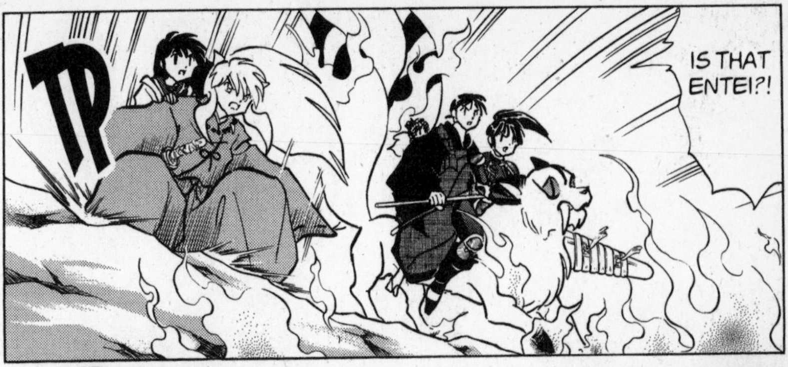
TP
IS THAT ENTEI?!

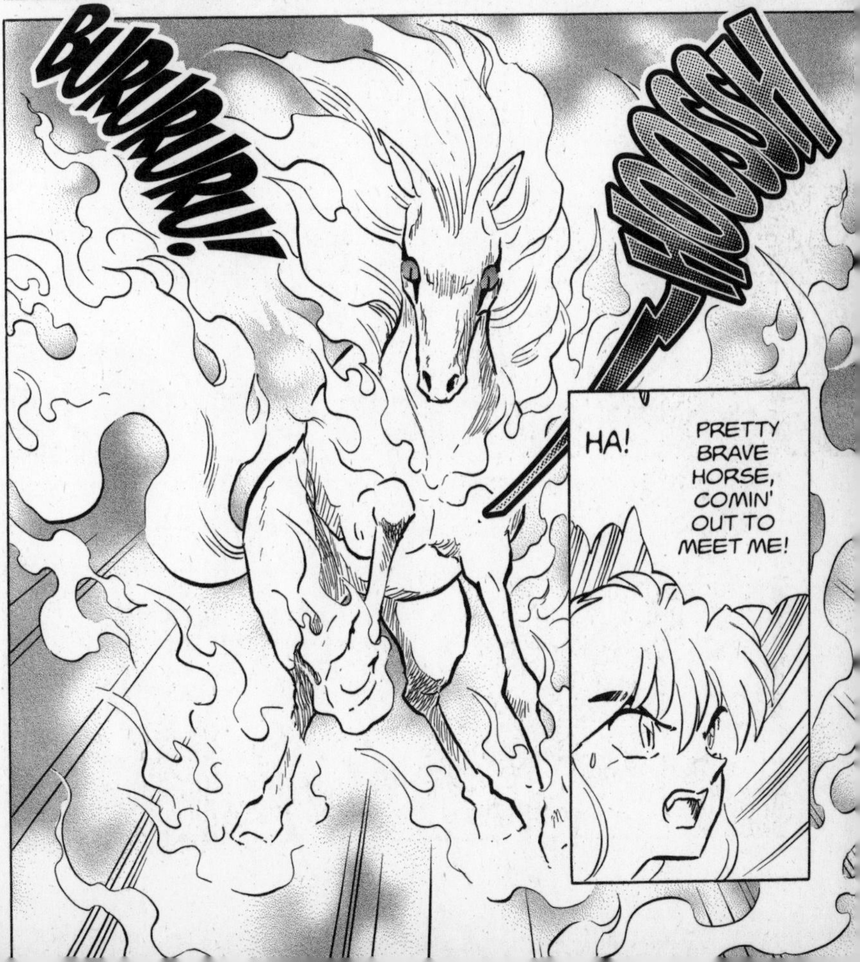
BURURURU!
WHOOSH
HA!
PRETTY BRAVE HORSE, COMIN' OUT TO MEET ME!

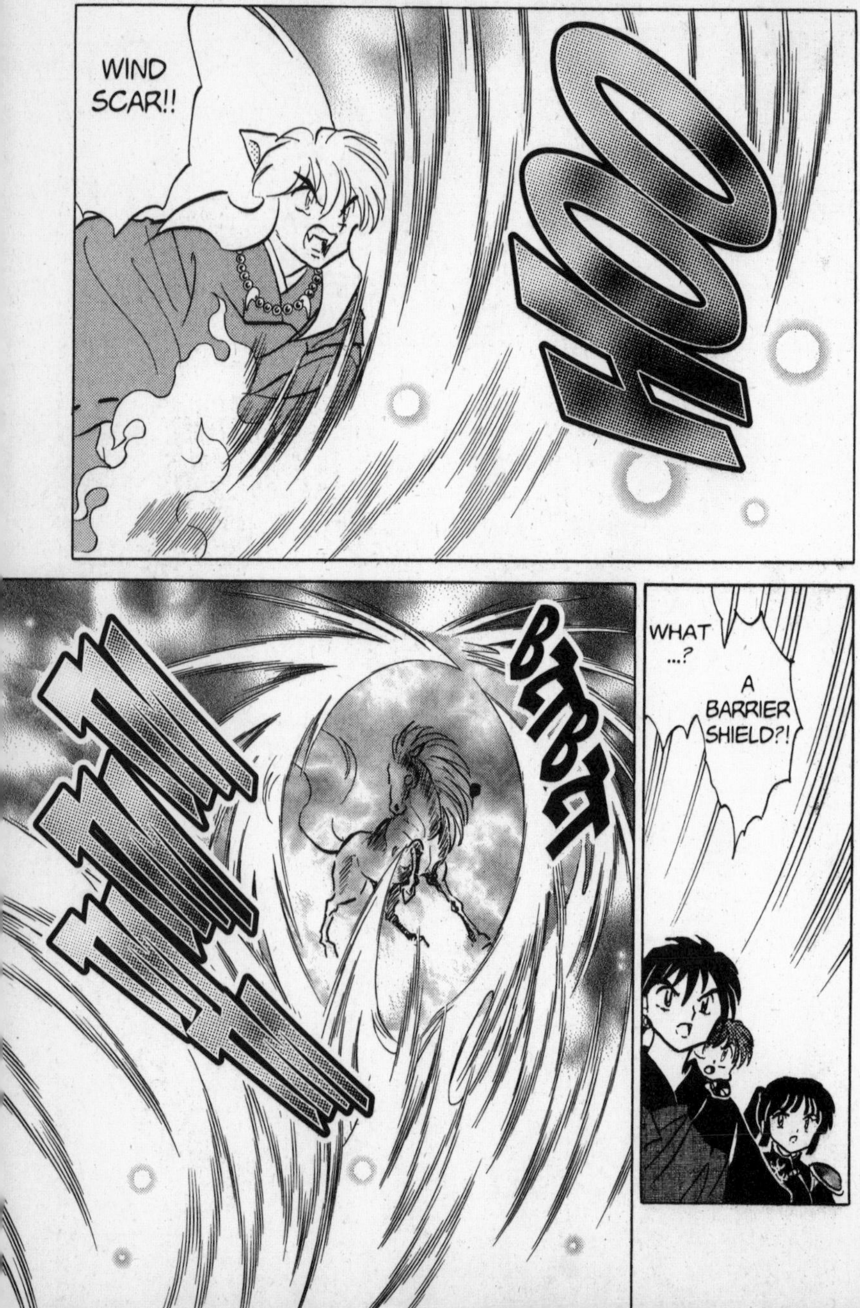
WIND SCAR!!
HOOO
BZBZT
WHAT ...?
A BARRIER SHIELD?!

HEH HEH HEH...

SUCH A RUDE GREETING, INUYASHA.

...

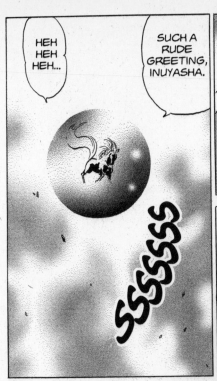

SSSSSSS

SOME-ONE...

...RIDING THE HORSE...

HEH HEH HEH...THIS HORSE MON-STER...

...SEEMS TO HAVE CHOSEN ME AS HIS MASTER...

BURURURU

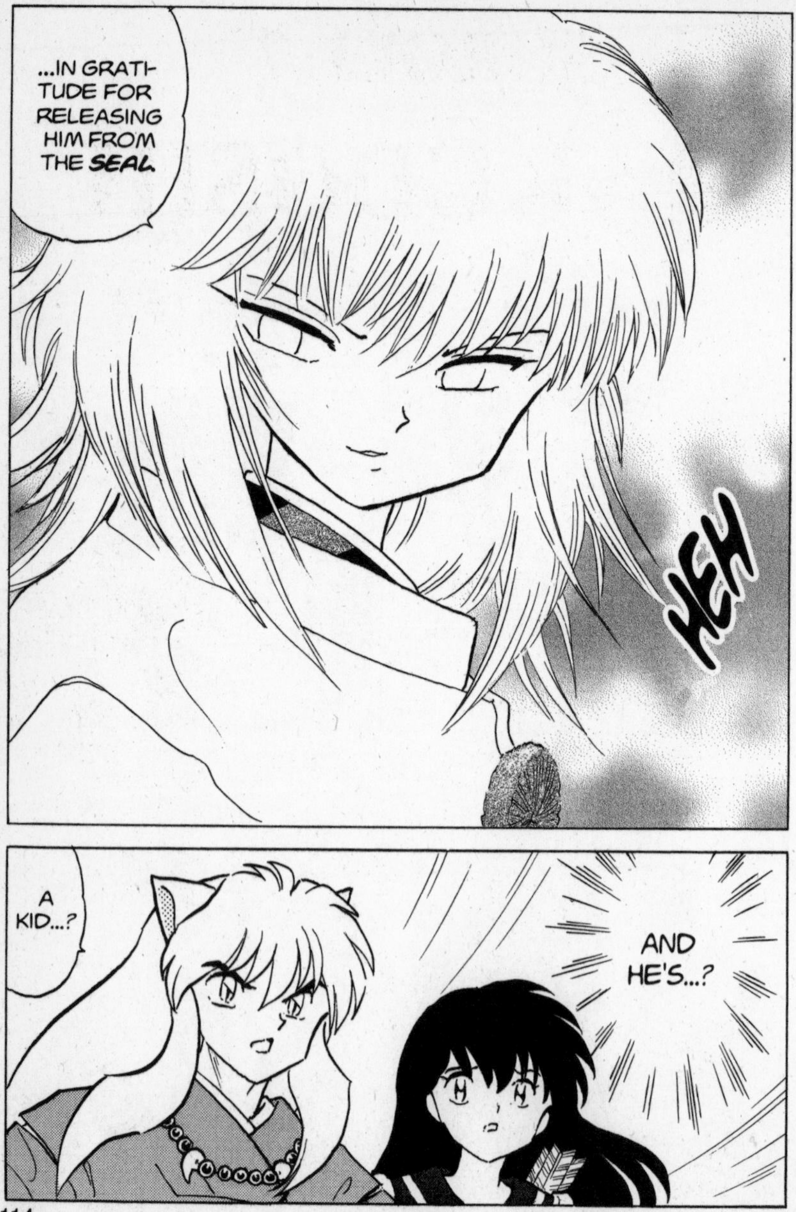
...IN GRATITUDE FOR RELEASING HIM FROM THE SEAL.
HEH
A KID...?
AND HE'S...?

SCROLL 7
HAKUDOSHI

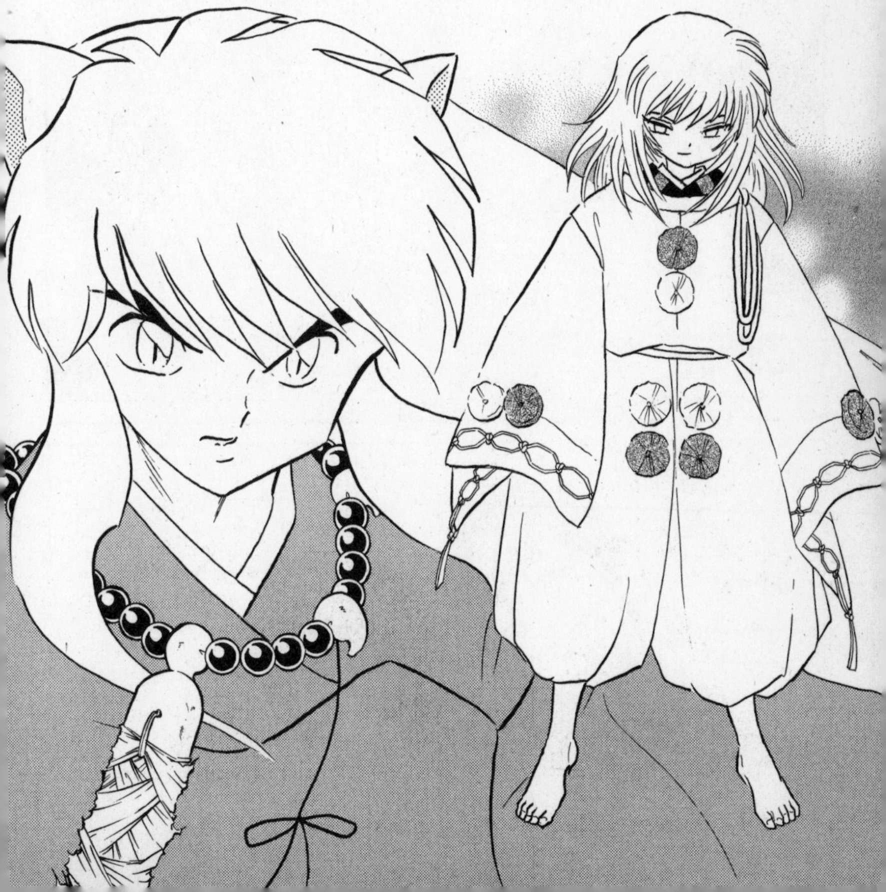

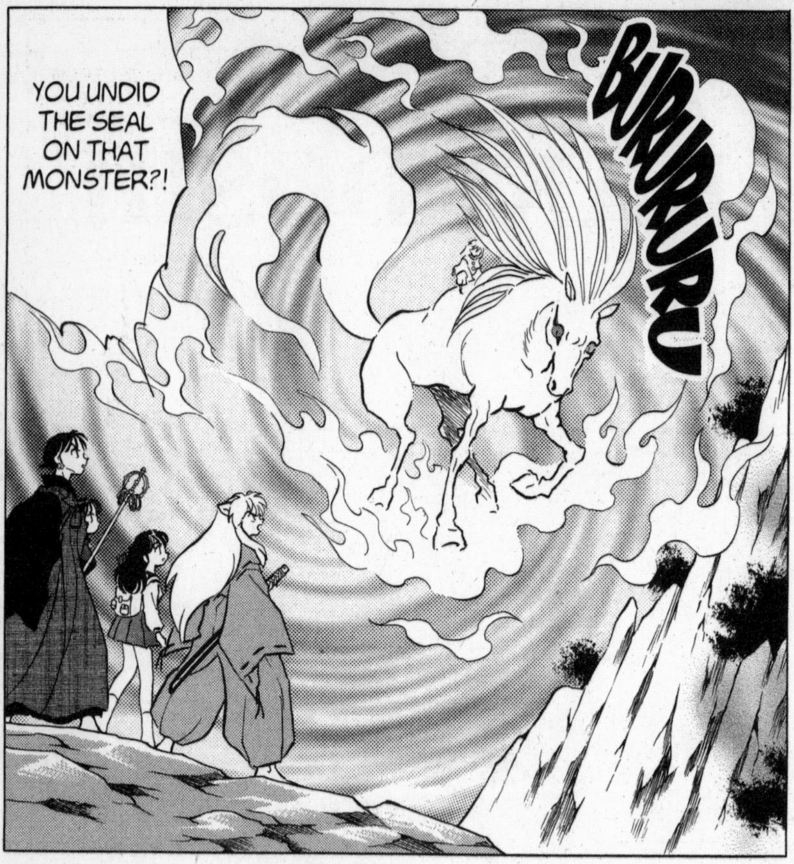
YOU UNDID THE SEAL ON THAT MONSTER?!
BURURURURU
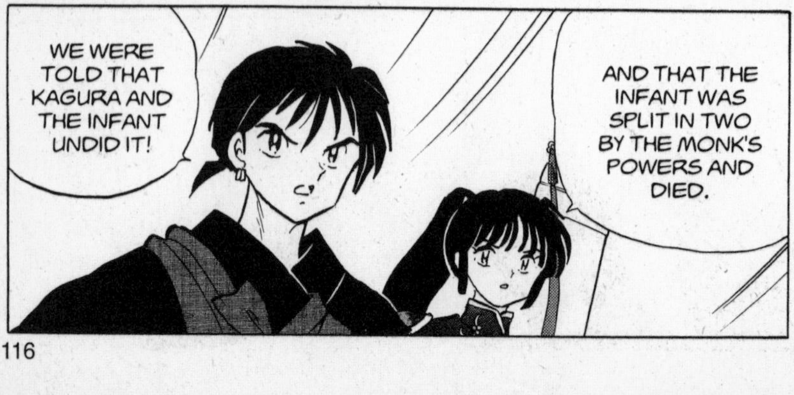
WE WERE TOLD THAT KAGURA AND THE INFANT UNDID IT!
AND THAT THE INFANT WAS SPLIT IN TWO BY THE MONK'S POWERS AND DIED.

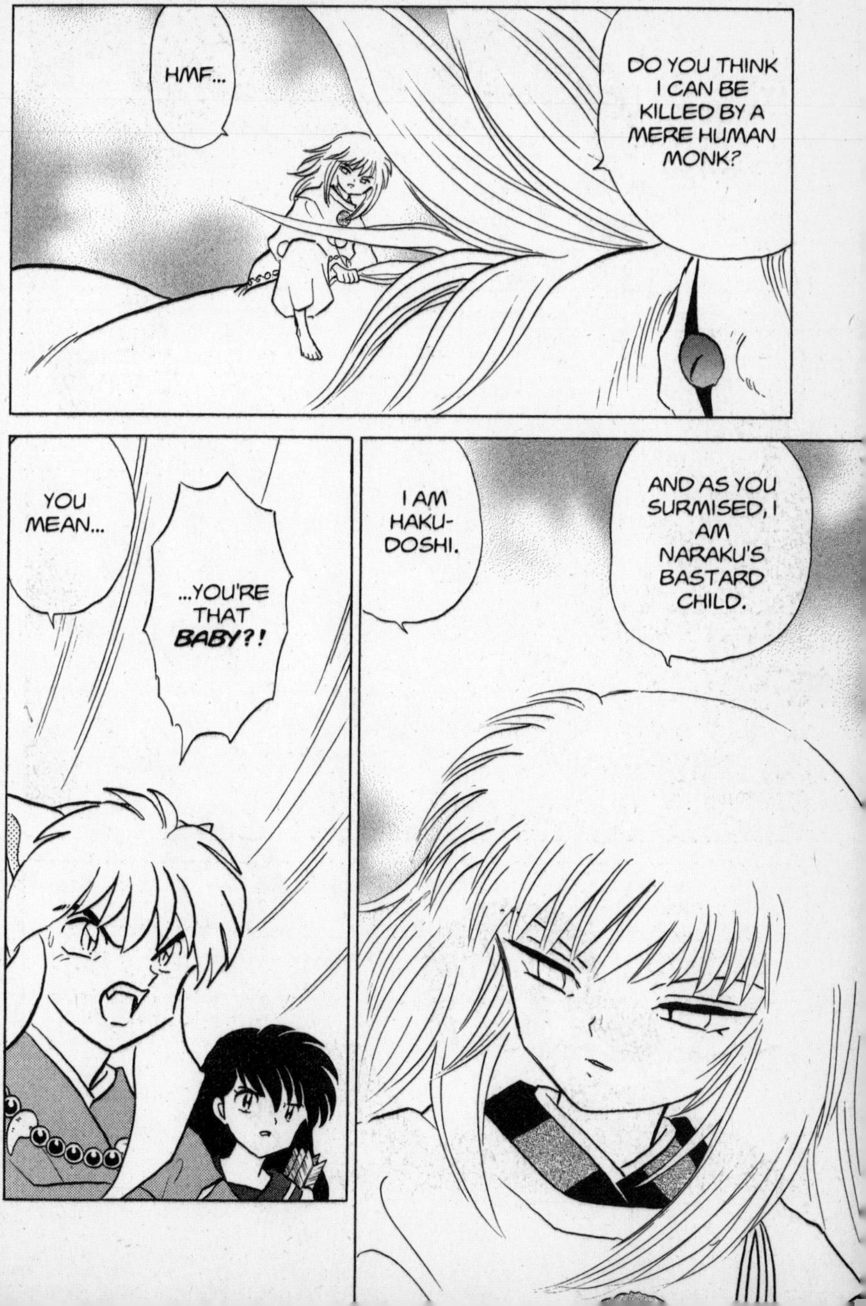
HMF...
DO YOU THINK I CAN BE KILLED BY A MERE HUMAN MONK?
YOU MEAN...
...YOU'RE THAT *BABY?!*
I AM HAKU-DOSHI.
AND AS YOU SURMISED, I AM NARAKU'S BASTARD CHILD.

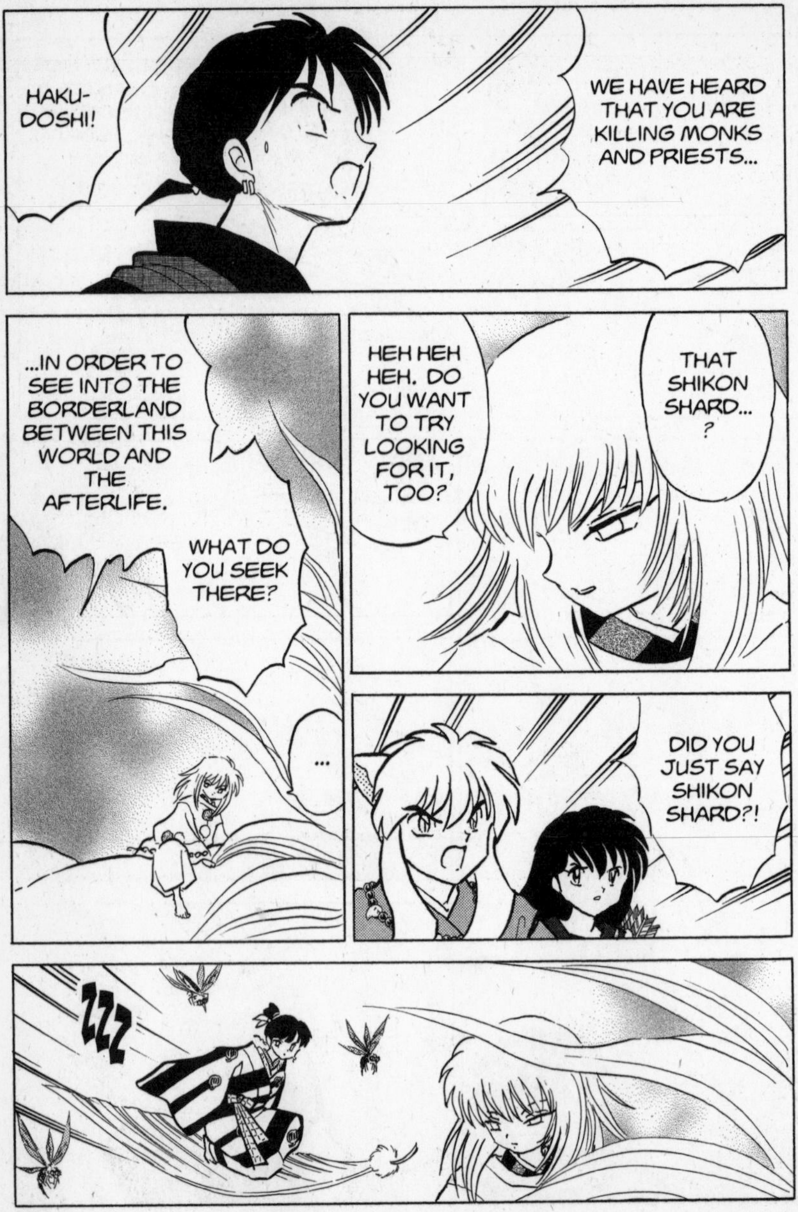
HAKU-DOSHI!
WE HAVE HEARD THAT YOU ARE KILLING MONKS AND PRIESTS...
...IN ORDER TO SEE INTO THE BORDERLAND BETWEEN THIS WORLD AND THE AFTERLIFE.
WHAT DO YOU SEEK THERE?
...
HEH HEH HEH. DO YOU WANT TO TRY LOOKING FOR IT, TOO?
THAT SHIKON SHARD...?
DID YOU JUST SAY SHIKON SHARD?!
ZZZ

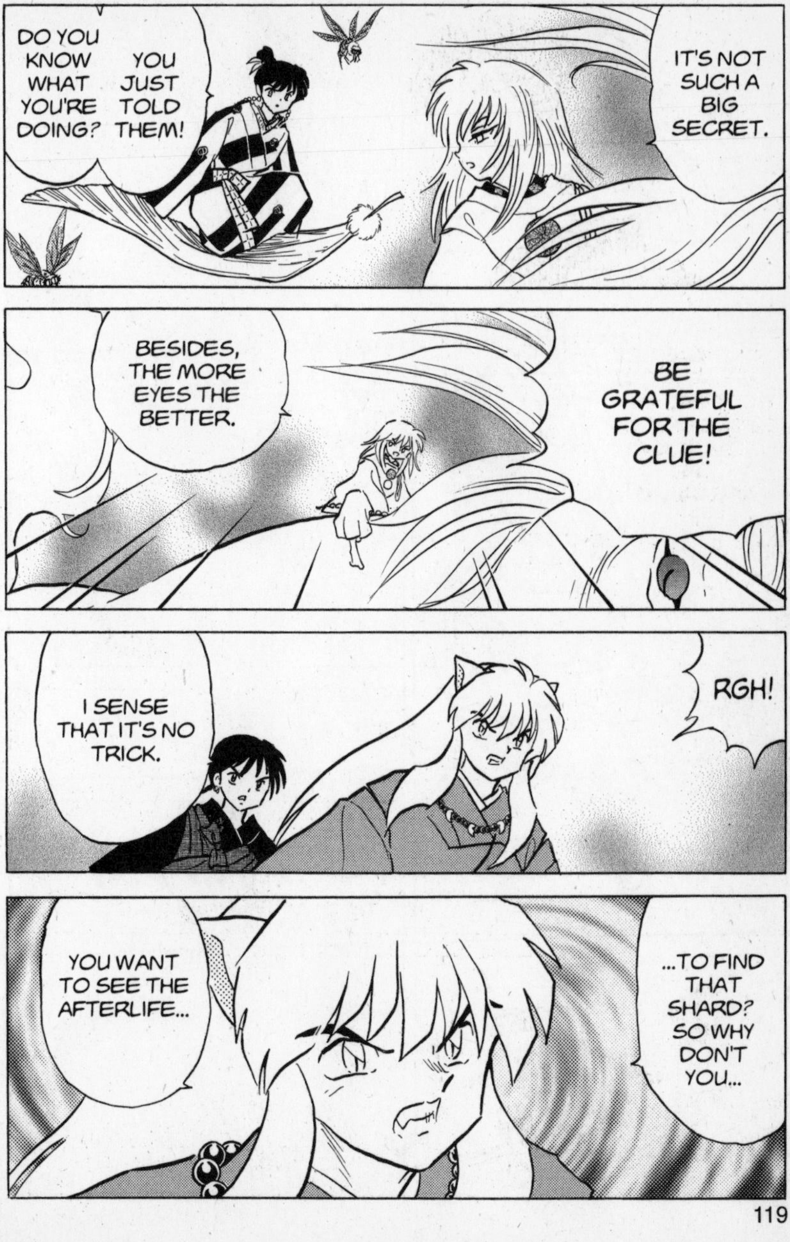
DO YOU KNOW WHAT YOU'RE DOING?
YOU JUST TOLD THEM!
IT'S NOT SUCH A BIG SECRET.
BESIDES, THE MORE EYES THE BETTER.
BE GRATEFUL FOR THE CLUE!
I SENSE THAT IT'S NO TRICK.
RGH!
YOU WANT TO SEE THE AFTERLIFE...
...TO FIND THAT SHARD? SO WHY DON'T YOU...

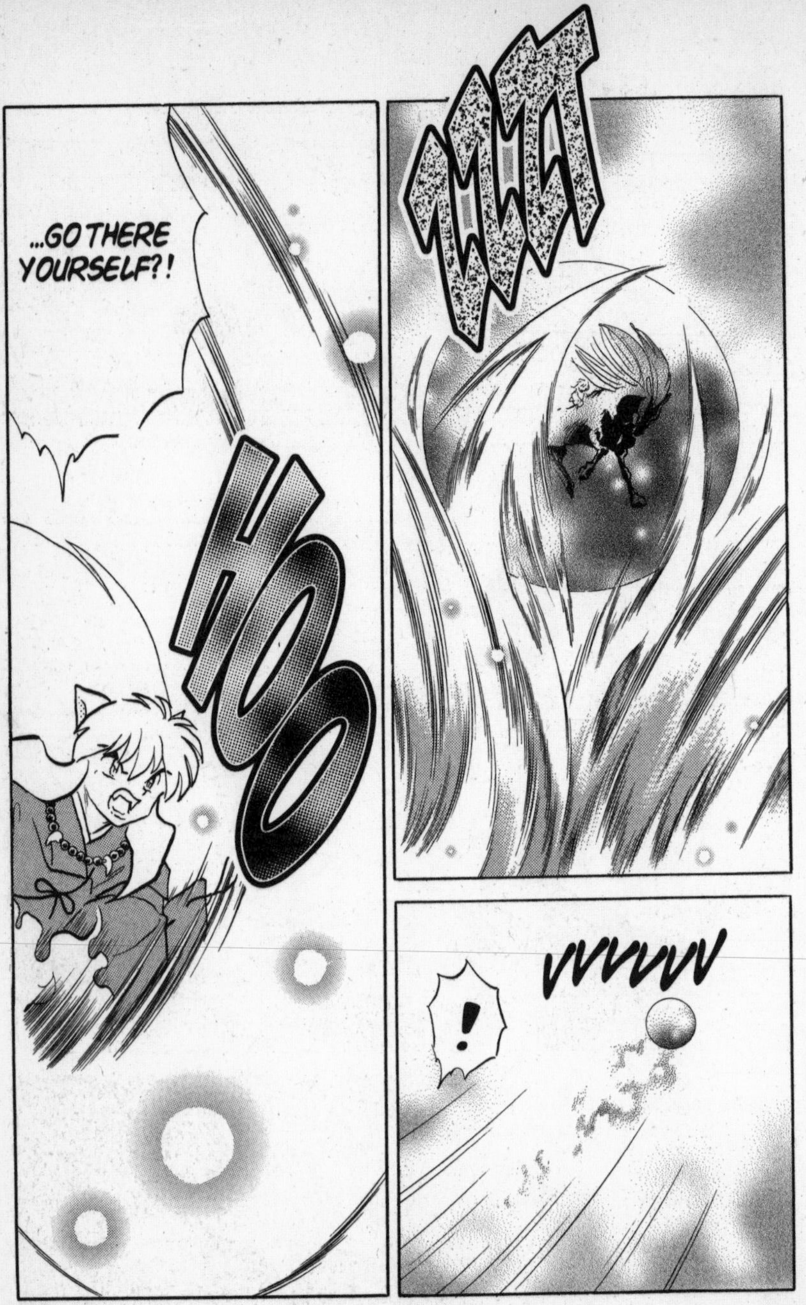

...GO THERE YOURSELF?!
HOOO
ZZZT
!
VVVVVV

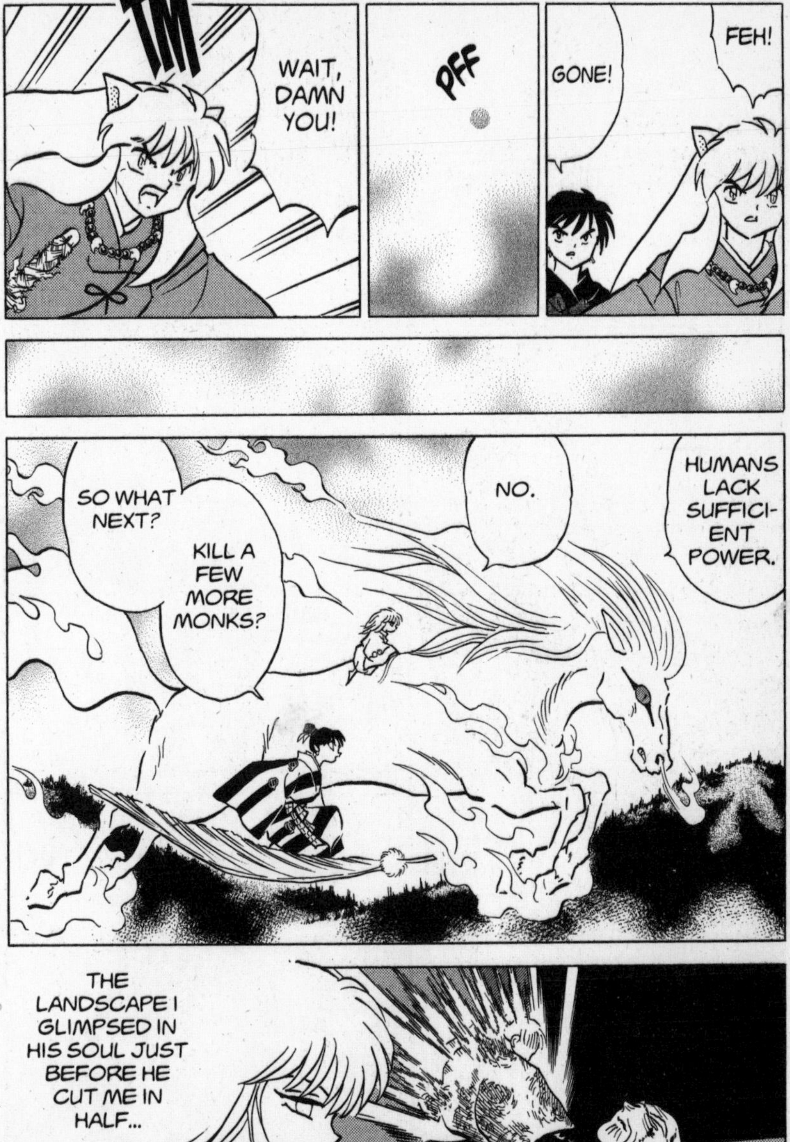
TM
WAIT, DAMN YOU!
PFF
GONE!
FEH!
SO WHAT NEXT?
KILL A FEW MORE MONKS?
NO.
HUMANS LACK SUFFICI-ENT POWER.
THE LANDSCAPE I GLIMPSED IN HIS SOUL JUST BEFORE HE CUT ME IN HALF...

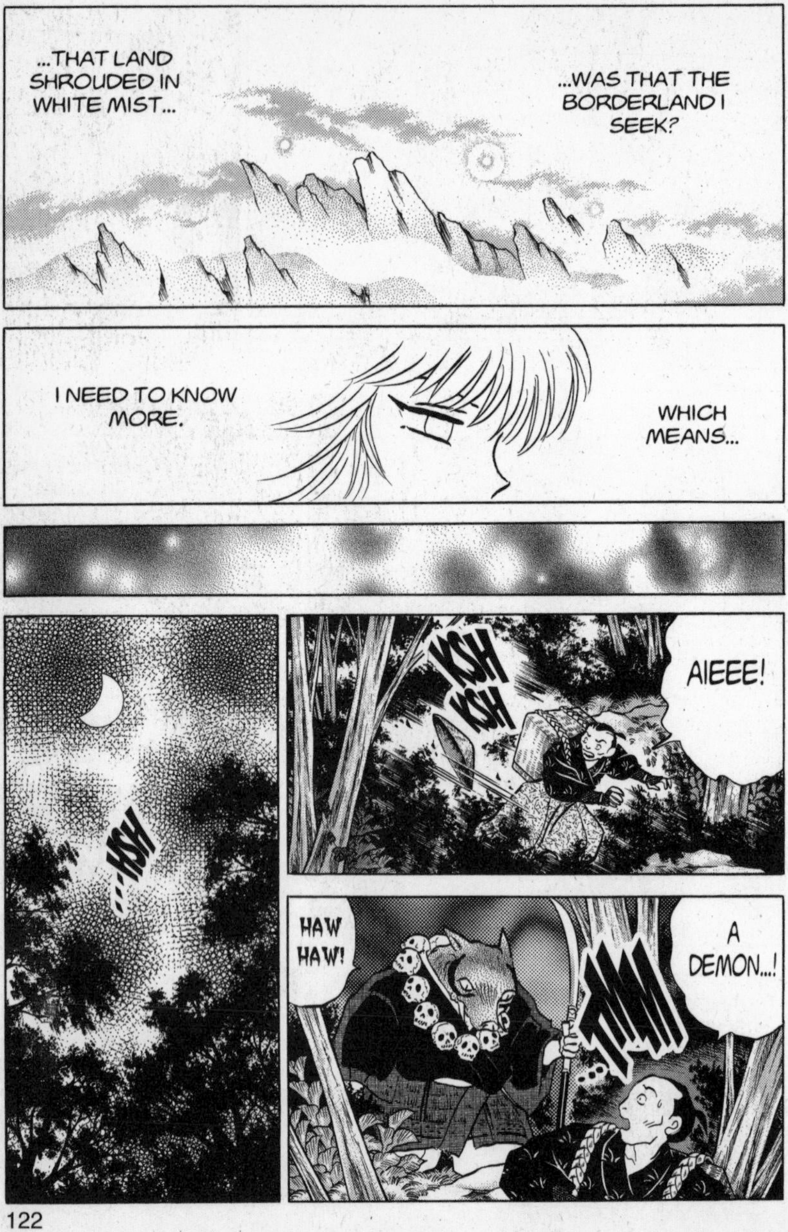
...WAS THAT THE BORDERLAND I SEEK?
...THAT LAND SHROUDED IN WHITE MIST...
WHICH MEANS...
I NEED TO KNOW MORE.
KSH KSH
AIEEE!
...KSH
A DEMON...!
THUMP
HAW HAW!

SHUK

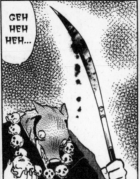

GEH HEH HEH...

KRAK

KRAKK

TOOM

MOOSH

TP

HERE YOU GO.

FLIP

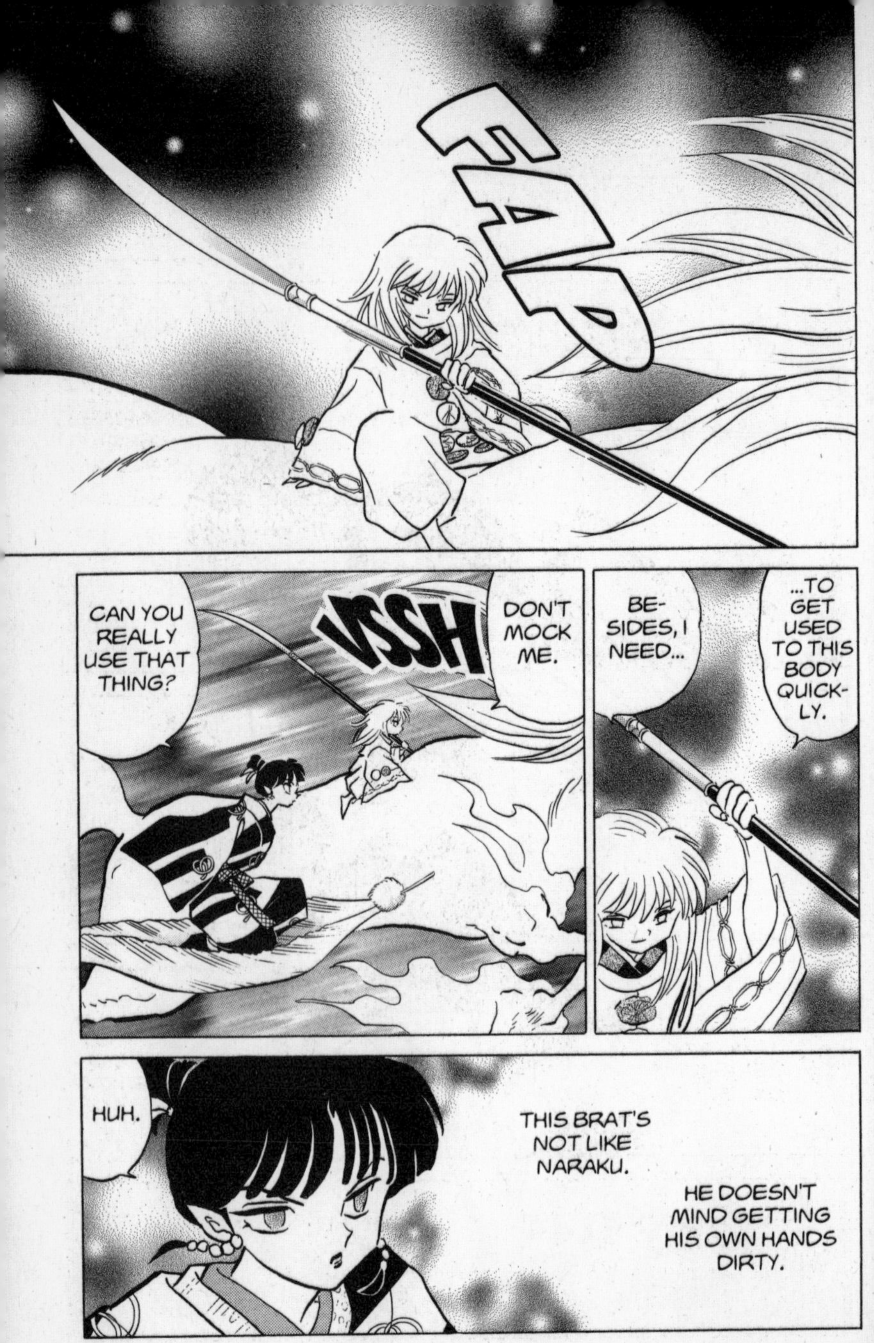
FAP
CAN YOU REALLY USE THAT THING?
VSSH
DON'T MOCK ME.
BE-SIDES, I NEED...
...TO GET USED TO THIS BODY QUICK-LY.
HUH.
THIS BRAT'S NOT LIKE NARAKU.
HE DOESN'T MIND GETTING HIS OWN HANDS DIRTY.

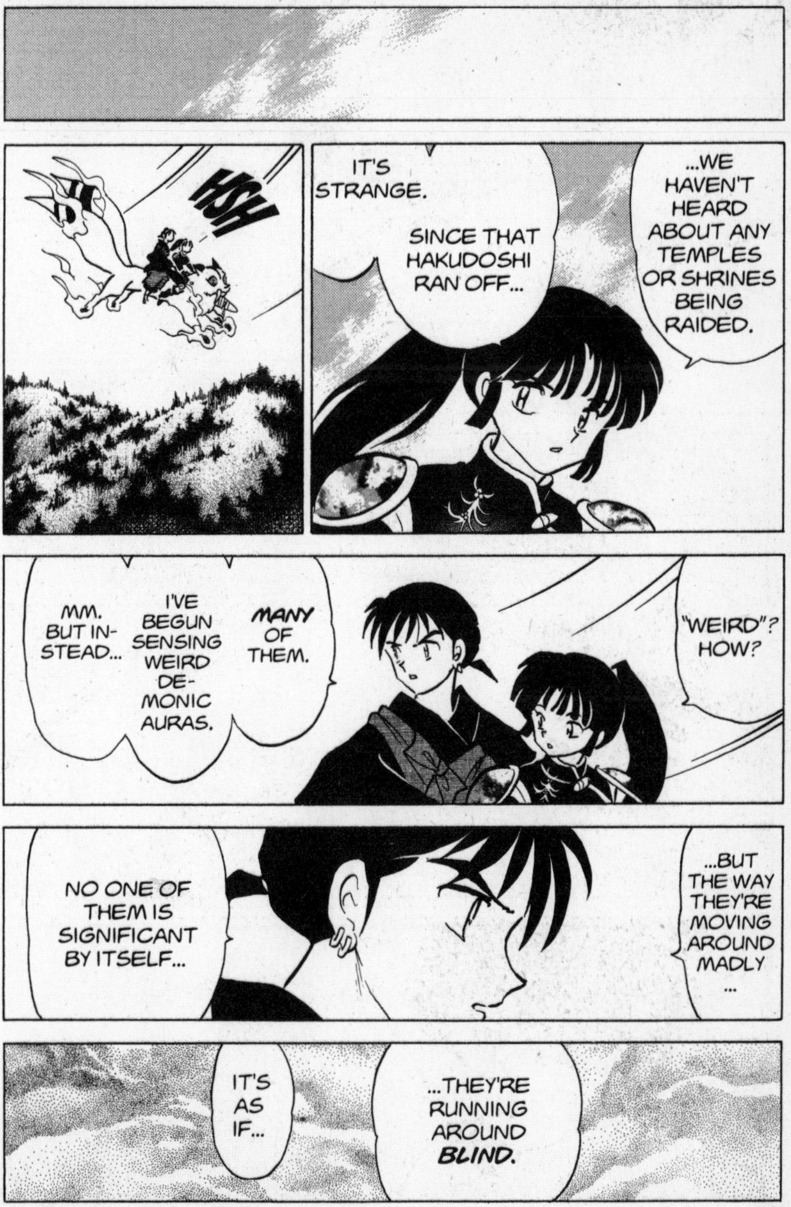
HSH
IT'S STRANGE.
SINCE THAT HAKUDOSHI RAN OFF...
...WE HAVEN'T HEARD ABOUT ANY TEMPLES OR SHRINES BEING RAIDED.
MM. BUT IN-STEAD...
I'VE BEGUN SENSING WEIRD DE-MONIC AURAS.
MANY OF THEM.
"WEIRD"? HOW?
NO ONE OF THEM IS SIGNIFICANT BY ITSELF...
...BUT THE WAY THEY'RE MOVING AROUND MADLY ...
IT'S AS IF...
...THEY'RE RUNNING AROUND BLIND.

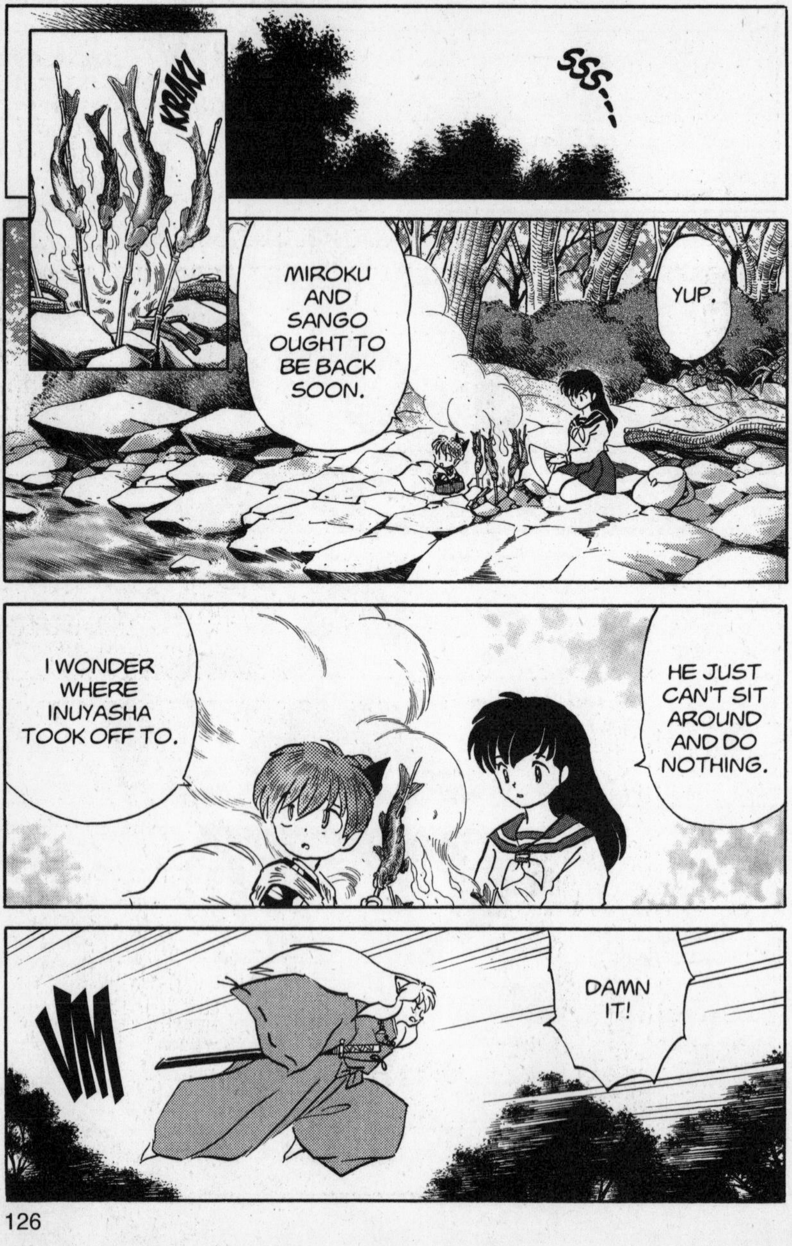
KRAK!
SSS...
MIROKU AND SANGO OUGHT TO BE BACK SOON.
YUP.
I WONDER WHERE INUYASHA TOOK OFF TO.
HE JUST CAN'T SIT AROUND AND DO NOTHING.
VM
DAMN IT!

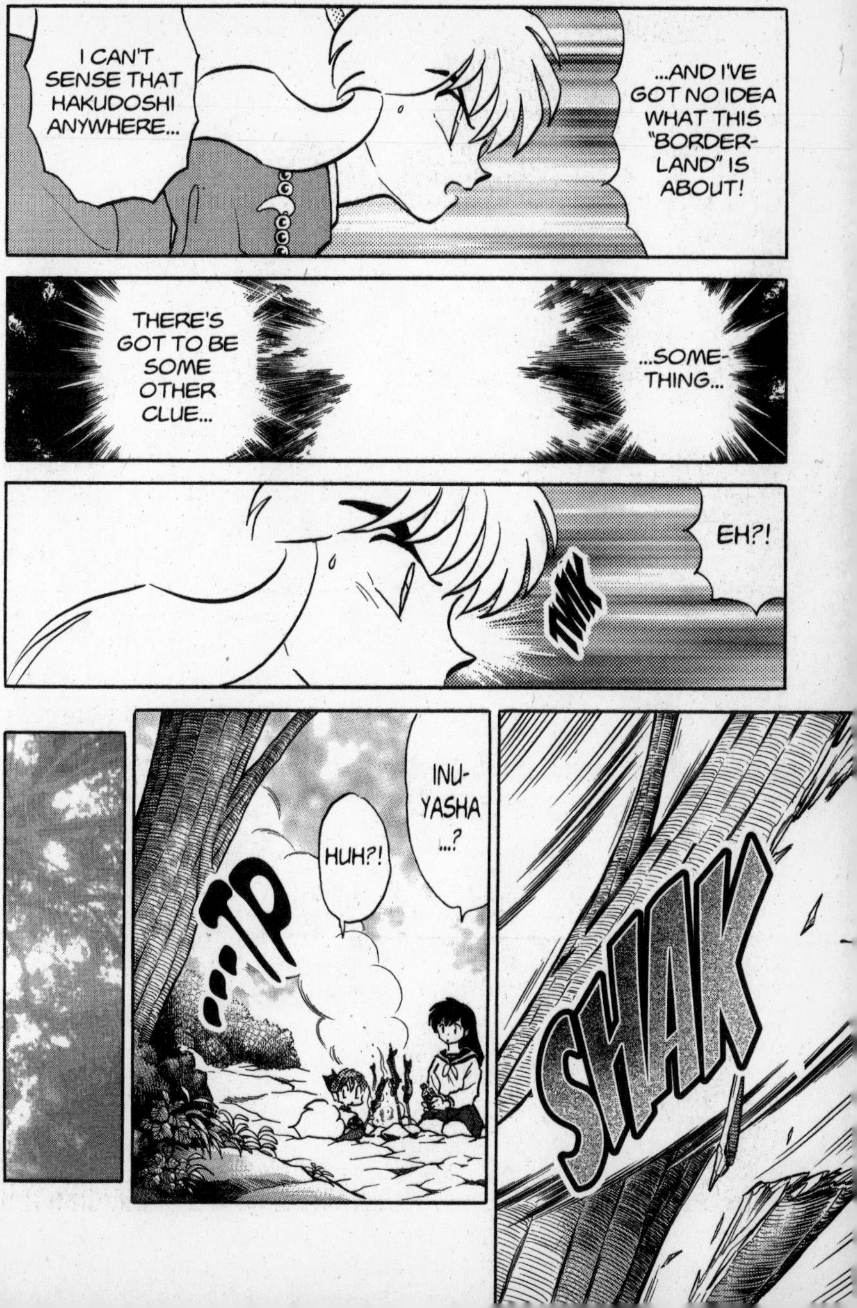
I CAN'T SENSE THAT HAKUDOSHI ANYWHERE...
...AND I'VE GOT NO IDEA WHAT THIS "BORDER-LAND" IS ABOUT!
THERE'S GOT TO BE SOME OTHER CLUE...
...SOME-THING...
EH?!
TWIK
...TP
HUH?!
INU-YASHA ...?
SHAK

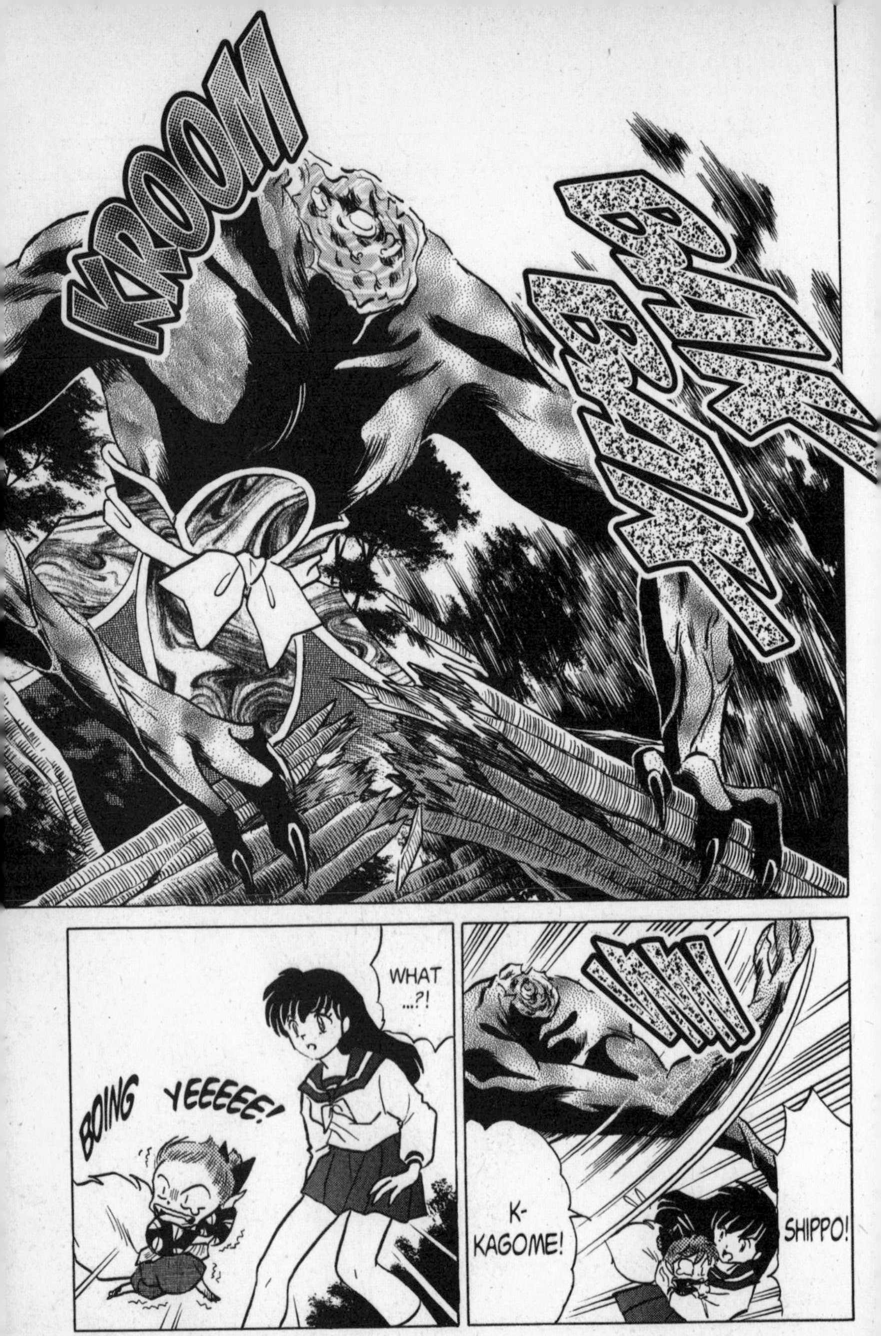
KROOM
WHAT ...?!
BOING
YEEEEE!
K-
KAGOME!
SHIPPO!

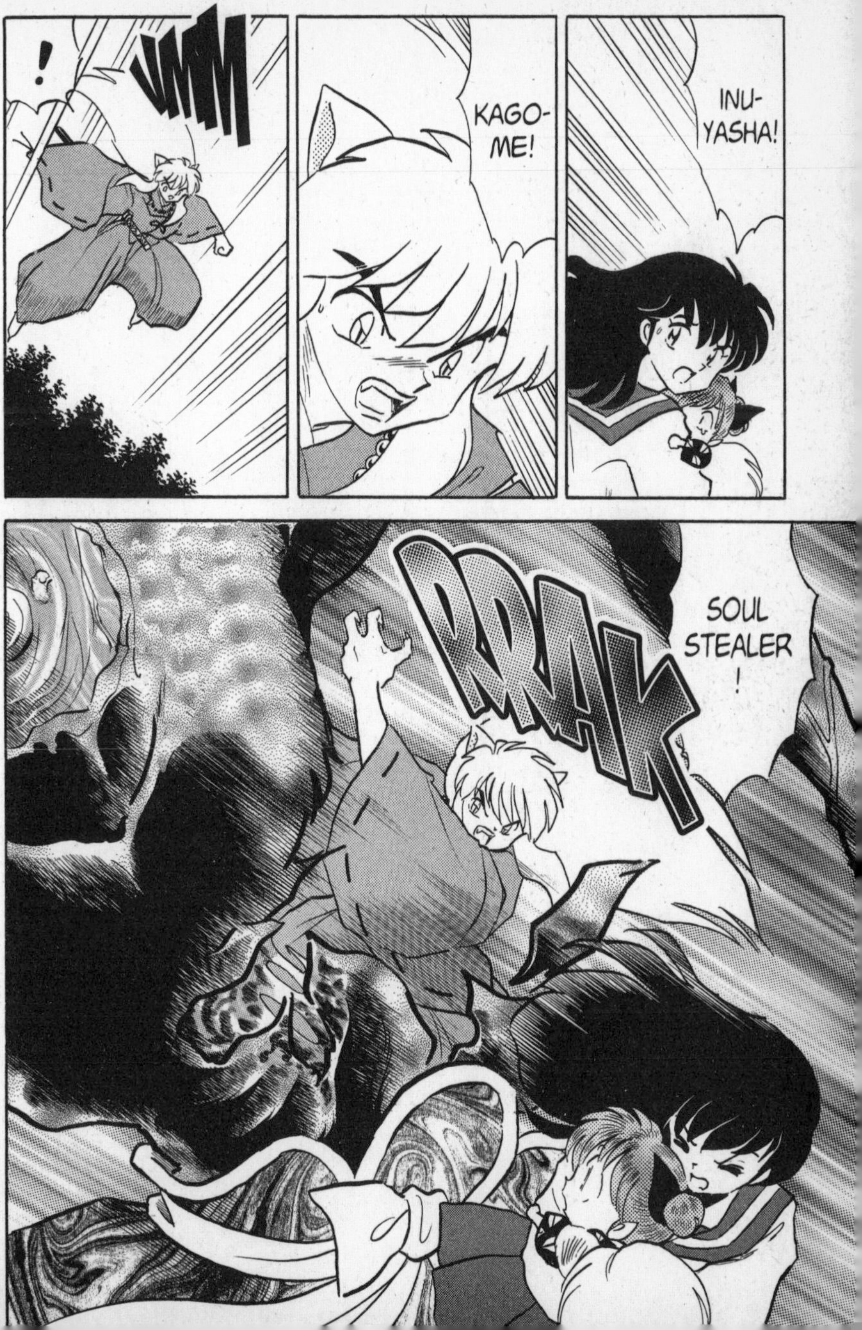
!
VMM
KAGO-
ME!
INU-
YASHA!
RRRAK
SOUL
STEALER
!

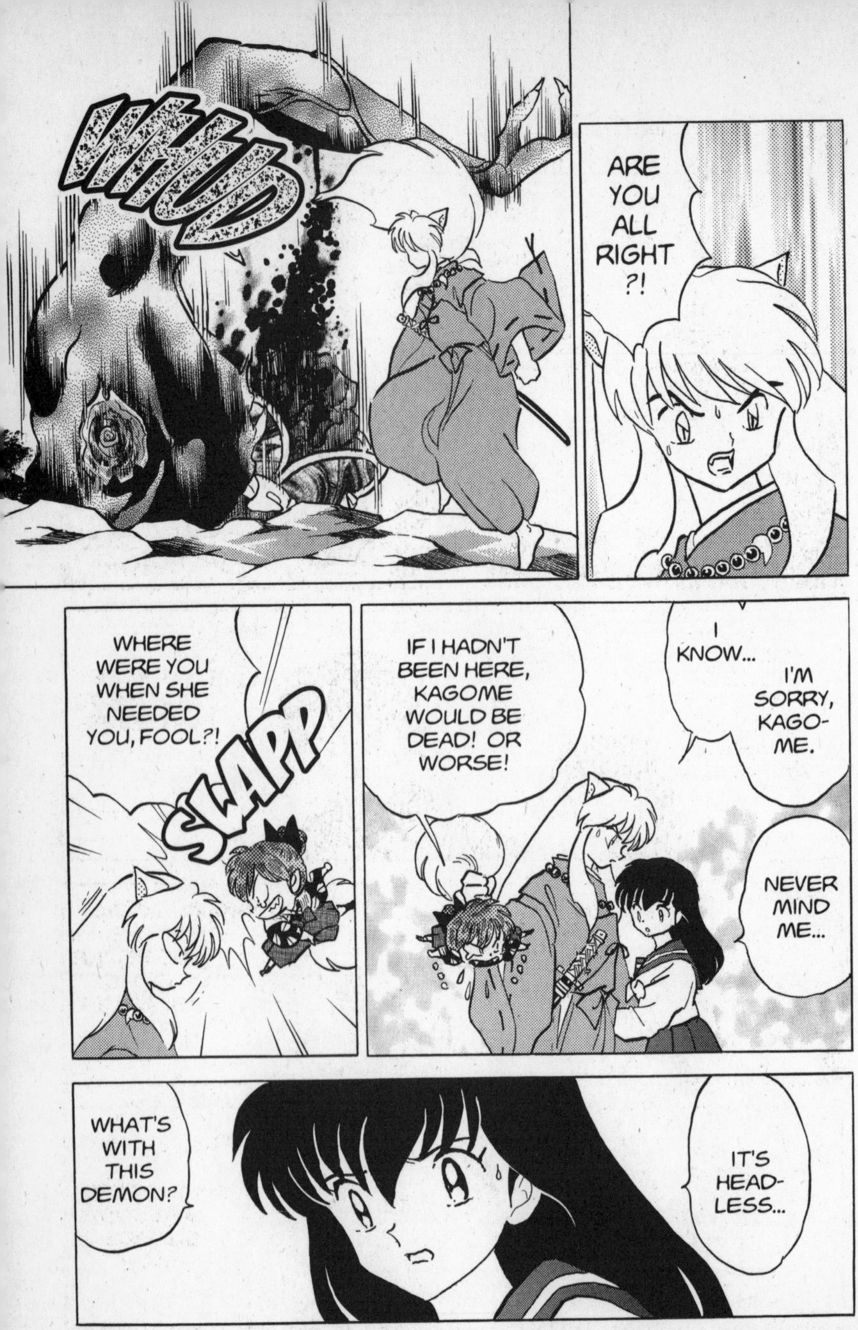
WHUD
ARE YOU ALL RIGHT ?!
WHERE WERE YOU WHEN SHE NEEDED YOU, FOOL?!
SLAPP
IF I HADN'T BEEN HERE, KAGOME WOULD BE DEAD! OR WORSE!
I KNOW...
I'M SORRY, KAGO-ME.
NEVER MIND ME...
WHAT'S WITH THIS DEMON?
IT'S HEAD-LESS...

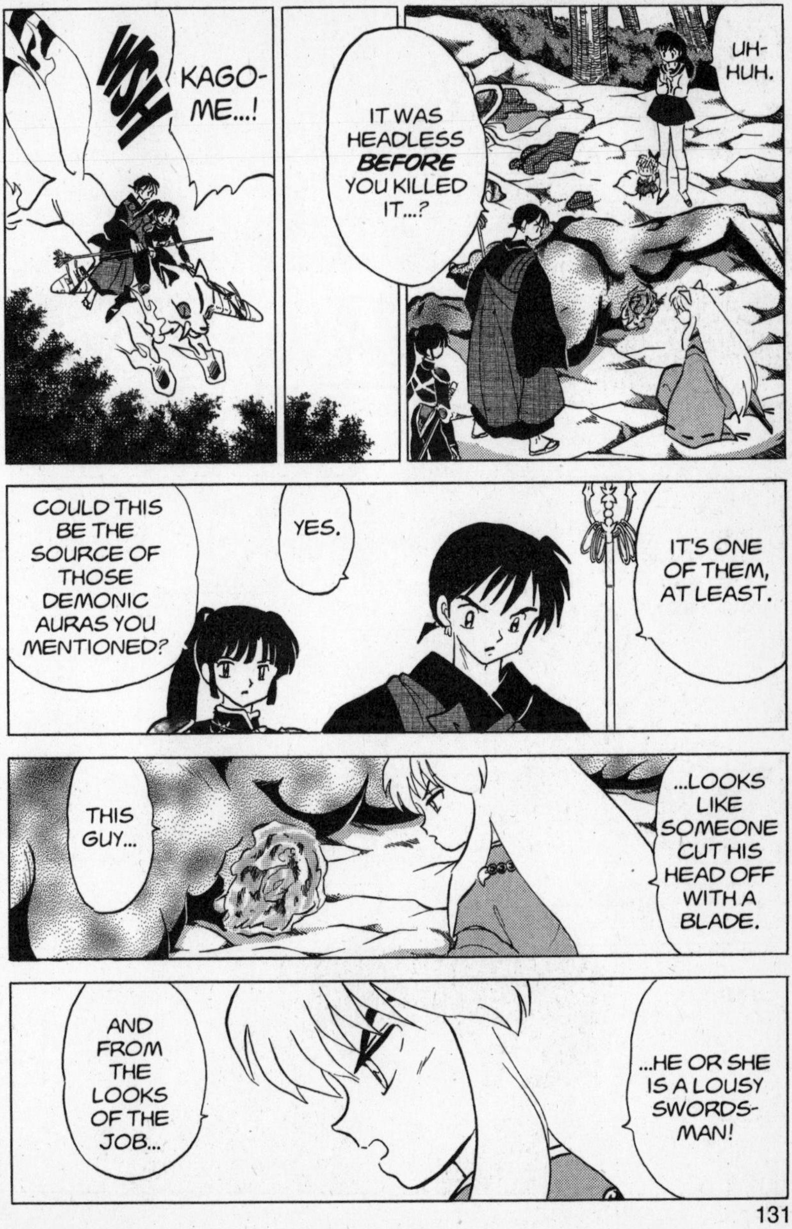
WSH
KAGO-ME...!
IT WAS HEADLESS *BEFORE* YOU KILLED IT...?
UH-HUH.
COULD THIS BE THE SOURCE OF THOSE DEMONIC AURAS YOU MENTIONED?
YES.
IT'S ONE OF THEM, AT LEAST.
THIS GUY...
...LOOKS LIKE SOMEONE CUT HIS HEAD OFF WITH A BLADE.
AND FROM THE LOOKS OF THE JOB...
...HE OR SHE IS A LOUSY SWORDS-MAN!

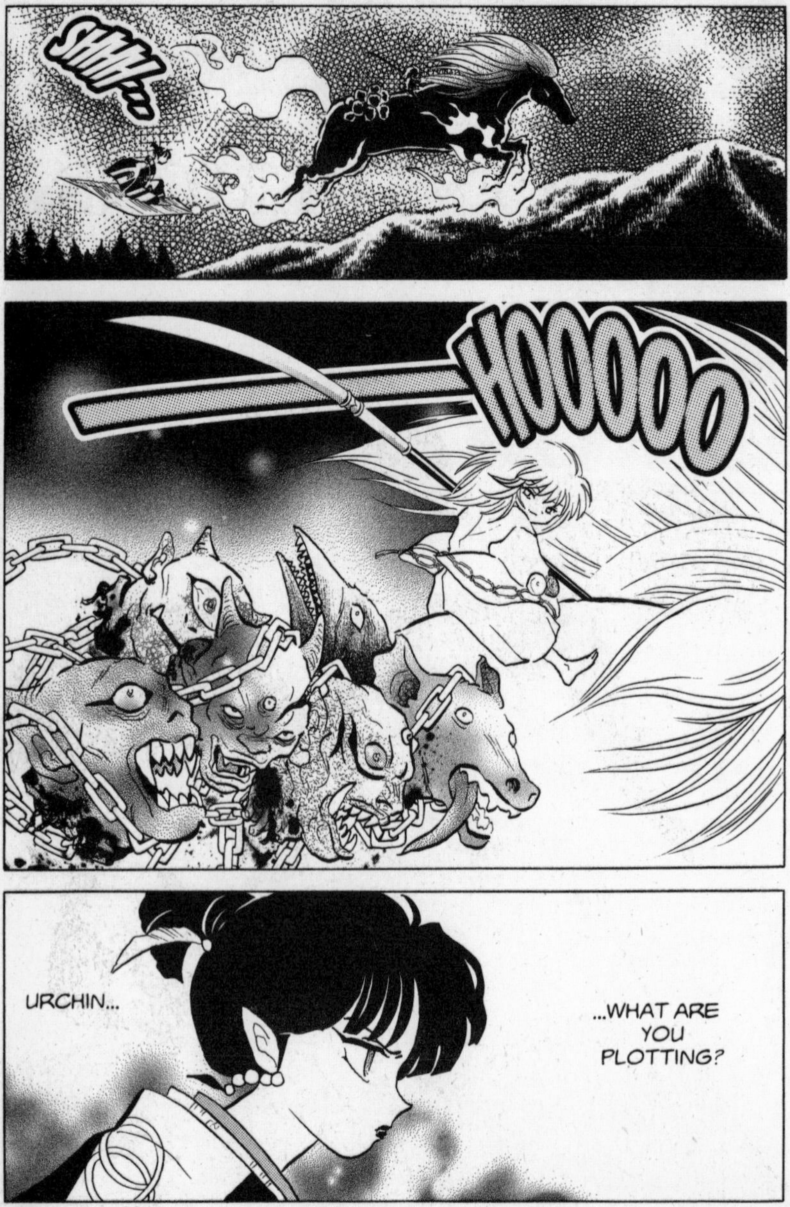
SHHH...
HOOOOO
URCHIN...
...WHAT ARE YOU PLOTTING?

SCROLL 8
THE HEADLESS DEMONS

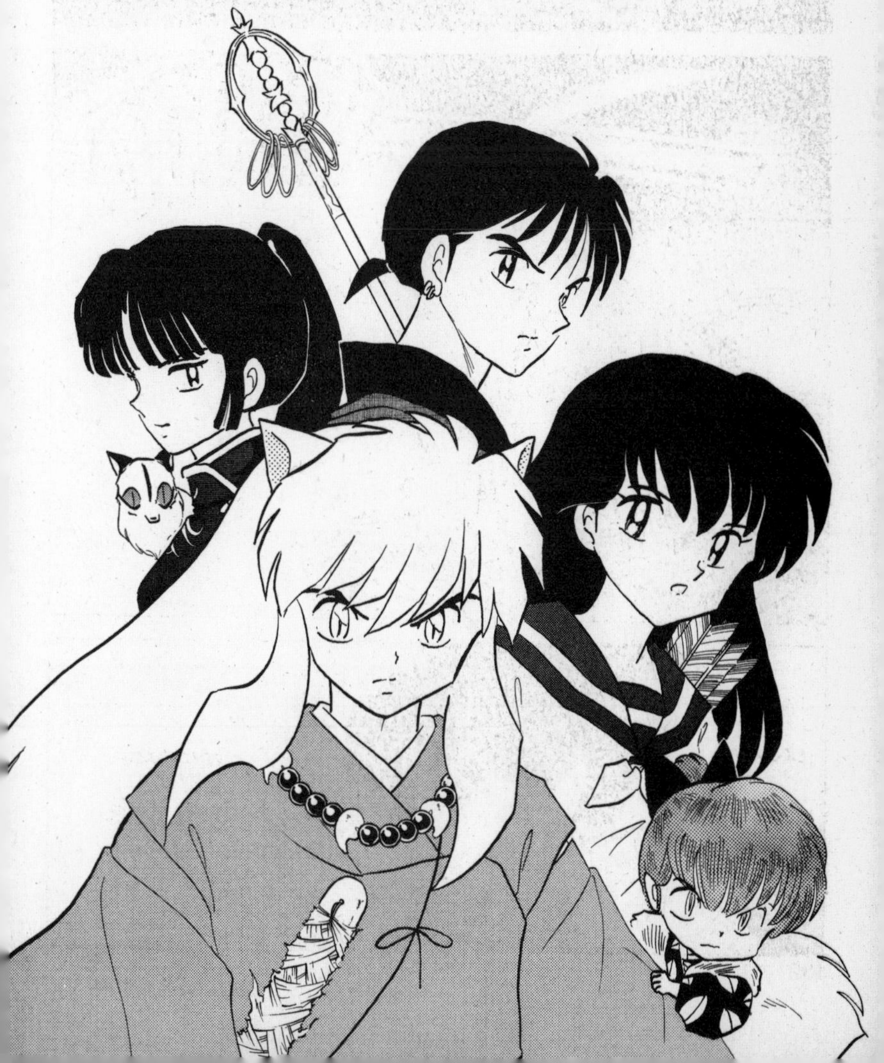

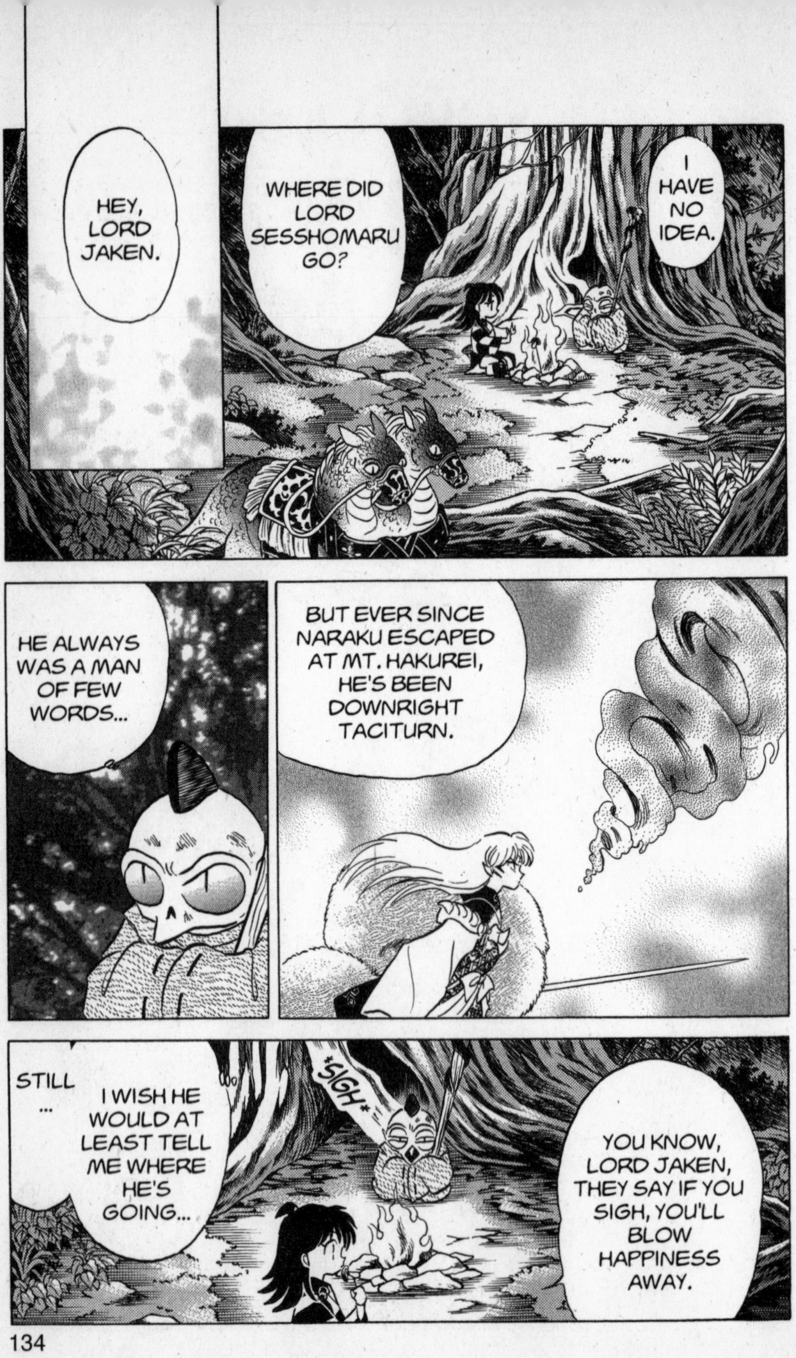
HEY, LORD JAKEN.
WHERE DID LORD SESSHOMARU GO?
I HAVE NO IDEA.
HE ALWAYS WAS A MAN OF FEW WORDS...
BUT EVER SINCE NARAKU ESCAPED AT MT. HAKUREI, HE'S BEEN DOWNRIGHT TACITURN.
STILL ...
SIGH
I WISH HE WOULD AT LEAST TELL ME WHERE HE'S GOING...
YOU KNOW, LORD JAKEN, THEY SAY IF YOU SIGH, YOU'LL BLOW HAPPINESS AWAY.

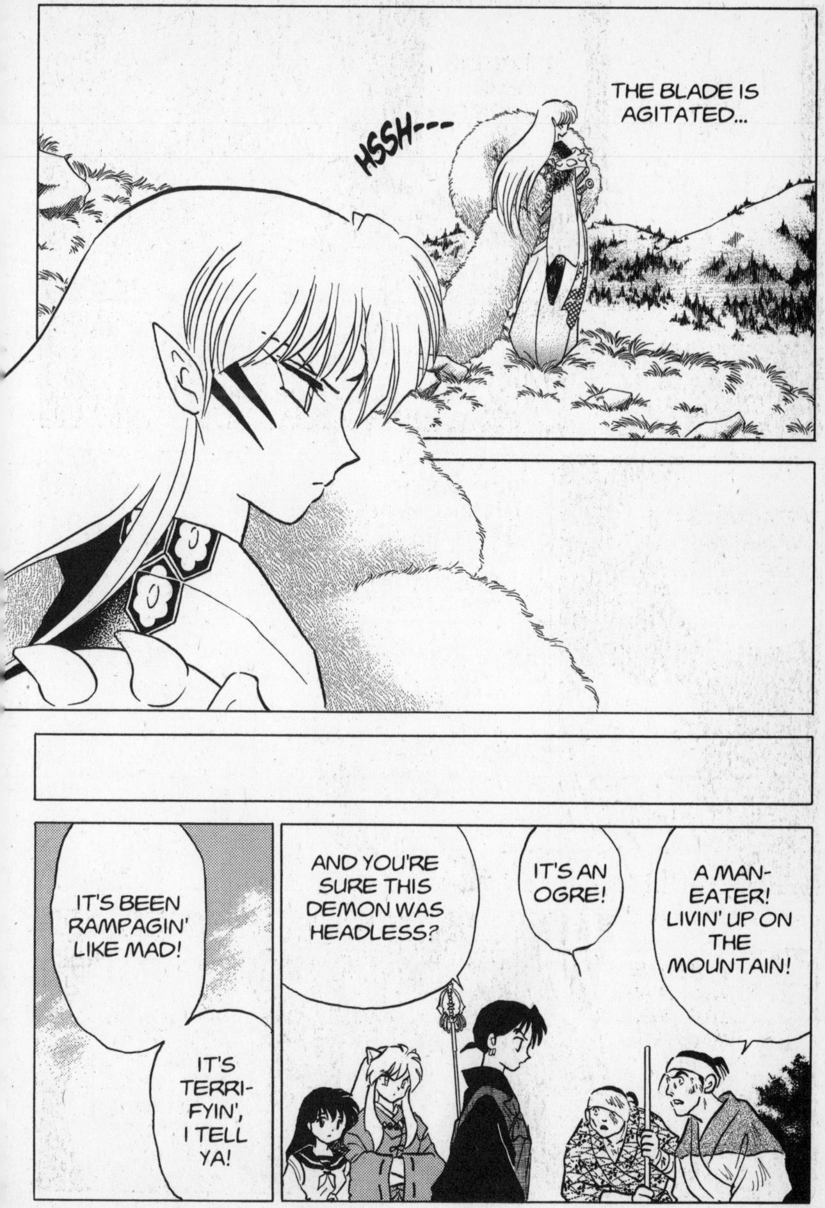
HSSH---
THE BLADE IS AGITATED...
IT'S BEEN RAMPAGIN' LIKE MAD!
IT'S TERRI-FYIN', I TELL YA!
AND YOU'RE SURE THIS DEMON WAS HEADLESS?
IT'S AN OGRE!
A MAN-EATER! LIVIN' UP ON THE MOUNTAIN!

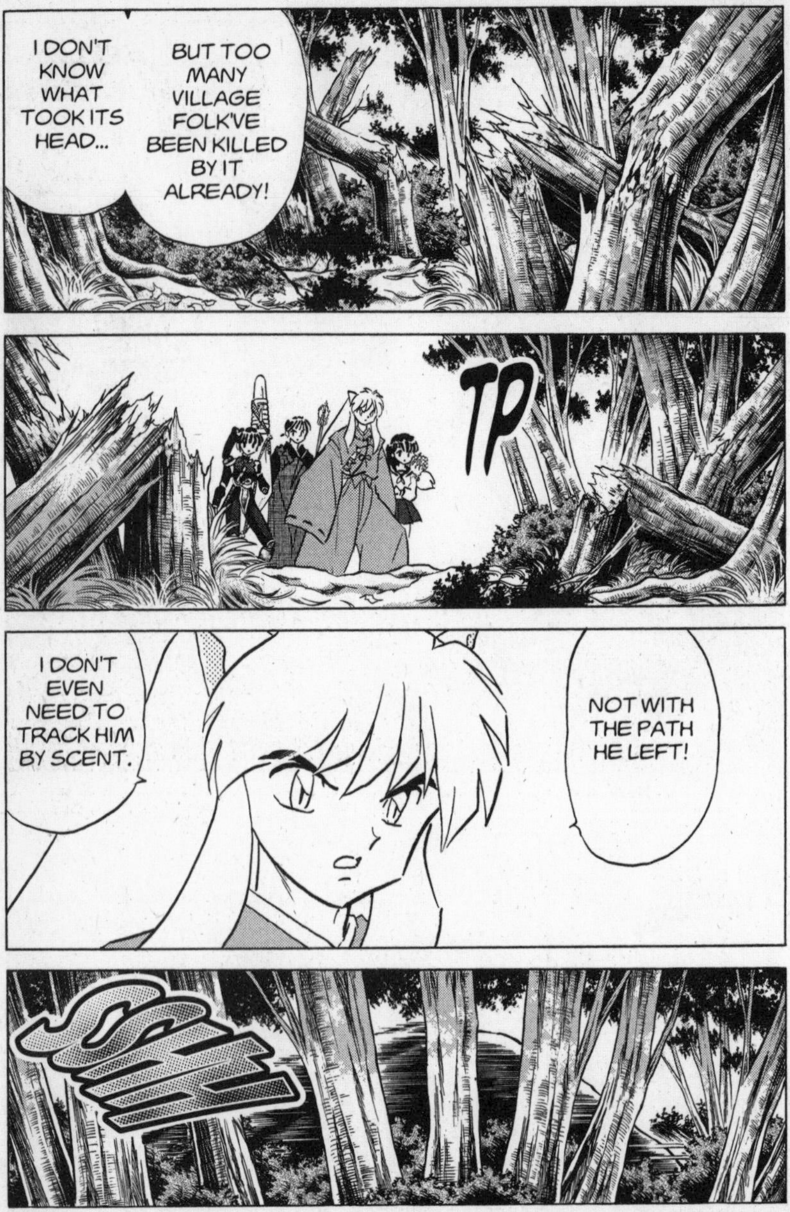
I DON'T KNOW WHAT TOOK ITS HEAD...
BUT TOO MANY VILLAGE FOLK'VE BEEN KILLED BY IT ALREADY!
TP
I DON'T EVEN NEED TO TRACK HIM BY SCENT.
NOT WITH THE PATH HE LEFT!
SSH

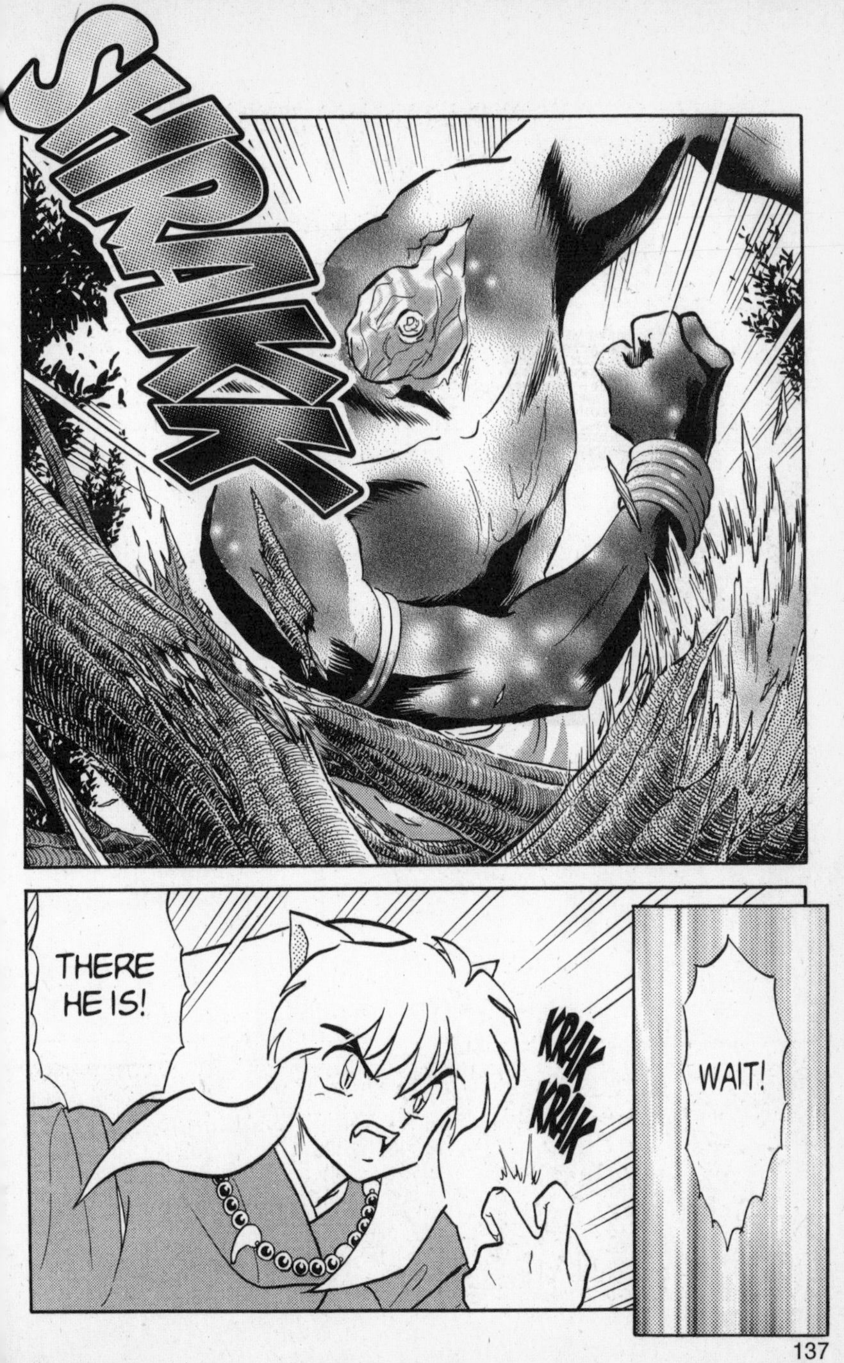
SHRAK
THERE HE IS!
KRAK KRAK
WAIT!

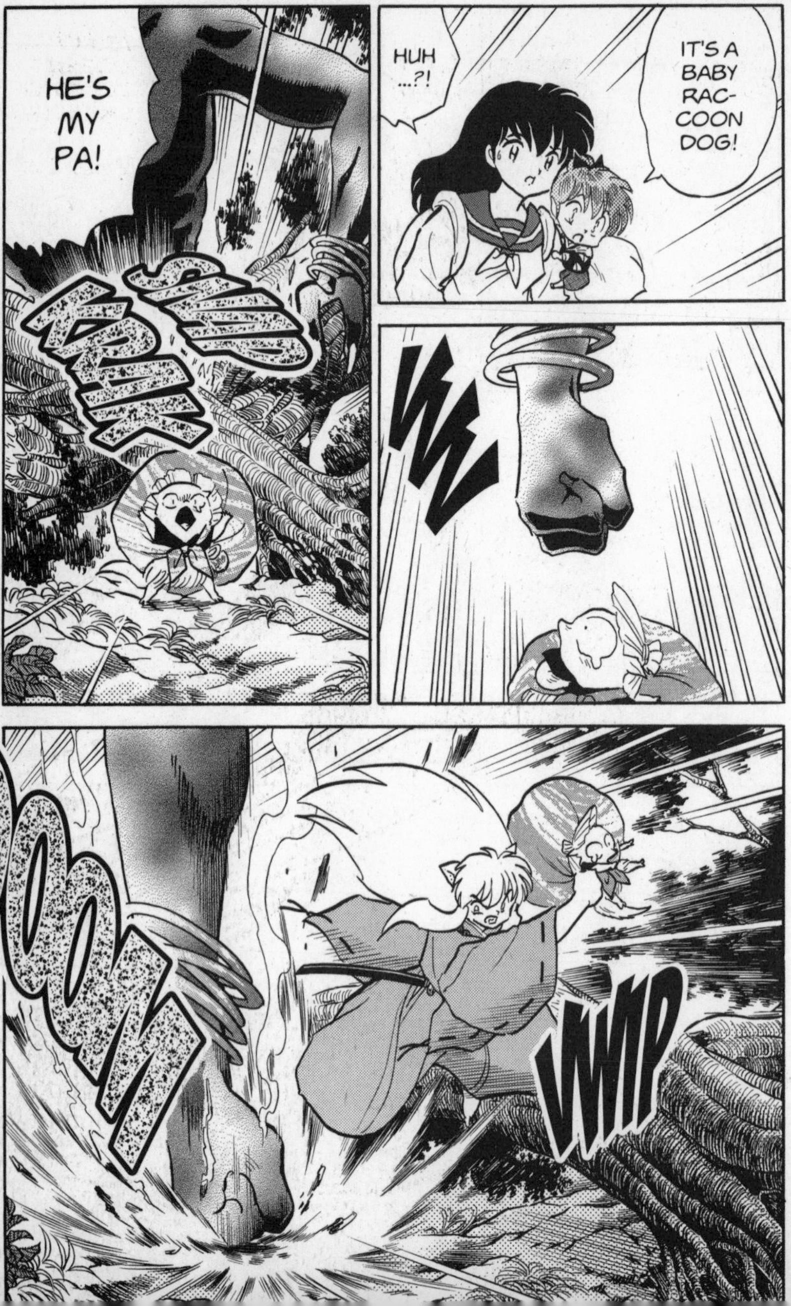
HE'S MY PA!
SNAP
KRAK
HUH ...?!
IT'S A BABY RACCOON DOG!
DOOOM

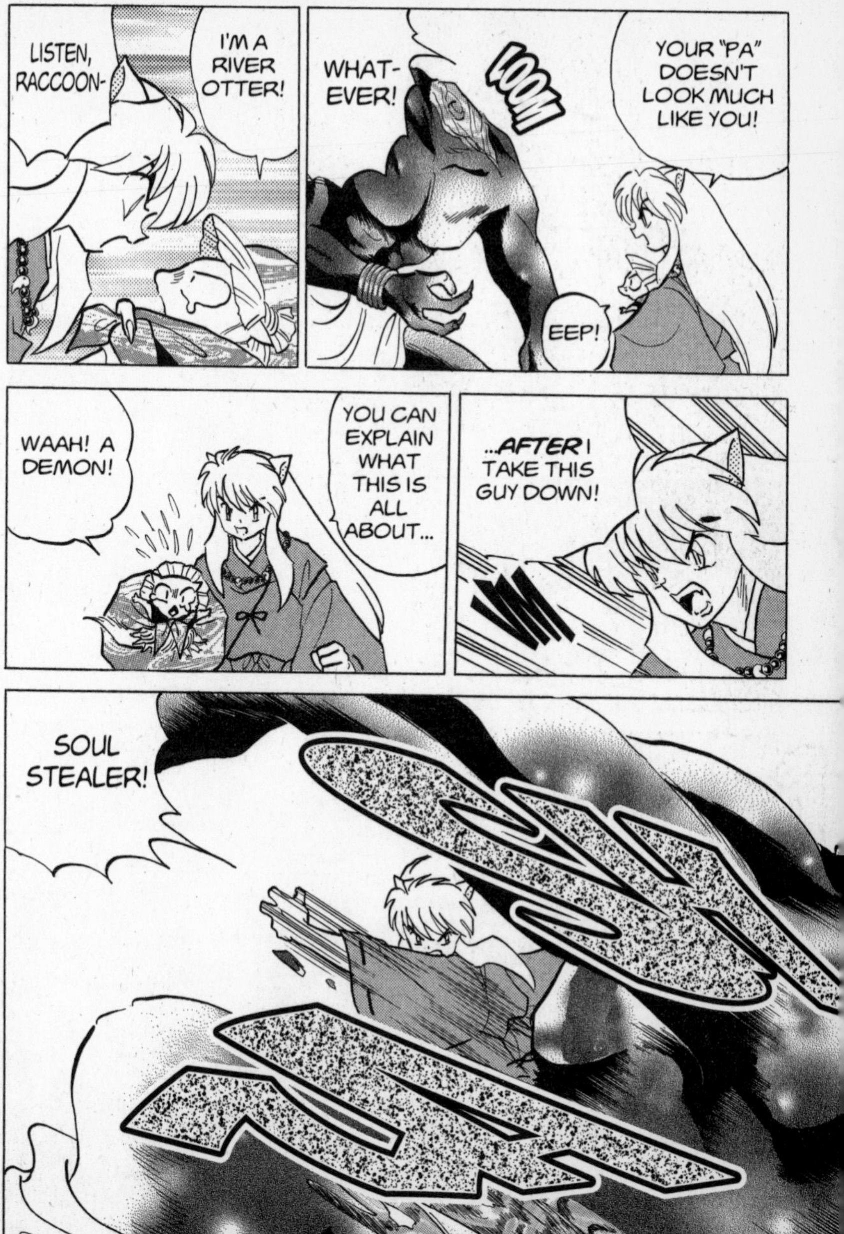
LISTEN, RACCOON-
I'M A RIVER OTTER!
WHAT-EVER!
LOOM
YOUR "PA" DOESN'T LOOK MUCH LIKE YOU!
EEP!
WAAH! A DEMON!
YOU CAN EXPLAIN WHAT THIS IS ALL ABOUT...
...AFTER I TAKE THIS GUY DOWN!
SOUL STEALER!

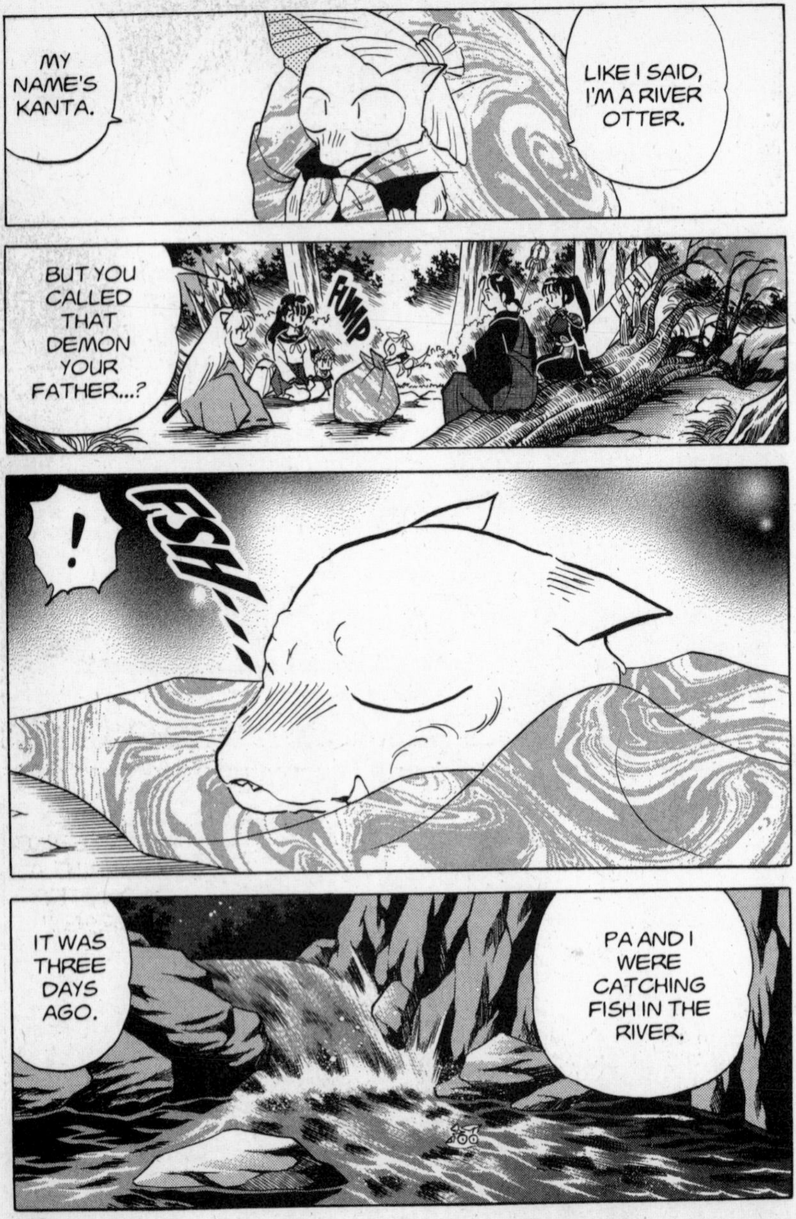
MY NAME'S KANTA.
LIKE I SAID, I'M A RIVER OTTER.
BUT YOU CALLED THAT DEMON YOUR FATHER...?
FUMP
!
FISH...
IT WAS THREE DAYS AGO.
PA AND I WERE CATCHING FISH IN THE RIVER.

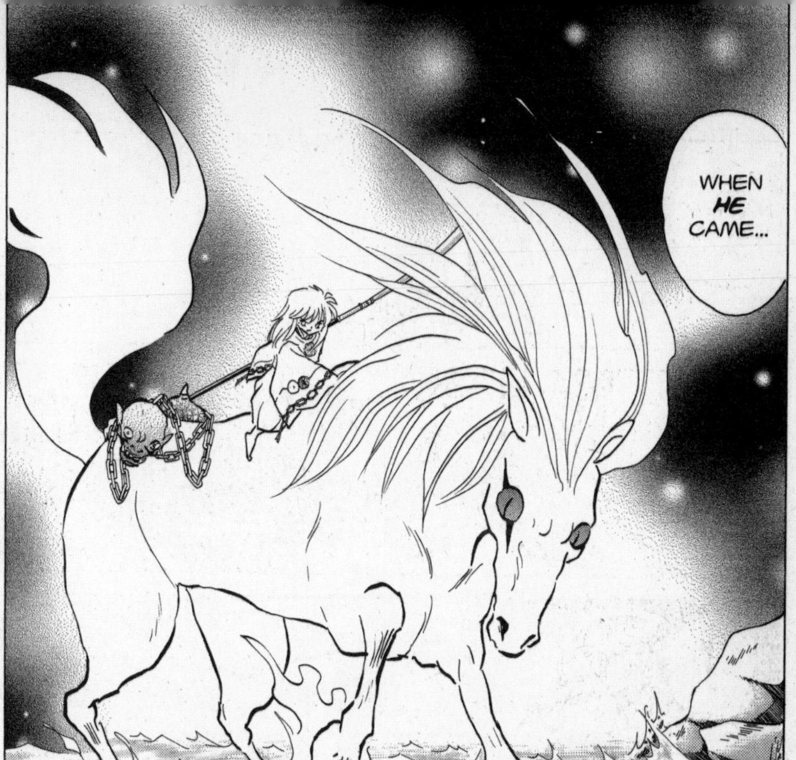
WHEN HE CAME...

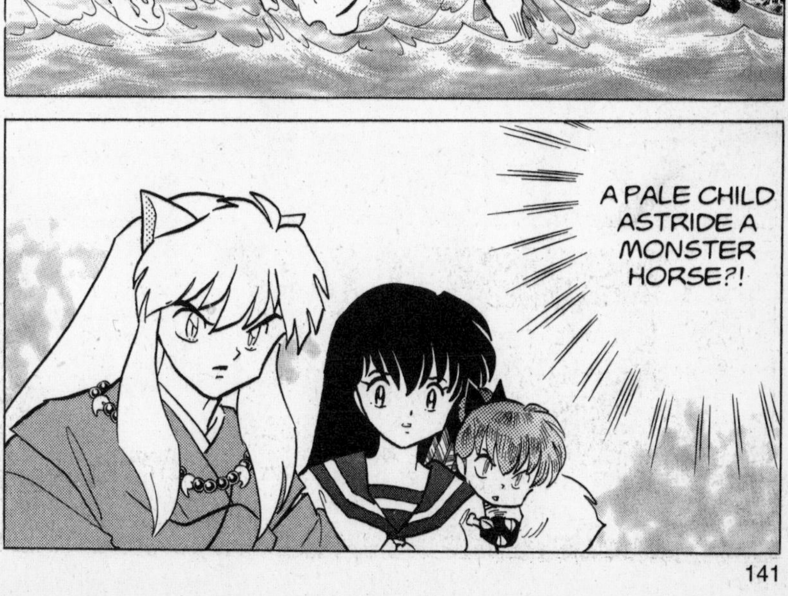
A PALE CHILD ASTRIDE A MONSTER HORSE?!

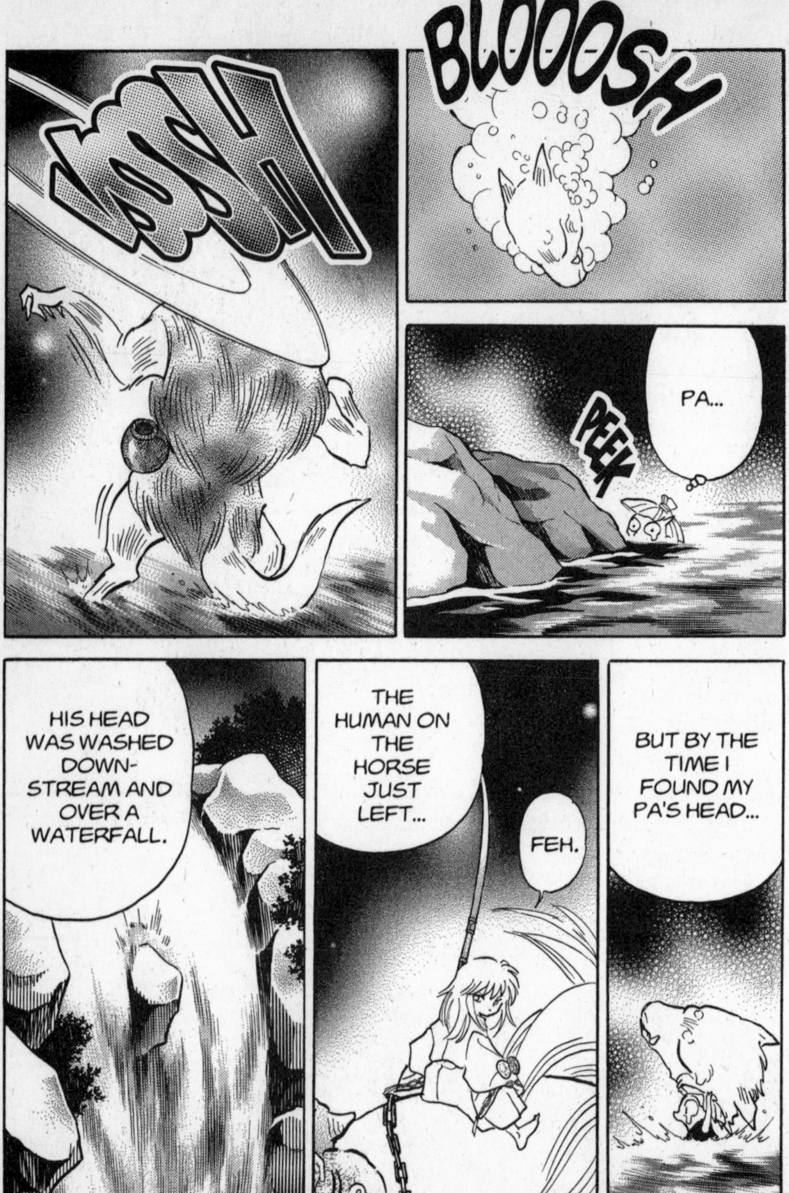
BLOOOSH
PEEK
PA...
HIS HEAD WAS WASHED DOWN-STREAM AND OVER A WATERFALL.
THE HUMAN ON THE HORSE JUST LEFT...
FEH.
BUT BY THE TIME I FOUND MY PA'S HEAD...

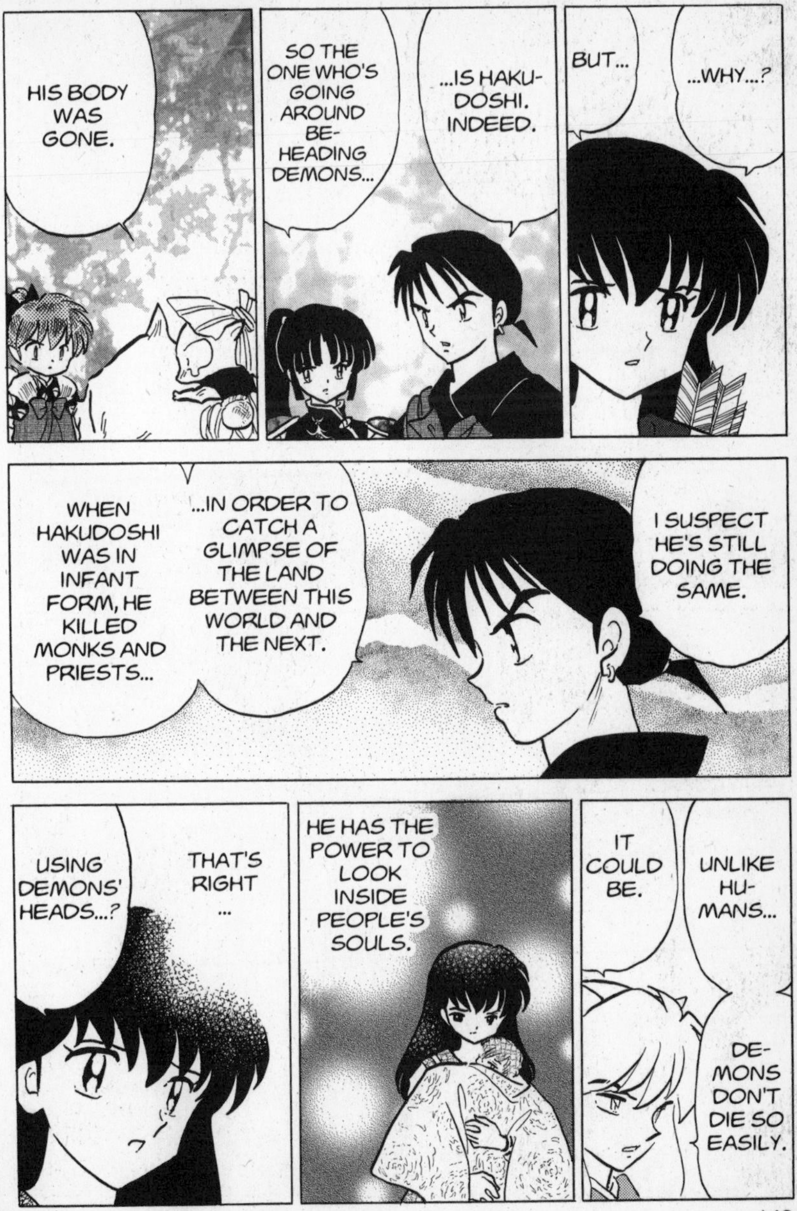
HIS BODY WAS GONE.
SO THE ONE WHO'S GOING AROUND BE-HEADING DEMONS...
...IS HAKU-DOSHI. INDEED.
BUT...
...WHY...?
WHEN HAKUDOSHI WAS IN INFANT FORM, HE KILLED MONKS AND PRIESTS...
...IN ORDER TO CATCH A GLIMPSE OF THE LAND BETWEEN THIS WORLD AND THE NEXT.
I SUSPECT HE'S STILL DOING THE SAME.
USING DEMONS' HEADS...?
THAT'S RIGHT ...
HE HAS THE POWER TO LOOK INSIDE PEOPLE'S SOULS.
IT COULD BE.
UNLIKE HU-MANS...
DE-MONS DON'T DIE SO EASILY.

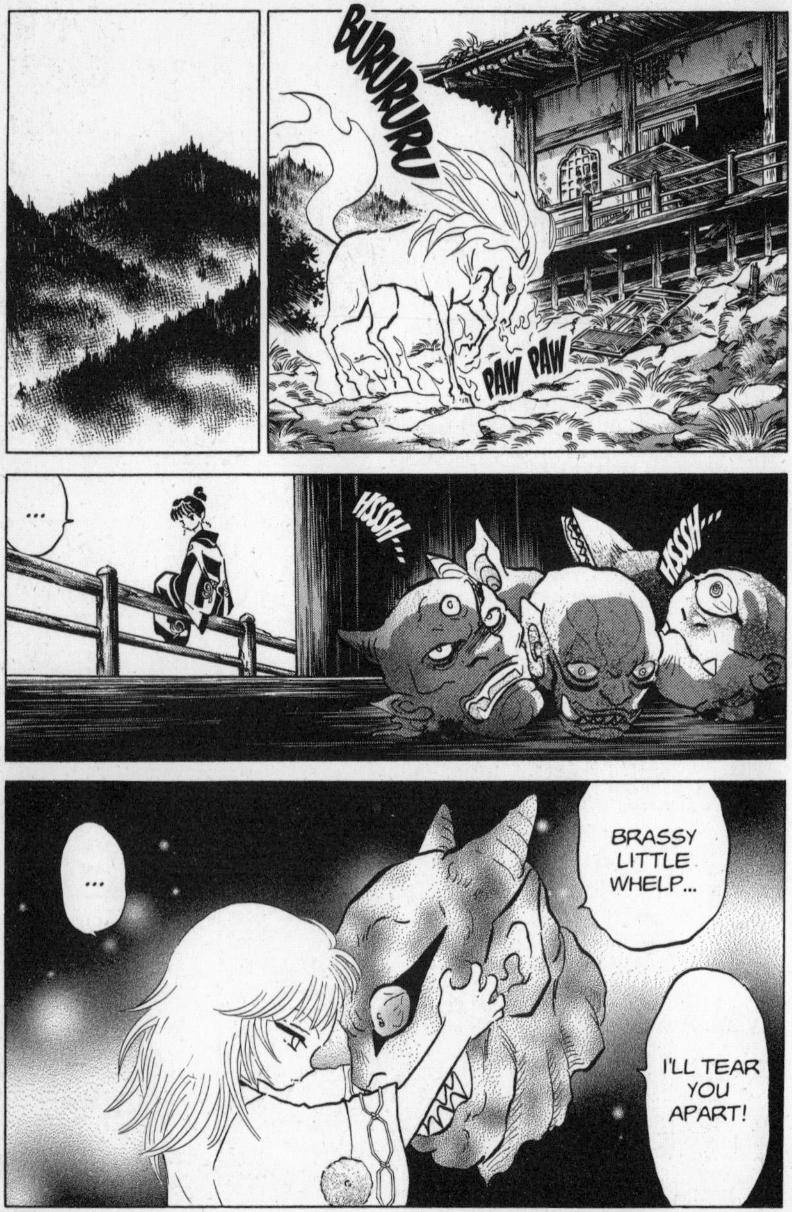
BURURURURU
PAW PAW
...
HSSSH...
HSSSH...
...
BRASSY LITTLE WHELP...
I'LL TEAR YOU APART!

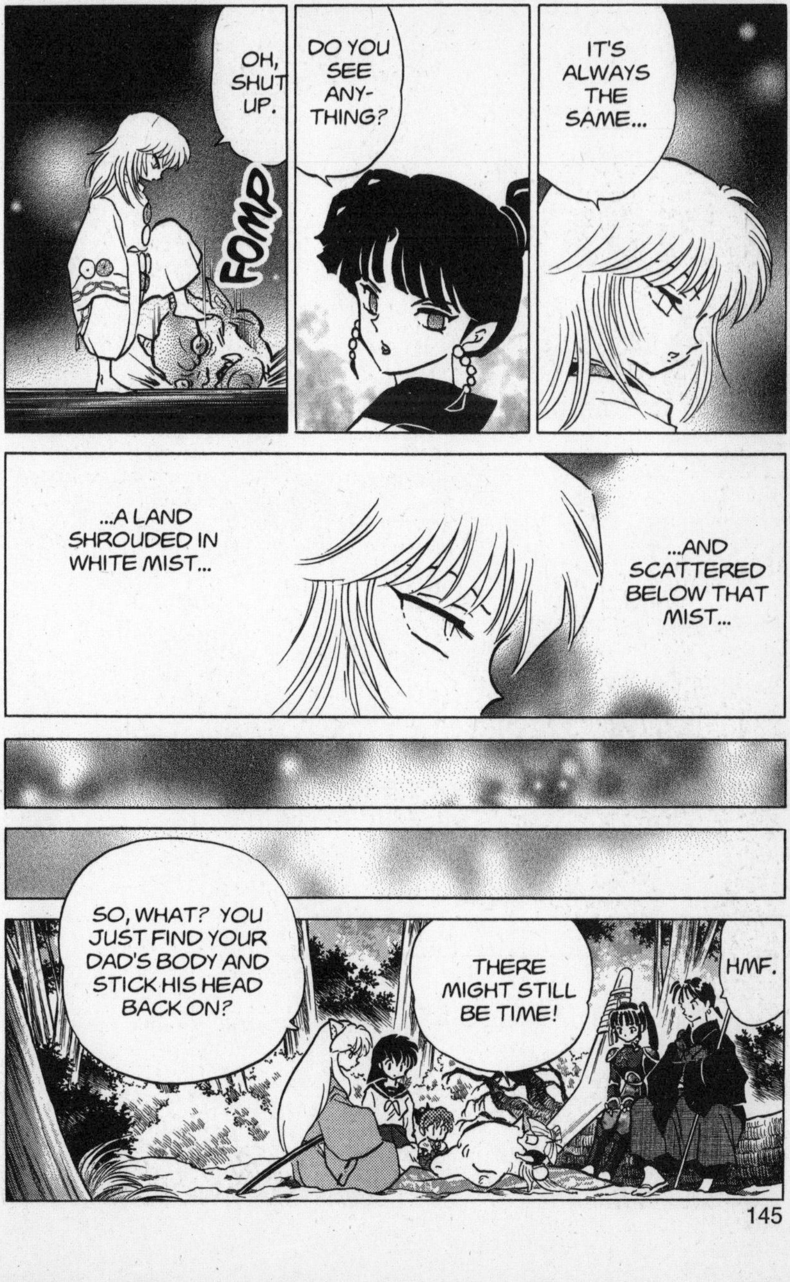
OH, SHUT UP.
FOMP
DO YOU SEE ANY-THING?
IT'S ALWAYS THE SAME...
...A LAND SHROUDED IN WHITE MIST...
...AND SCATTERED BELOW THAT MIST...
SO, WHAT? YOU JUST FIND YOUR DAD'S BODY AND STICK HIS HEAD BACK ON?
THERE MIGHT STILL BE TIME!
HMF.

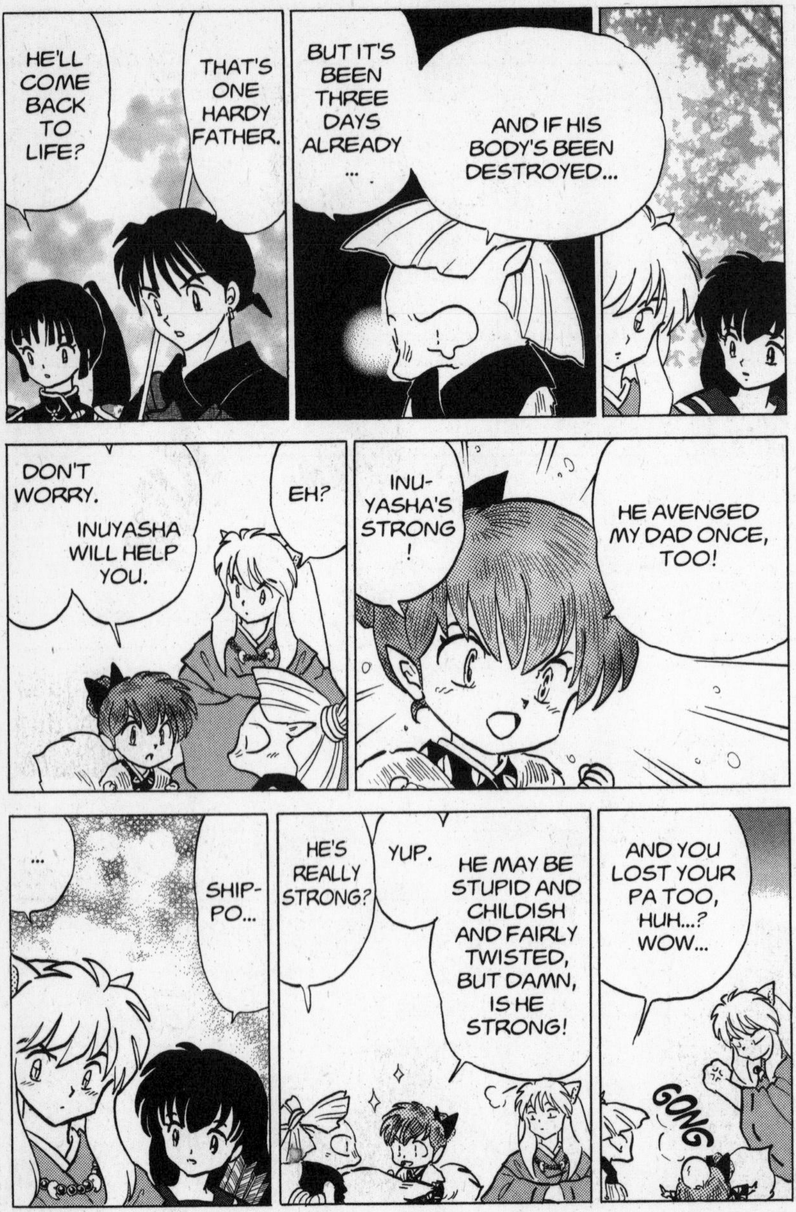
HE'LL COME BACK TO LIFE?
THAT'S ONE HARDY FATHER.
BUT IT'S BEEN THREE DAYS ALREADY ...
AND IF HIS BODY'S BEEN DESTROYED...
DON'T WORRY.
INUYASHA WILL HELP YOU.
EH?
INU-YASHA'S STRONG!
HE AVENGED MY DAD ONCE, TOO!
...
SHIP-PO...
HE'S REALLY STRONG?
YUP.
HE MAY BE STUPID AND CHILDISH AND FAIRLY TWISTED, BUT DAMN, IS HE STRONG!
AND YOU LOST YOUR PA TOO, HUH...? WOW...
GONG

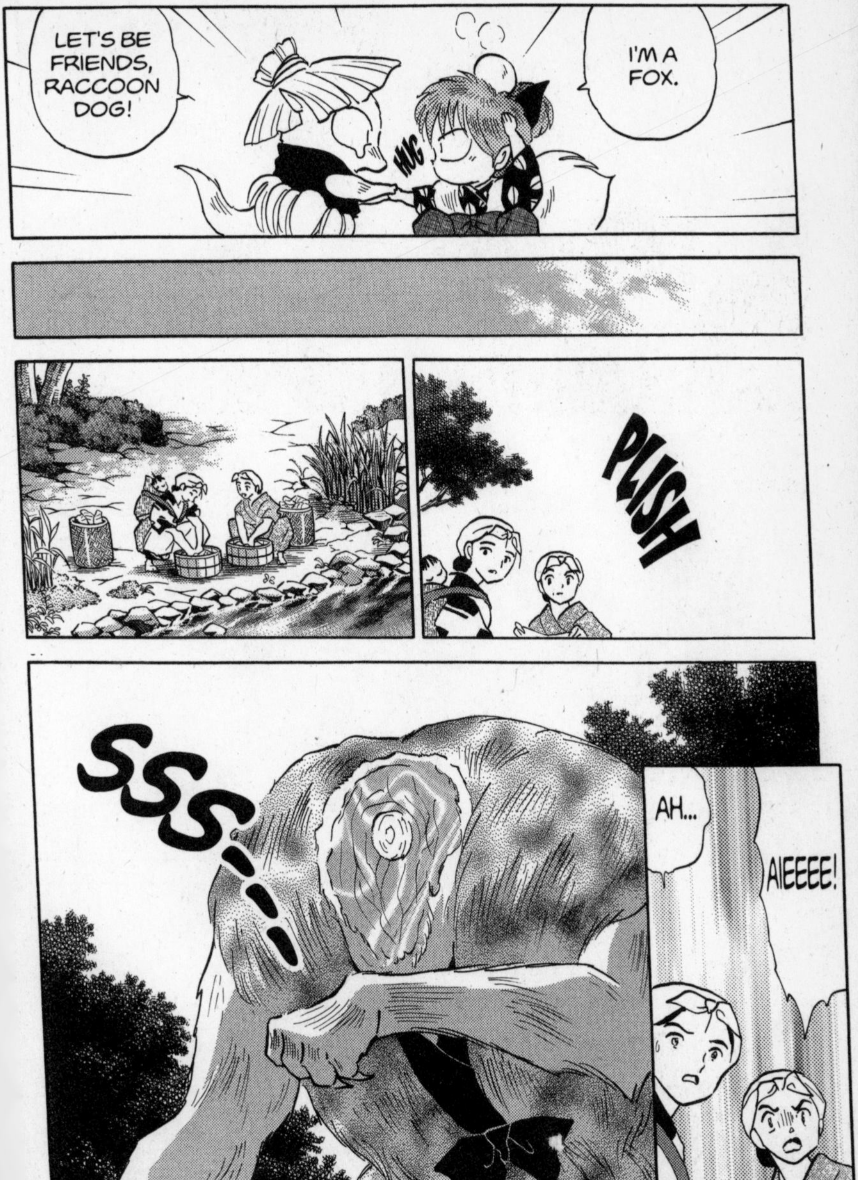
LET'S BE FRIENDS, RACCOON DOG!
HUG
I'M A FOX.
PLISH
SSS...
AH...
AIEEEE!

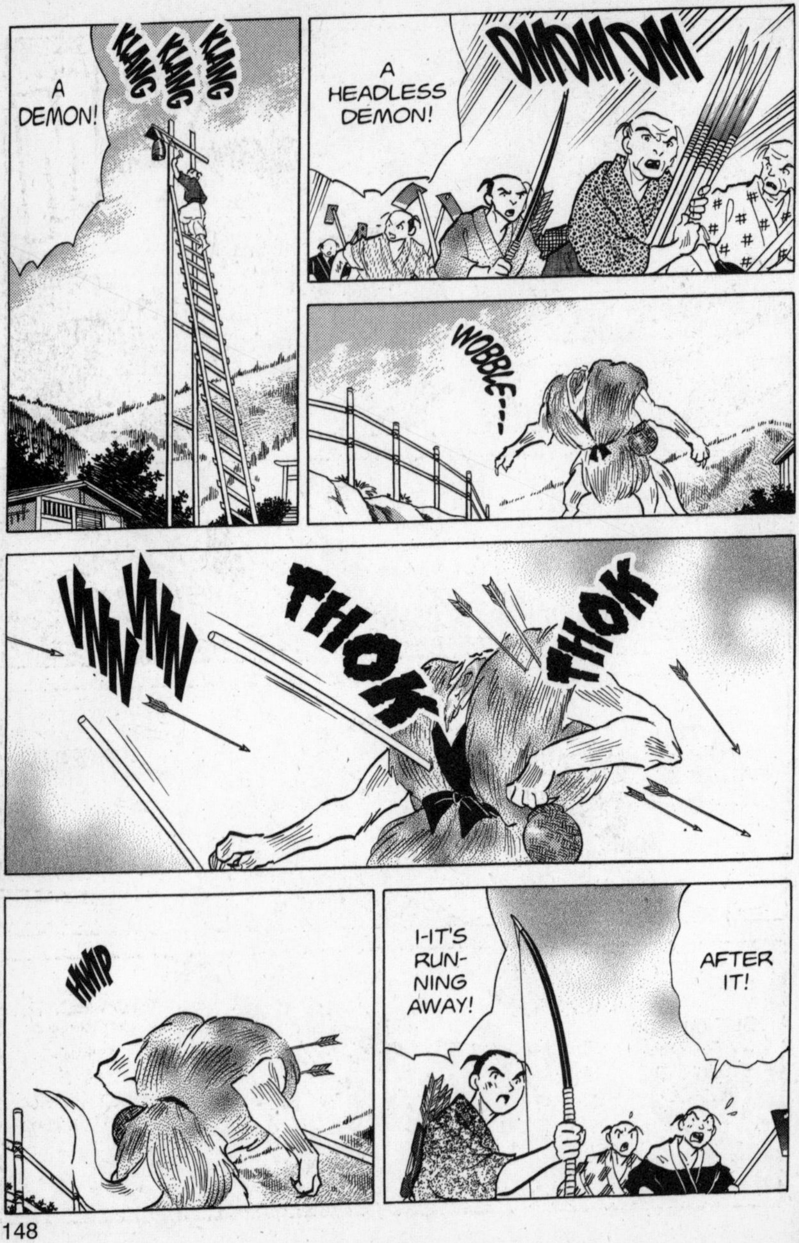
A DEMON!
KLANG KLANG KLANG
A HEADLESS DEMON!
DMDMDMDM
WOBBLE...
VMMN VMMN
THOK THOK
HWIP
I-IT'S RUN-NING AWAY!
AFTER IT!

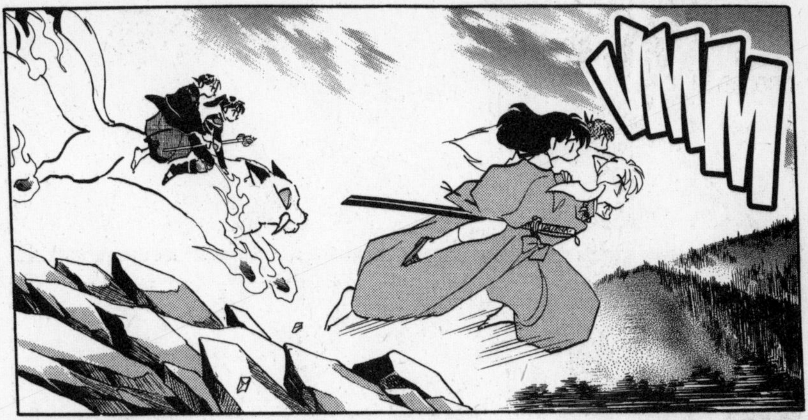
VMMM
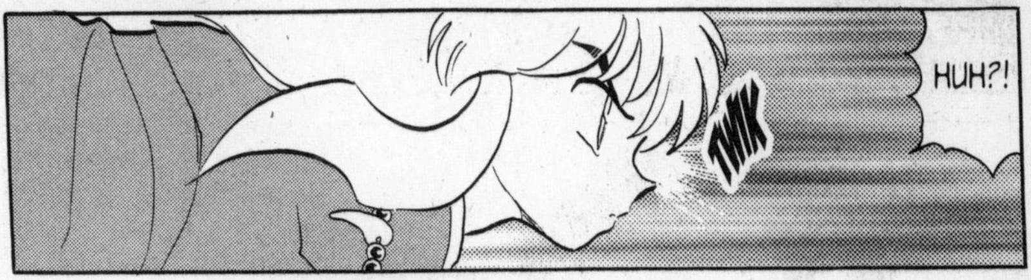
TWIK
HUH?!
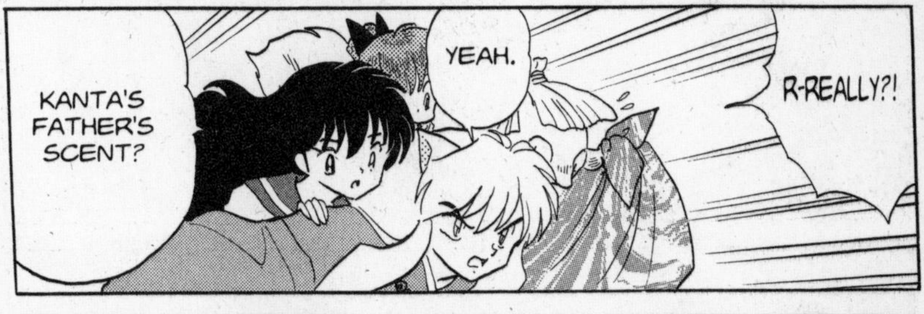
KANTA'S FATHER'S SCENT?
YEAH.
R-REALLY?!
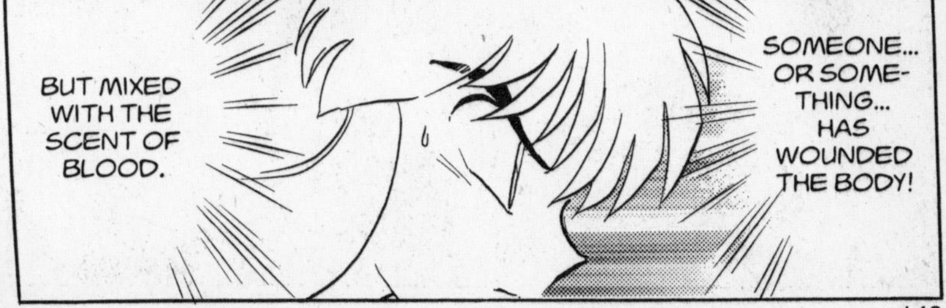
BUT MIXED WITH THE SCENT OF BLOOD.
SOMEONE... OR SOMETHING... HAS WOUNDED THE BODY!

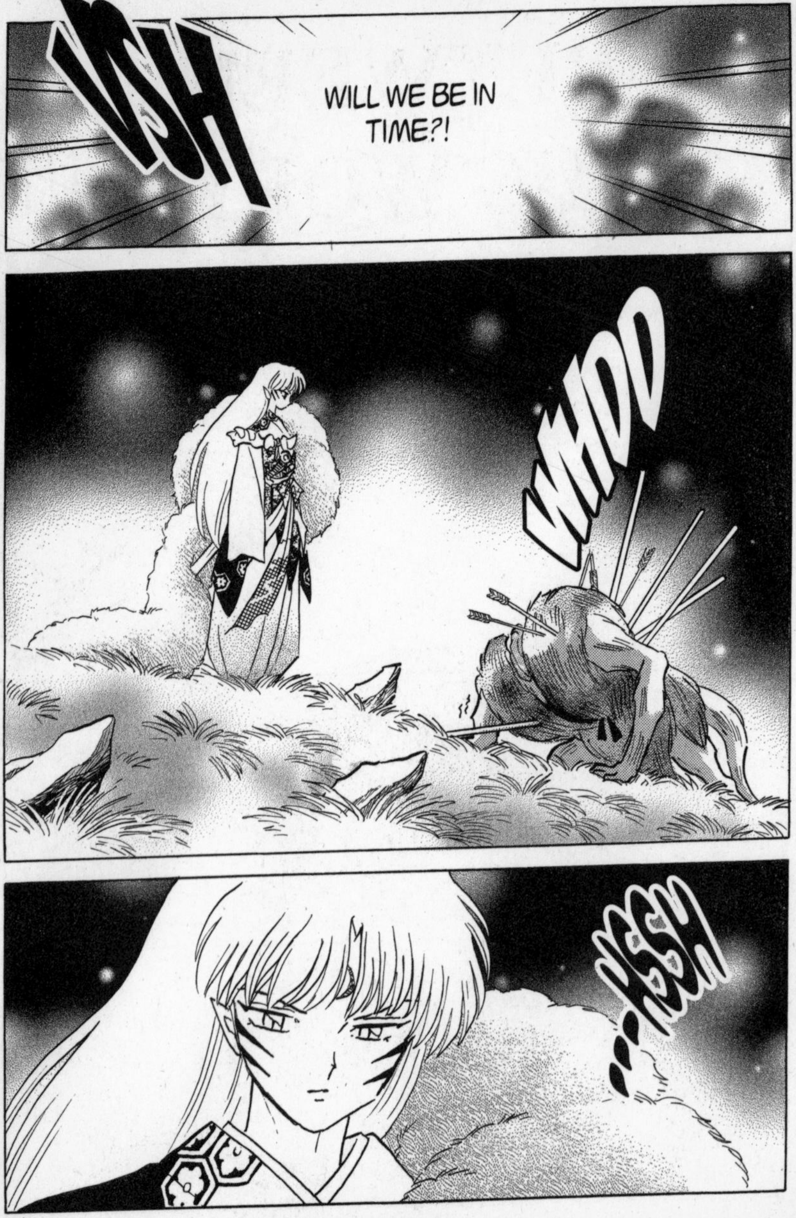
VSH
WILL WE BE IN TIME?!
WHDD
...HSSH

SCROLL 9

BETWEEN THIS WORLD AND THE NEXT

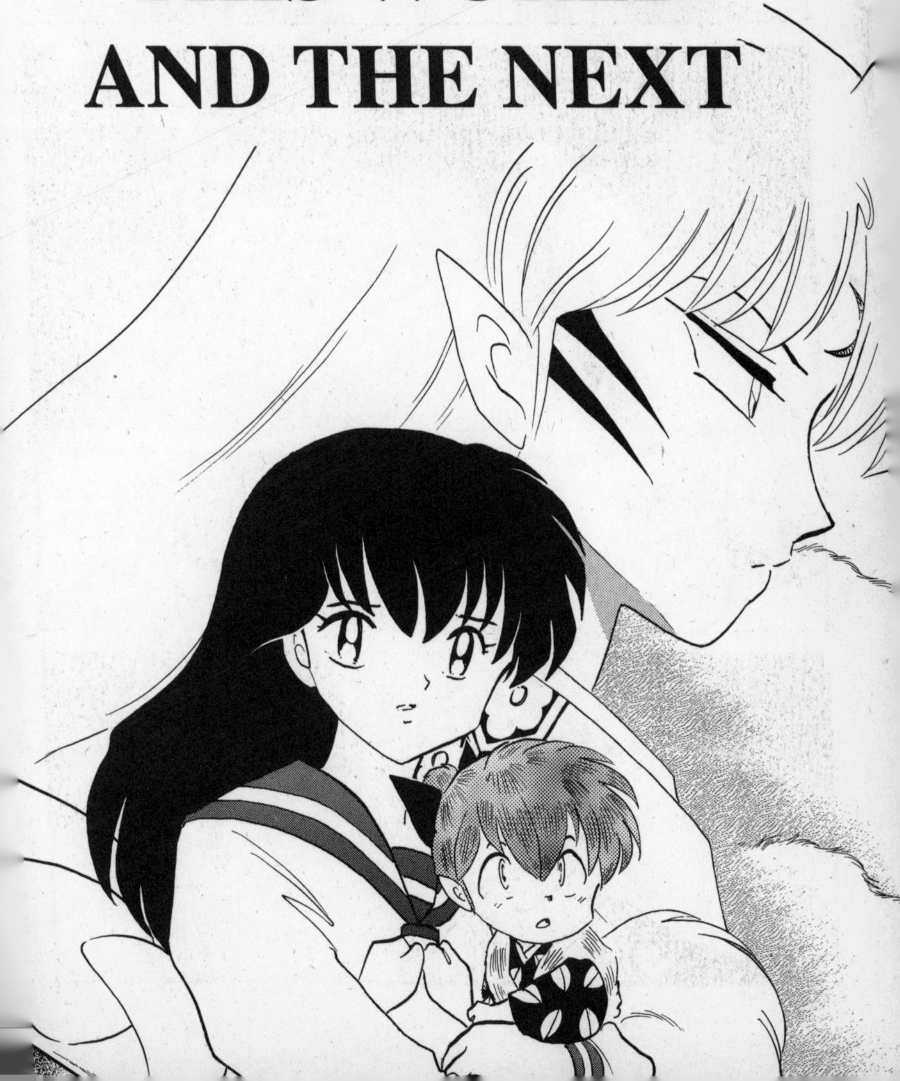

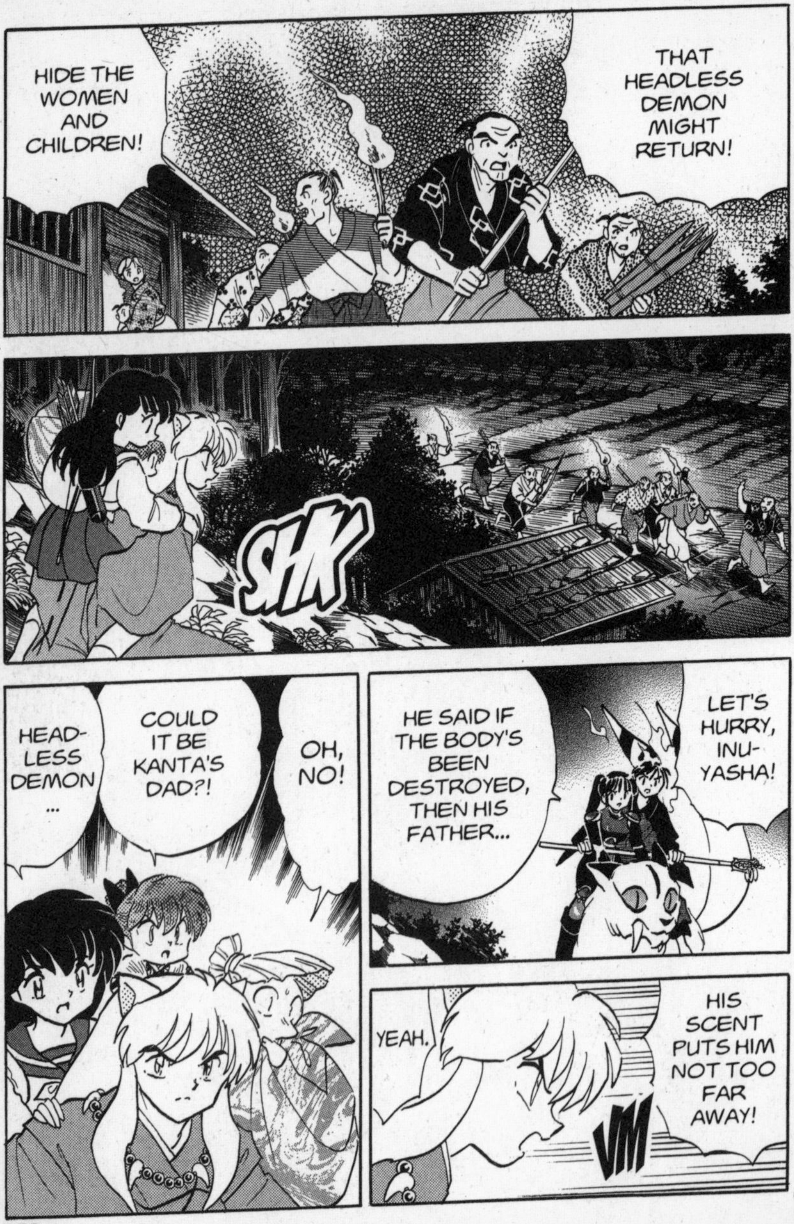
HIDE THE WOMEN AND CHILDREN!
THAT HEADLESS DEMON MIGHT RETURN!
SHK
HEADLESS DEMON ...
COULD IT BE KANTA'S DAD?!
OH, NO!
HE SAID IF THE BODY'S BEEN DESTROYED, THEN HIS FATHER...
LET'S HURRY, INUYASHA!
YEAH.
HIS SCENT PUTS HIM NOT TOO FAR AWAY!
VM

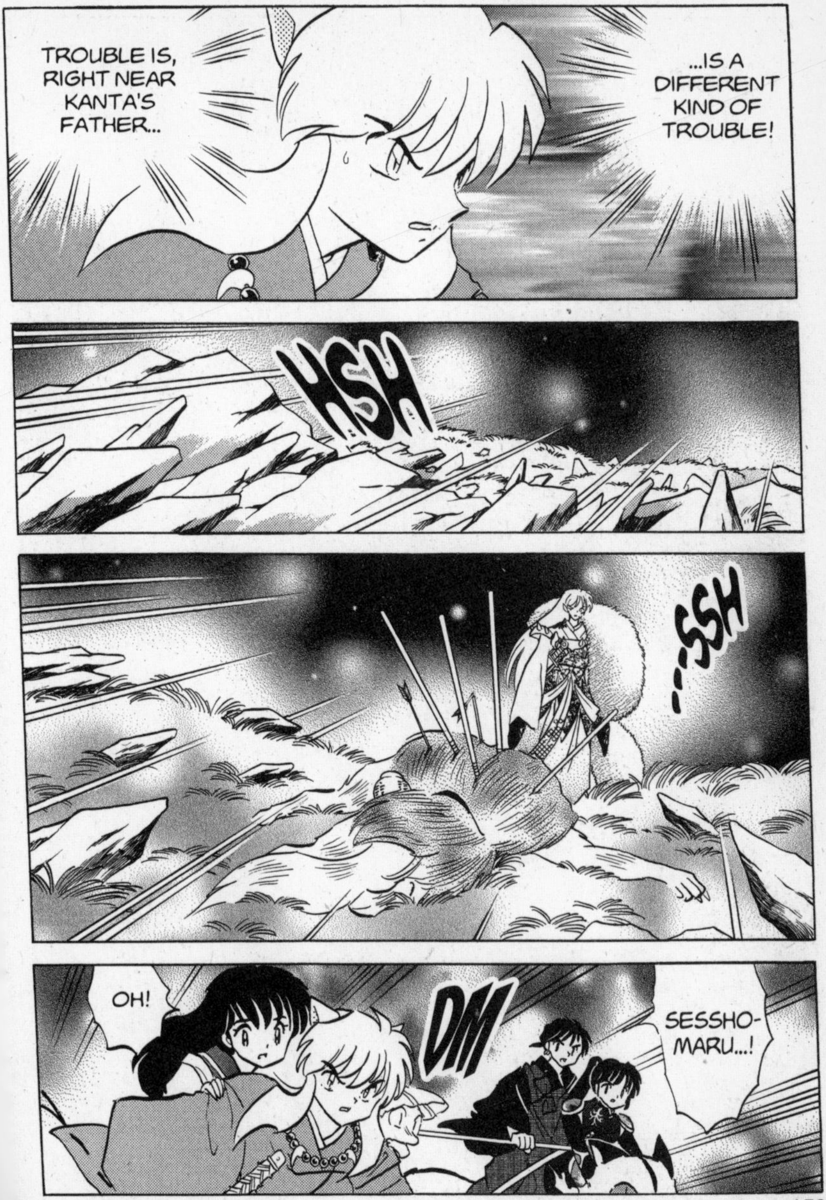
TROUBLE IS, RIGHT NEAR KANTA'S FATHER...
...IS A DIFFERENT KIND OF TROUBLE!
HSH
...SSH
OH!
DM
SESSHO-MARU...!

...

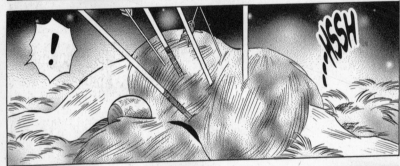

PSSH

OH...

PA--!

H-HANG ON, PA--!

LET'S GET HIS HEAD, KANTA!

YEAH.

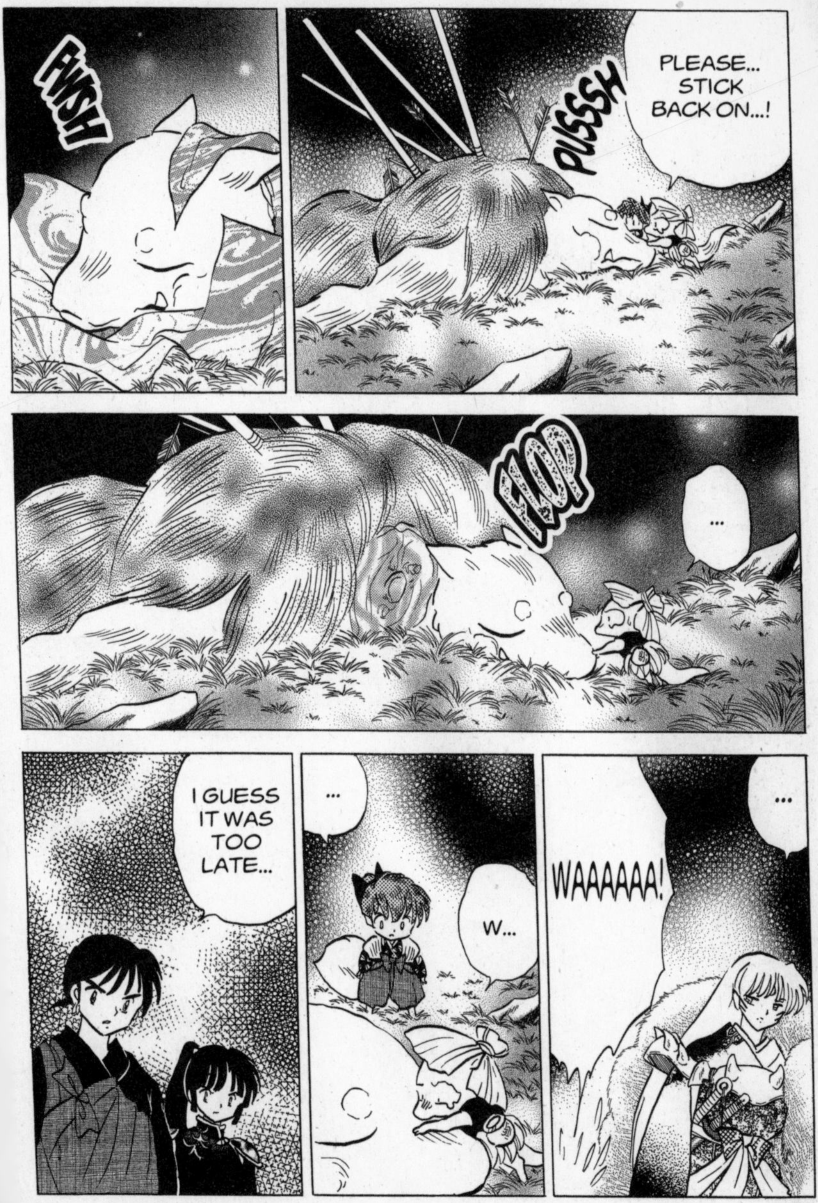
FWSH
PUSSSH
PLEASE... STICK BACK ON...!
HOP
...
I GUESS IT WAS TOO LATE...
...
W...
...
WAAAAAA!

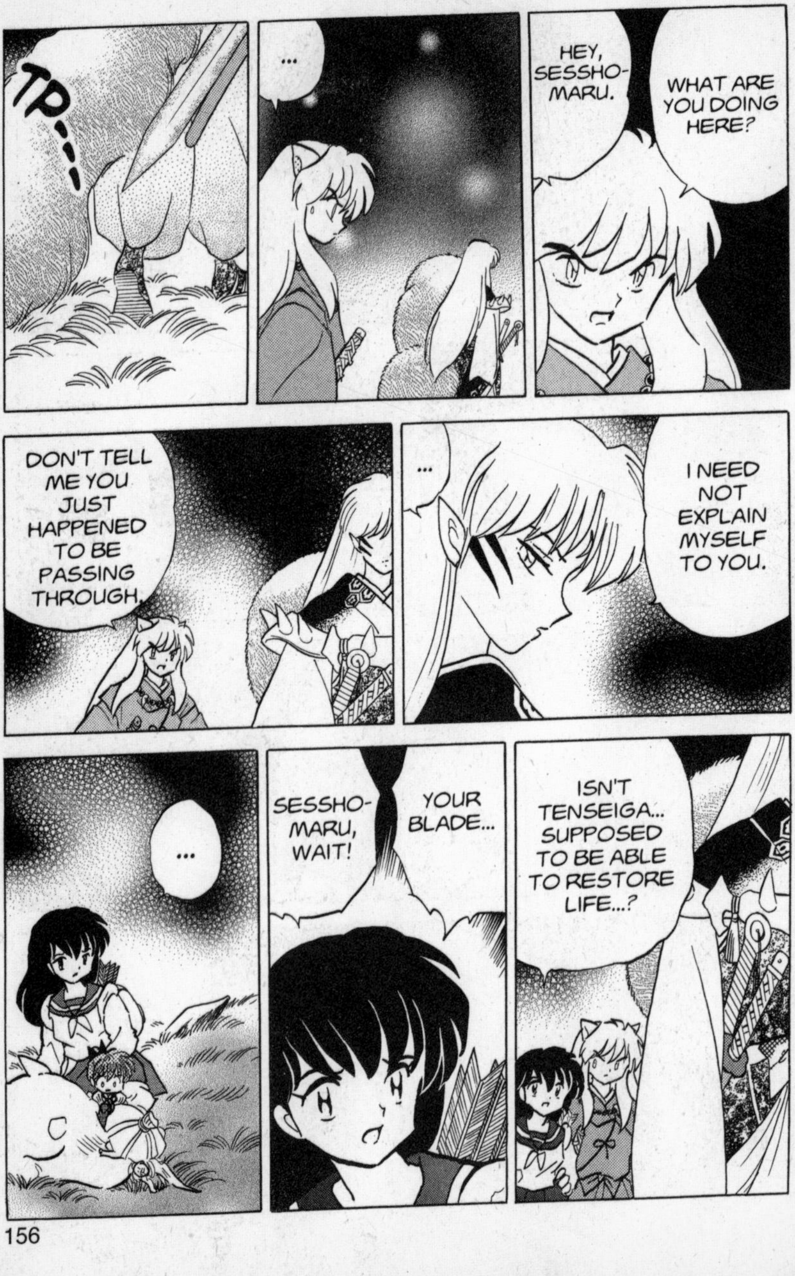
TP...
...
HEY, SESSHO-MARU.
WHAT ARE YOU DOING HERE?
DON'T TELL ME YOU JUST HAPPENED TO BE PASSING THROUGH.
...
I NEED NOT EXPLAIN MYSELF TO YOU.
...
SESSHO-MARU, WAIT!
YOUR BLADE...
ISN'T TENSEIGA... SUPPOSED TO BE ABLE TO RESTORE LIFE...?

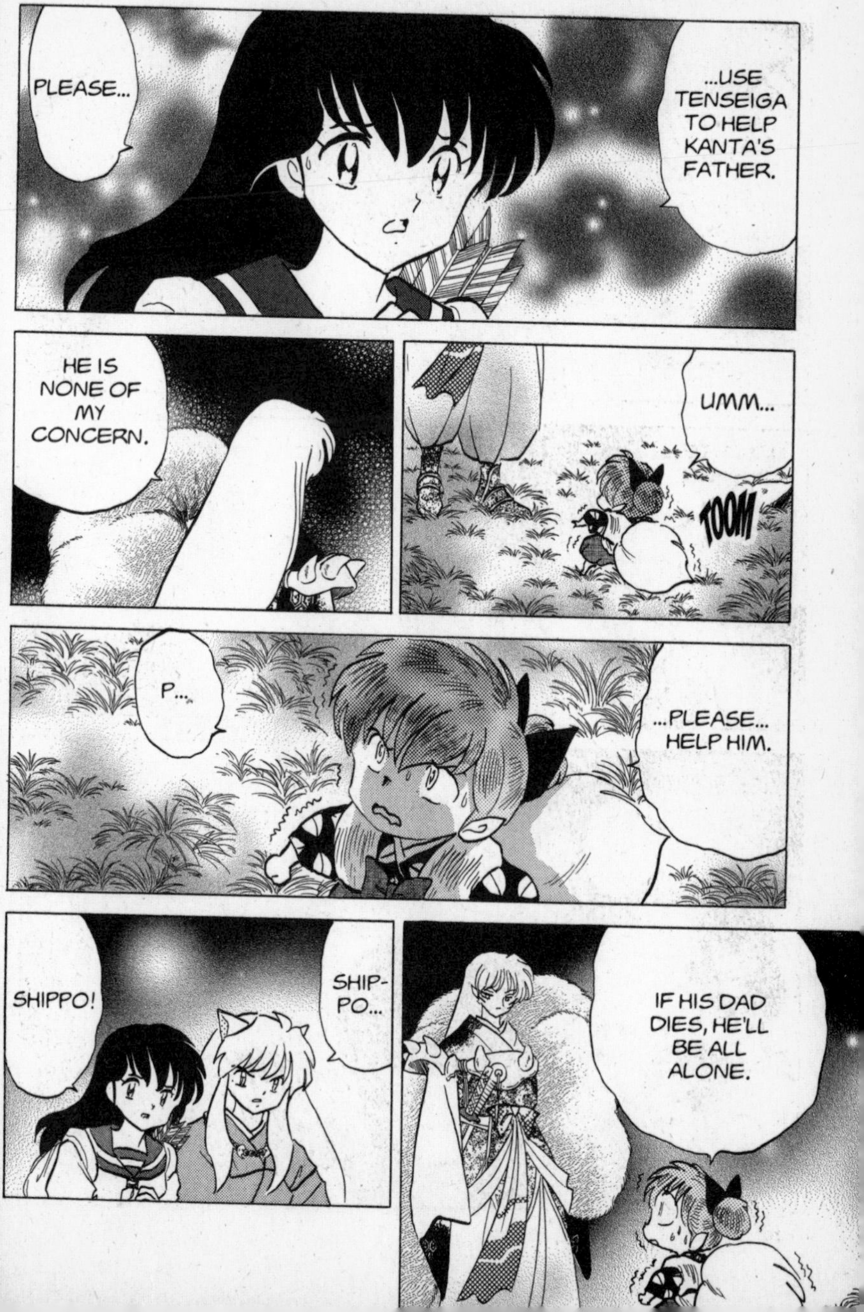
PLEASE...
...USE TENSEIGA TO HELP KANTA'S FATHER.
HE IS NONE OF MY CONCERN.
UMM...
TOOM
P...
...PLEASE... HELP HIM.
SHIPPO!
SHIP-PO...
IF HIS DAD DIES, HE'LL BE ALL ALONE.

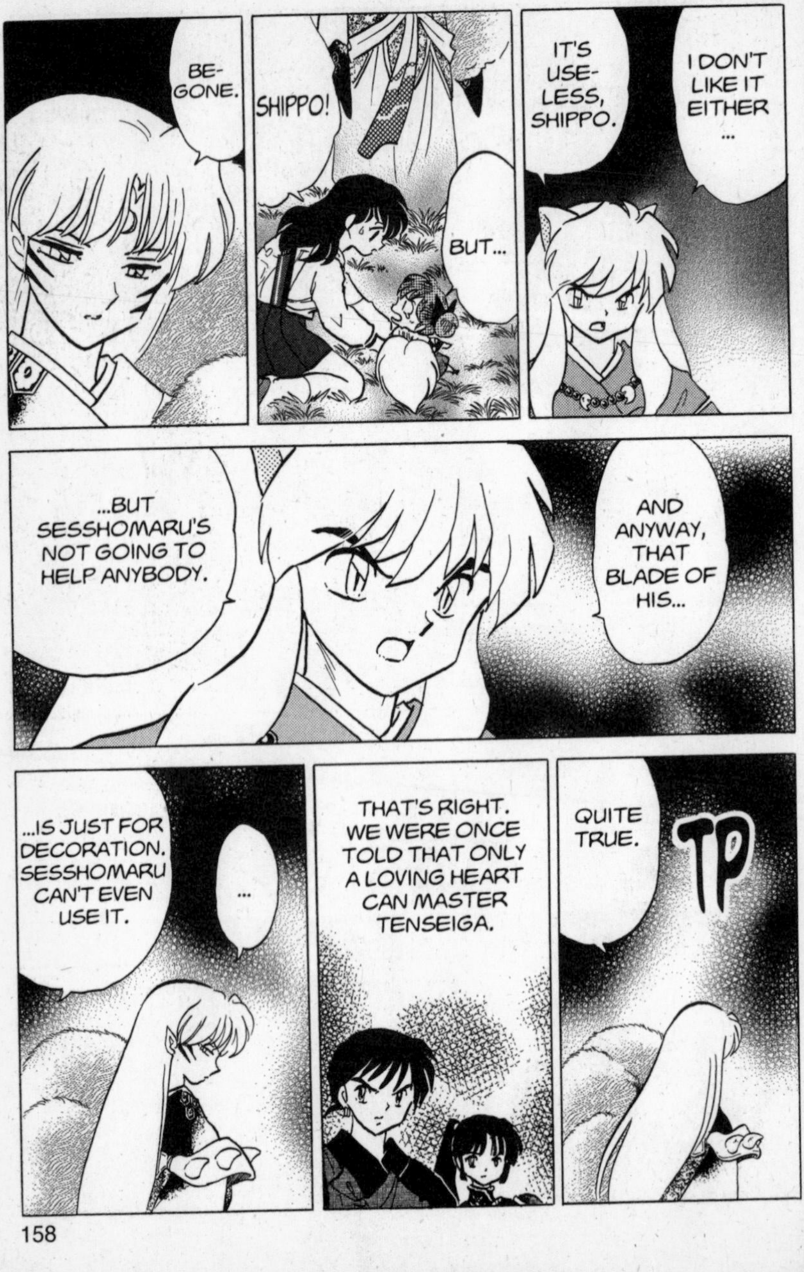
BE-GONE.
SHIPPO!
BUT...
IT'S USE-LESS, SHIPPO.
I DON'T LIKE IT EITHER ...
...BUT SESSHOMARU'S NOT GOING TO HELP ANYBODY.
AND ANYWAY, THAT BLADE OF HIS...
...IS JUST FOR DECORATION. SESSHOMARU CAN'T EVEN USE IT.
...
THAT'S RIGHT. WE WERE ONCE TOLD THAT ONLY A LOVING HEART CAN MASTER TENSEIGA.
QUITE TRUE.
TP

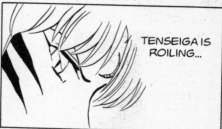

TENSEIGA IS ROILING...

IS IT TELLING ME TO SAVE HIM...?

...BUT WHY?

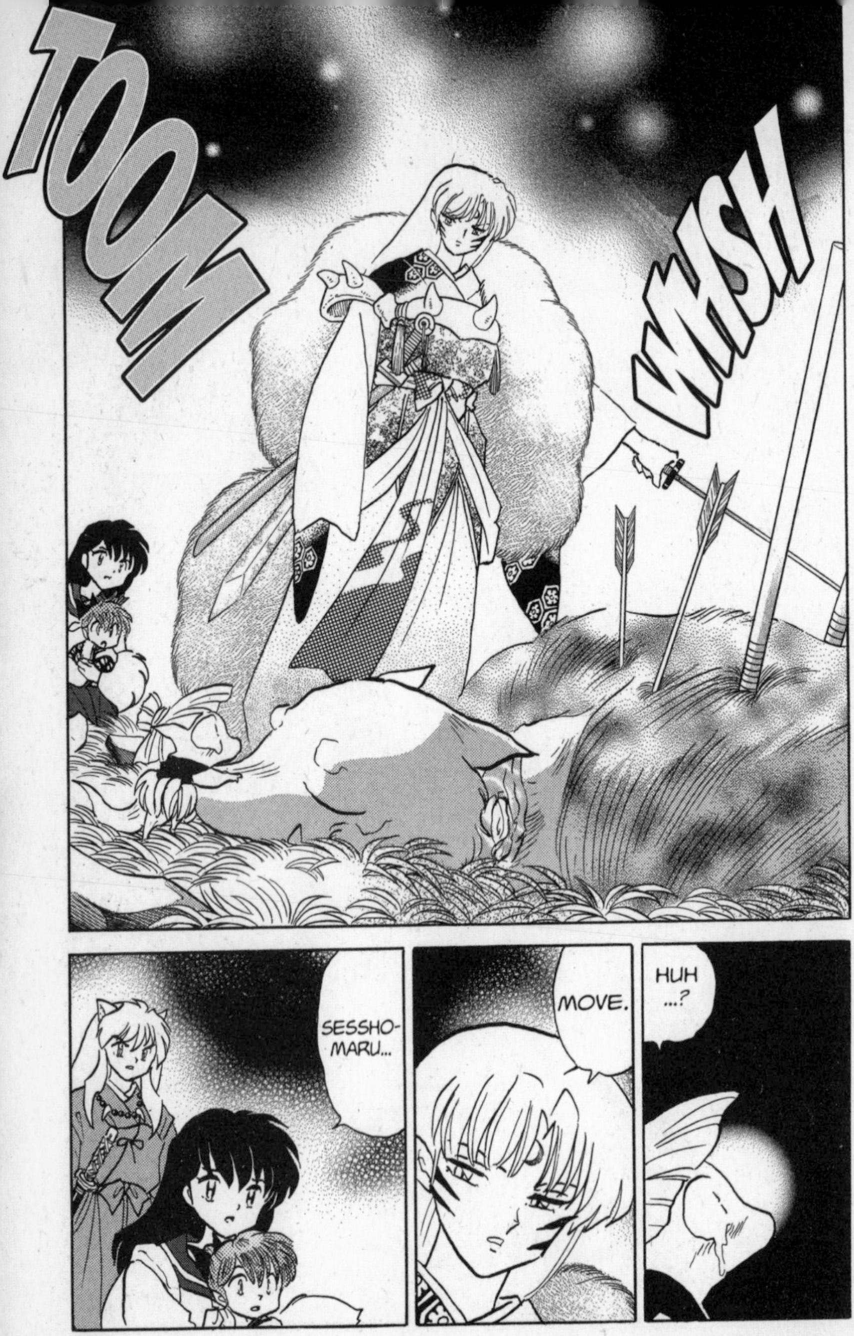
TOOM
WHISH
SESSHO-MARU...
MOVE.
HUH ...?

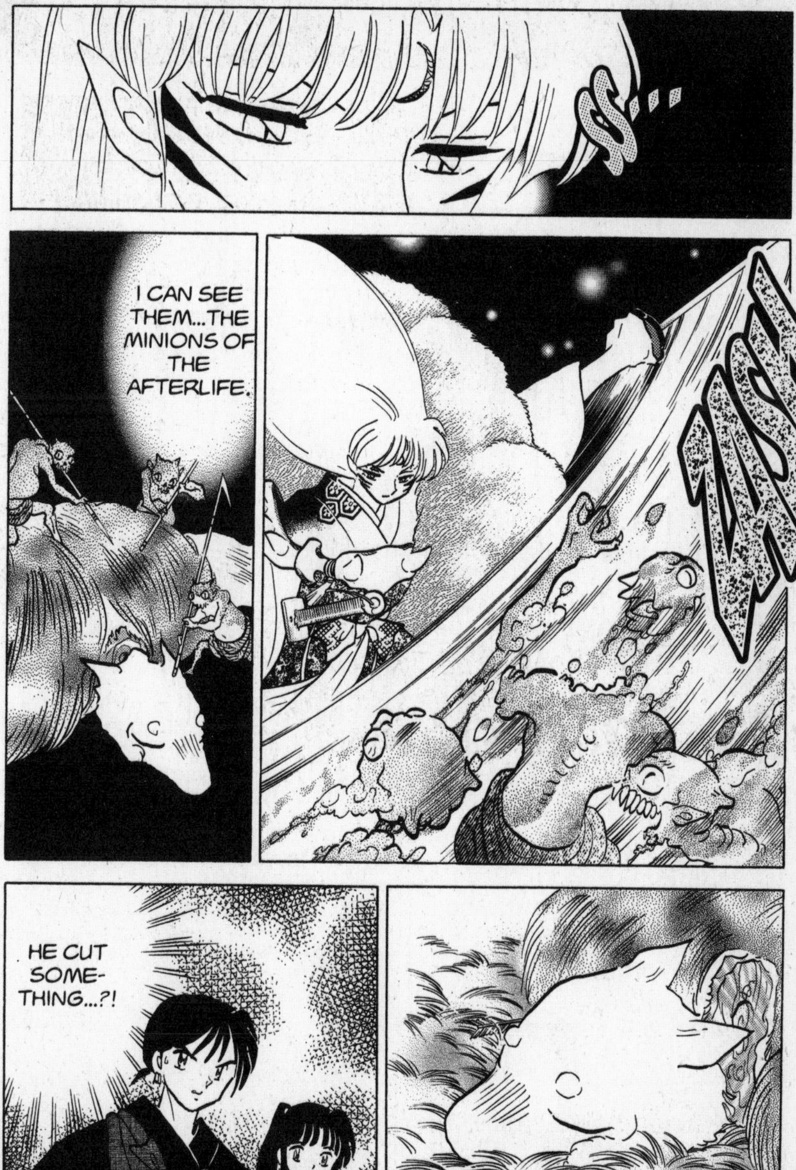
S...
I CAN SEE THEM...THE MINIONS OF THE AFTERLIFE.
ZWSH
HE CUT SOME-THING...?!

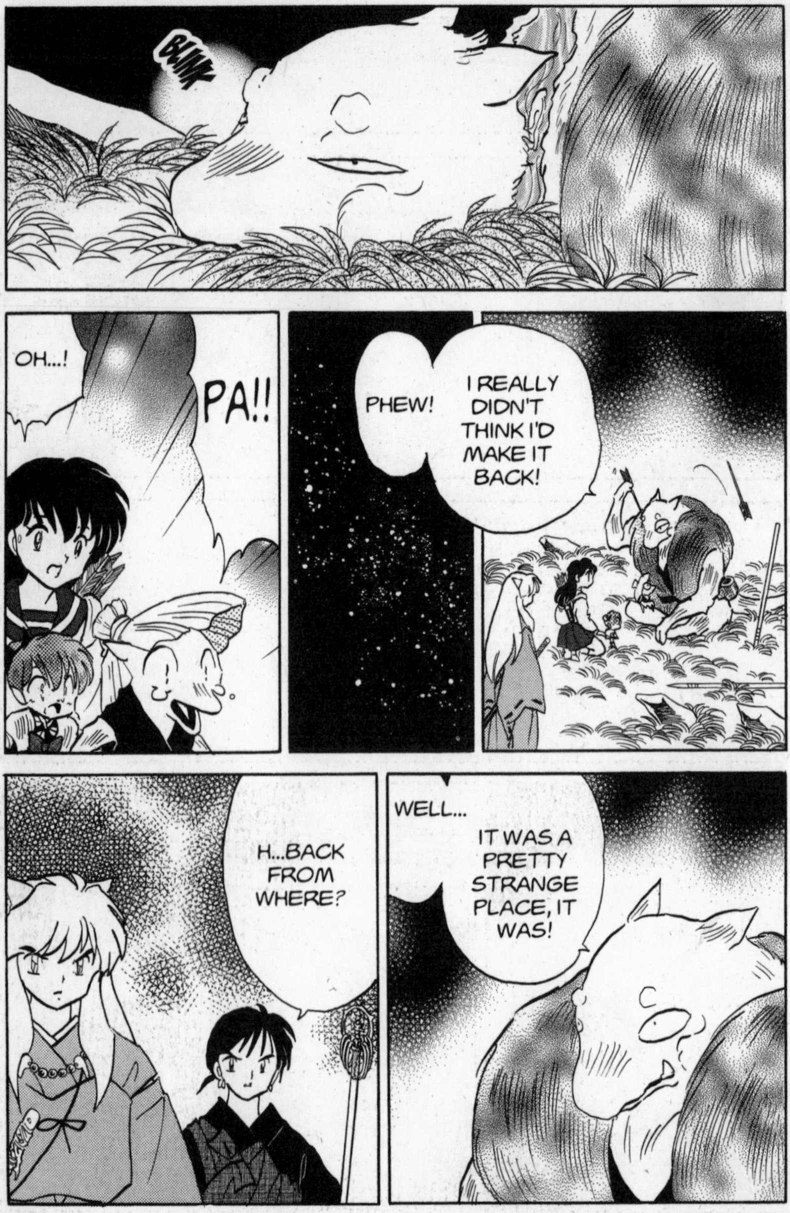
BLINK
OH...!
PA!!
PHEW!
I REALLY DIDN'T THINK I'D MAKE IT BACK!
H...BACK FROM WHERE?
WELL...
IT WAS A PRETTY STRANGE PLACE, IT WAS!

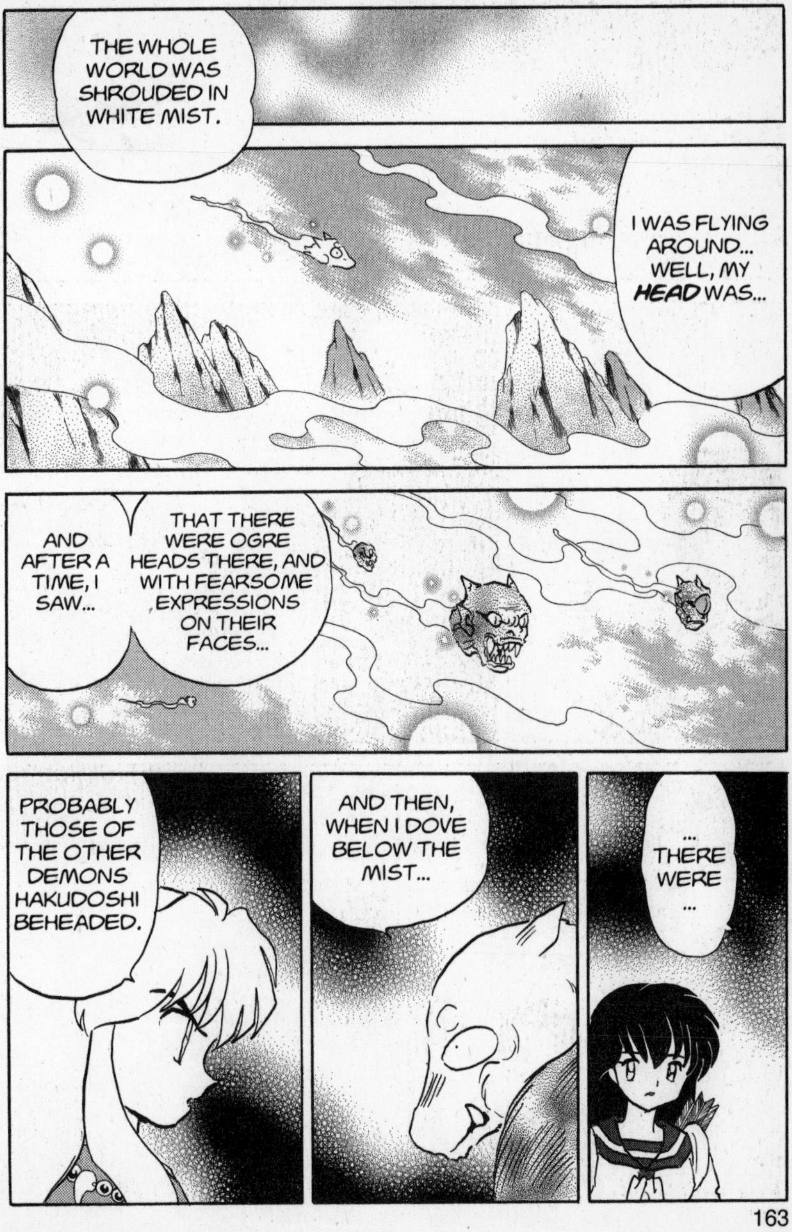
THE WHOLE WORLD WAS SHROUDED IN WHITE MIST.
I WAS FLYING AROUND... WELL, MY **HEAD** WAS...
AND AFTER A TIME, I SAW...
THAT THERE WERE OGRE HEADS THERE, AND WITH FEARSOME EXPRESSIONS ON THEIR FACES...
PROBABLY THOSE OF THE OTHER DEMONS HAKUDOSHI BEHEADED.
AND THEN, WHEN I DOVE BELOW THE MIST...
... THERE WERE ...

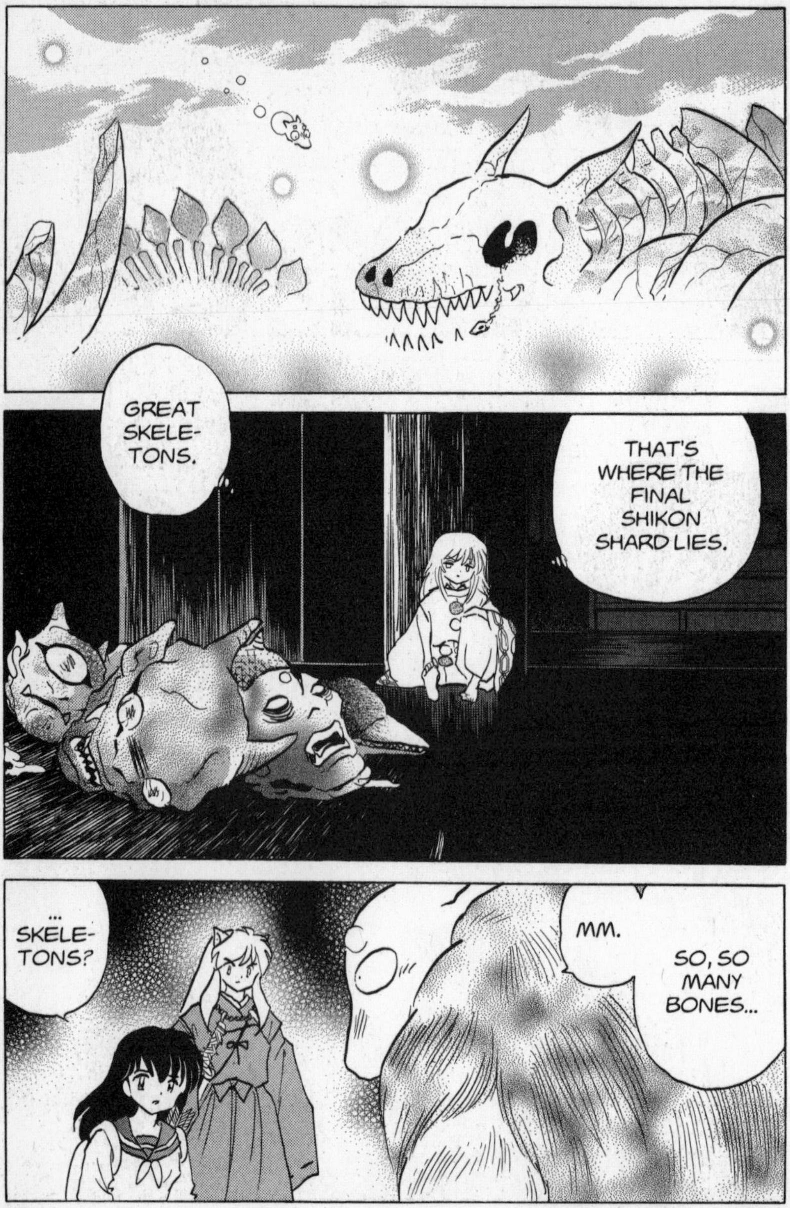
GREAT SKELE- TONS.
THAT'S WHERE THE FINAL SHIKON SHARD LIES.
... SKELE- TONS?
MM.
SO, SO MANY BONES...

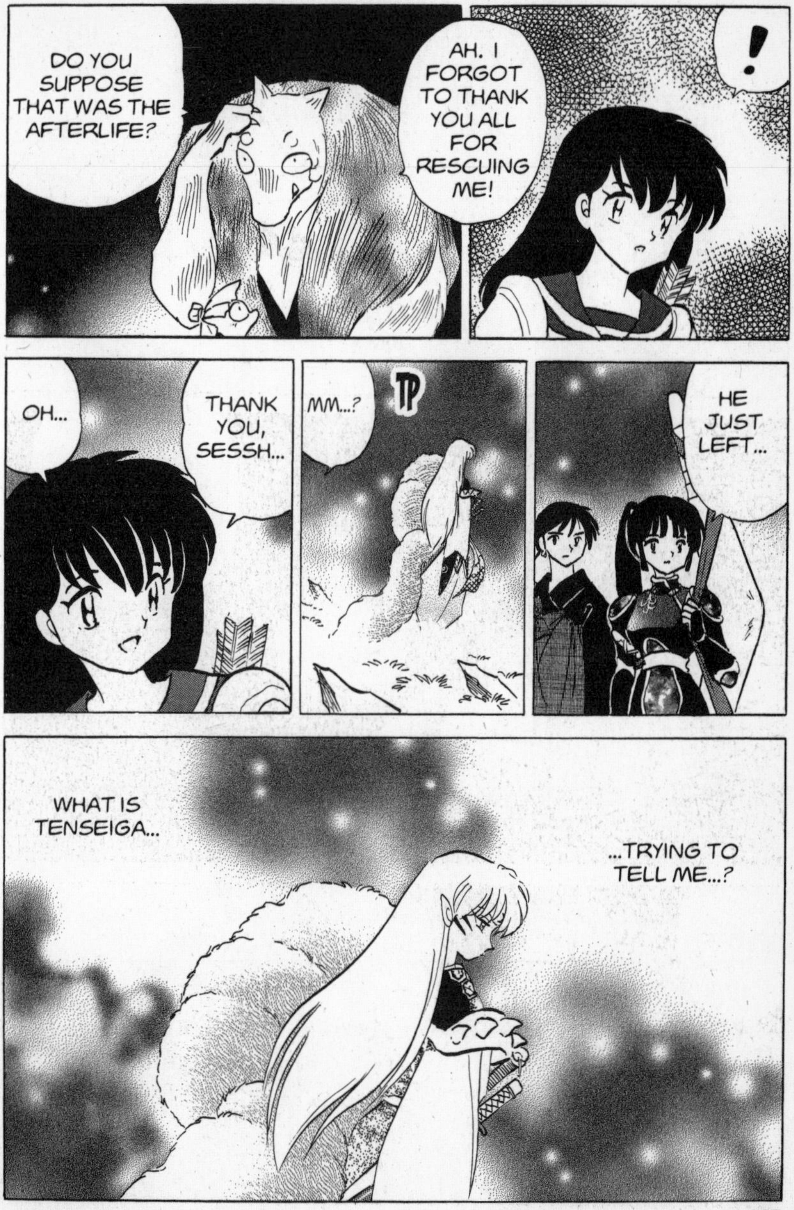
DO YOU SUPPOSE THAT WAS THE AFTERLIFE?
AH. I FORGOT TO THANK YOU ALL FOR RESCUING ME!
!
OH...
THANK YOU, SESSH...
MM...?
TP
HE JUST LEFT...
WHAT IS TENSEIGA...
...TRYING TO TELL ME...?

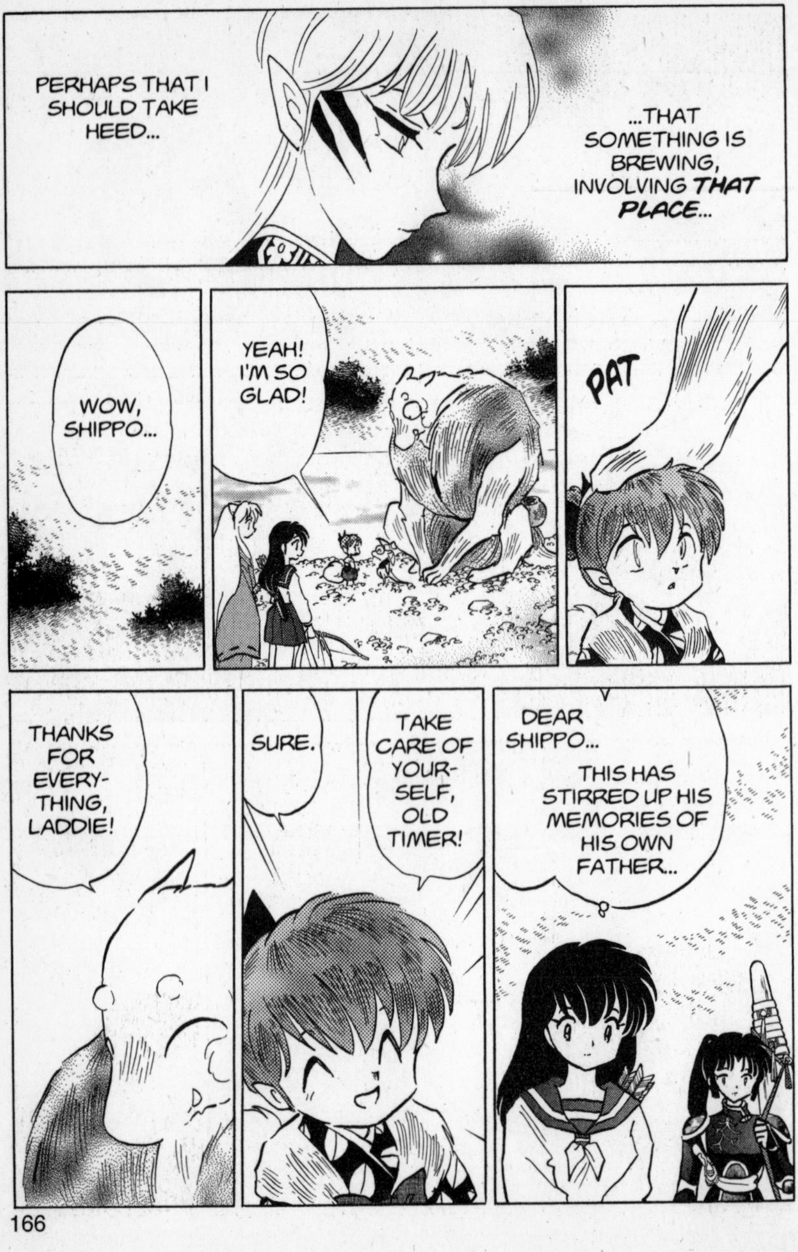
PERHAPS THAT I SHOULD TAKE HEED...
...THAT SOMETHING IS BREWING, INVOLVING ***THAT PLACE***...
WOW, SHIPPO...
YEAH! I'M SO GLAD!
PAT
THANKS FOR EVERY-THING, LADDIE!
SURE.
TAKE CARE OF YOUR-SELF, OLD TIMER!
DEAR SHIPPO...
THIS HAS STIRRED UP HIS MEMORIES OF HIS OWN FATHER...

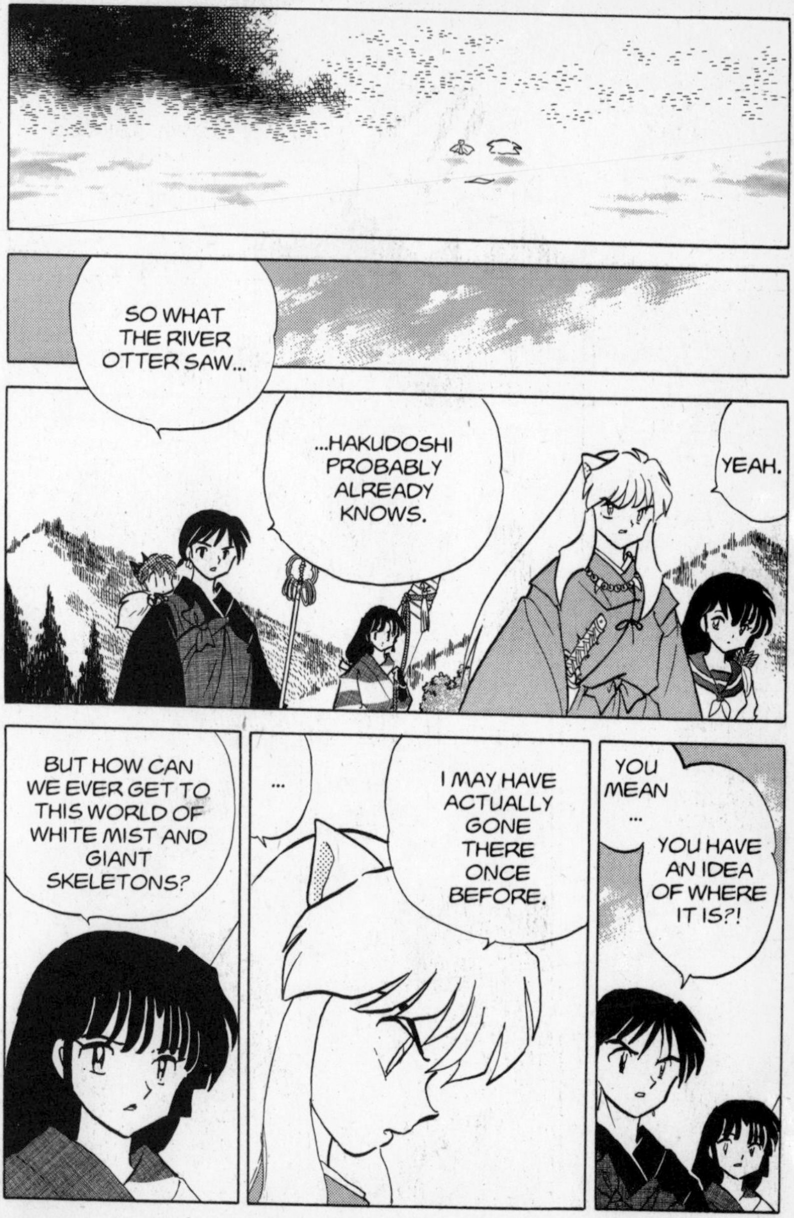
SO WHAT THE RIVER OTTER SAW...
...HAKUDOSHI PROBABLY ALREADY KNOWS.
YEAH.
BUT HOW CAN WE EVER GET TO THIS WORLD OF WHITE MIST AND GIANT SKELETONS?
...
I MAY HAVE ACTUALLY GONE THERE ONCE BEFORE.
YOU MEAN ...
YOU HAVE AN IDEA OF WHERE IT IS?!

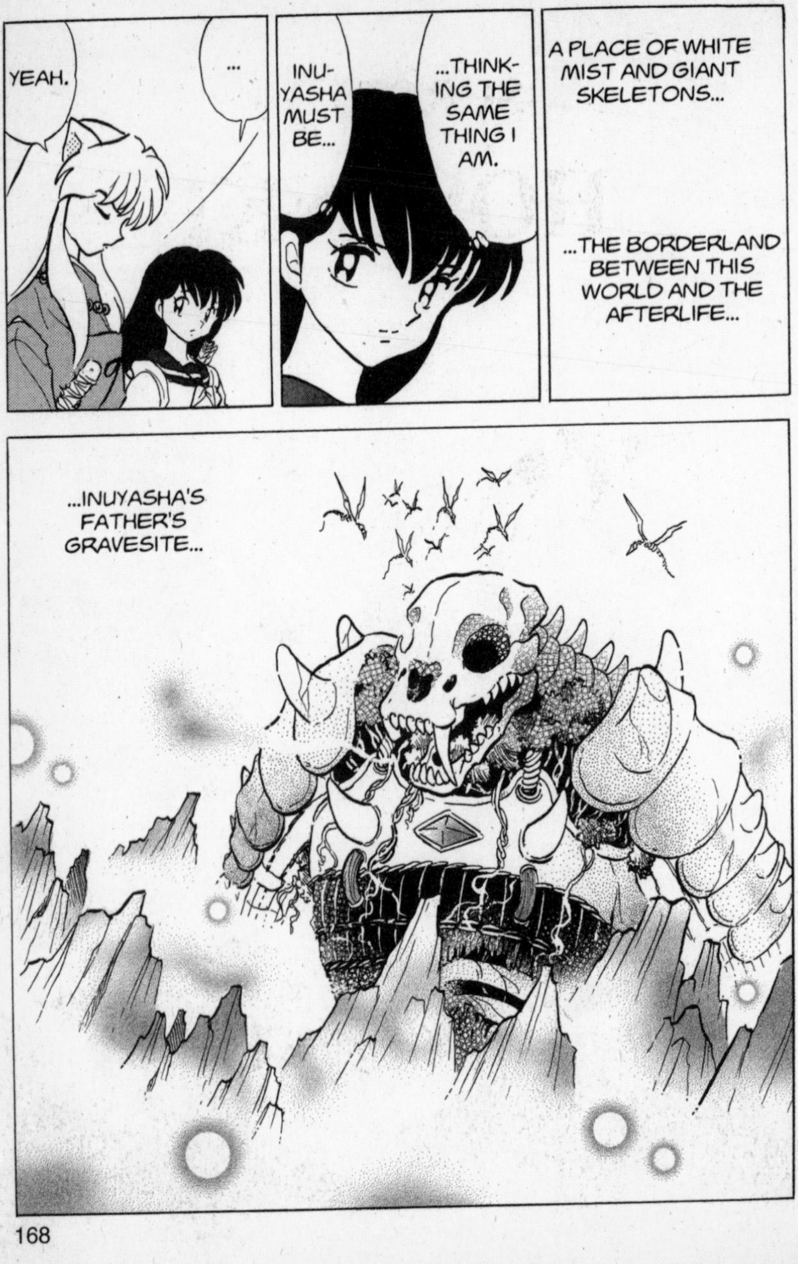
YEAH.
...
INU-YASHA MUST BE...
...THINK-ING THE SAME THING I AM.
A PLACE OF WHITE MIST AND GIANT SKELETONS...
...THE BORDERLAND BETWEEN THIS WORLD AND THE AFTERLIFE...
...INUYASHA'S FATHER'S GRAVESITE...

SCROLL 10

HOSENKI

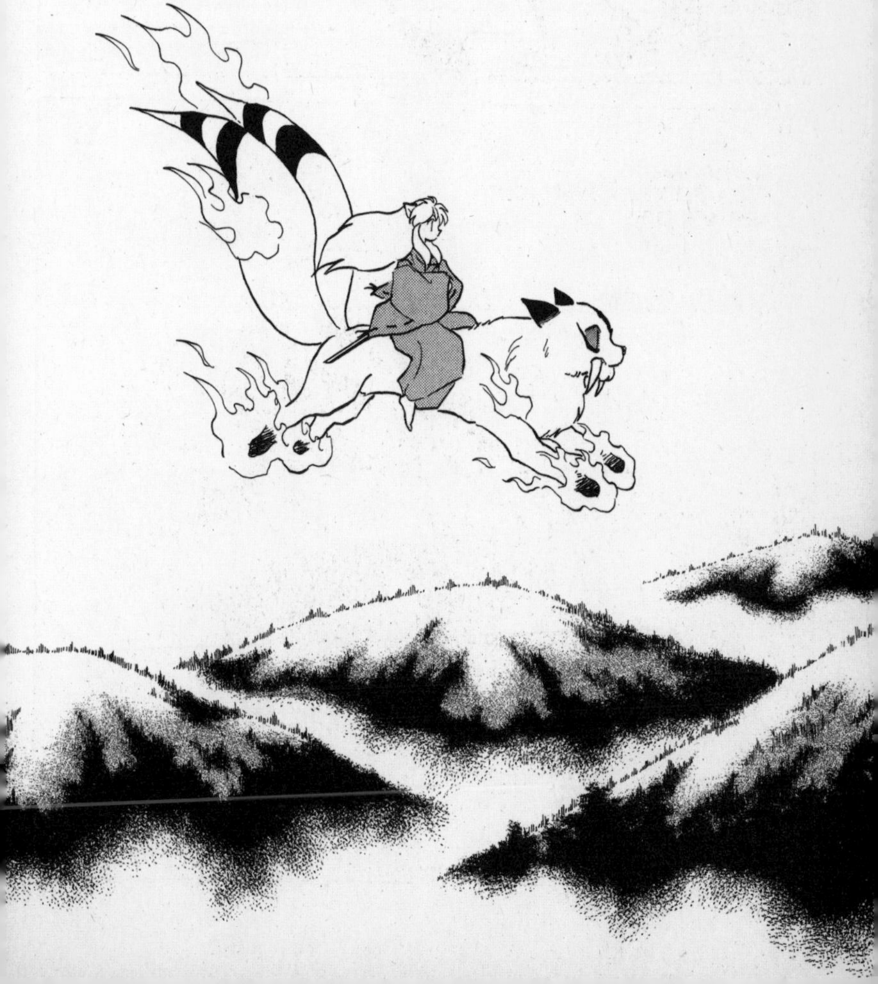

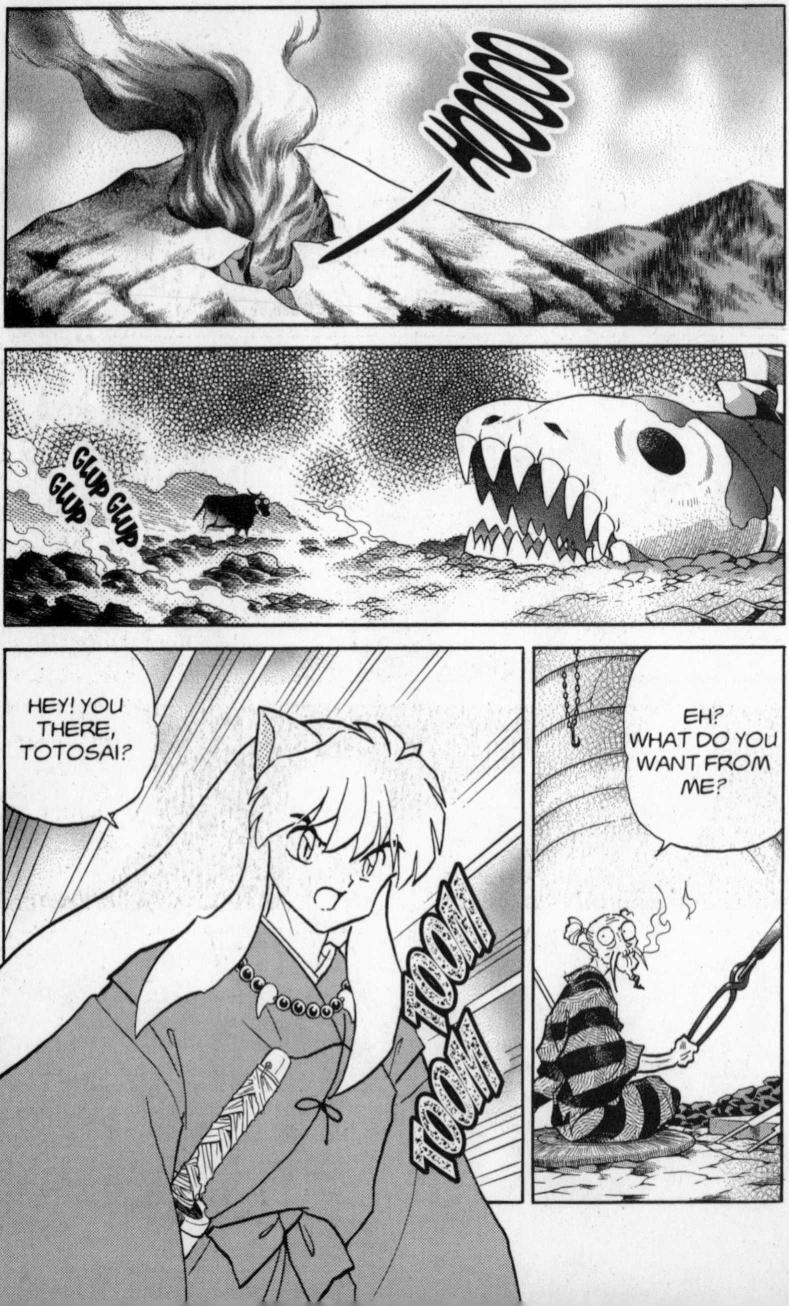
HOOOOO
GLUP GLUP
GLUP
HEY! YOU THERE, TOTOSAI?
TOOM TOOM
TOOM
EH? WHAT DO YOU WANT FROM ME?

FROM YOU, NOTHING. WHERE'S MYOGA?

RUDE AS EVER, I SEE.

SSSSUCK MOOP MOOP MOOP

YOU DELIBER-ATELY CAME LOOKING FOR ME?

IT CAN'T BE FOR ANY-THING GOOD.

SIGH-

SLAP

SPLAT

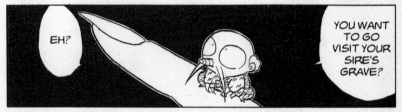

EH?

YOU WANT TO GO VISIT YOUR SIRE'S GRAVE?

TAKE ME THERE. THERE'S SOMETHING I NEED TO KNOW.

...BUT...

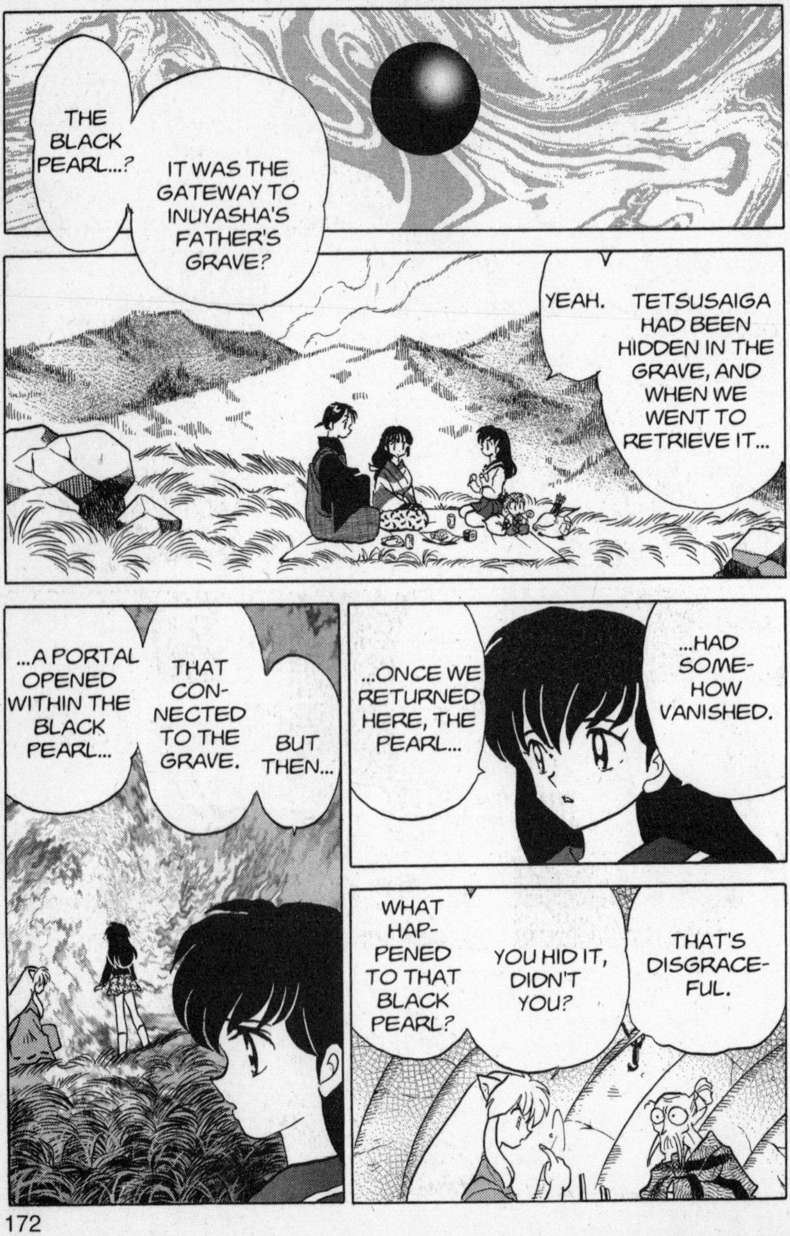

THE BLACK PEARL...?
IT WAS THE GATEWAY TO INUYASHA'S FATHER'S GRAVE?
YEAH.
TETSUSAIGA HAD BEEN HIDDEN IN THE GRAVE, AND WHEN WE WENT TO RETRIEVE IT...
...A PORTAL OPENED WITHIN THE BLACK PEARL...
THAT CONNECTED TO THE GRAVE.
BUT THEN...
...ONCE WE RETURNED HERE, THE PEARL...
...HAD SOMEHOW VANISHED.
WHAT HAPPENED TO THAT BLACK PEARL?
YOU HID IT, DIDN'T YOU?
THAT'S DISGRACEFUL.

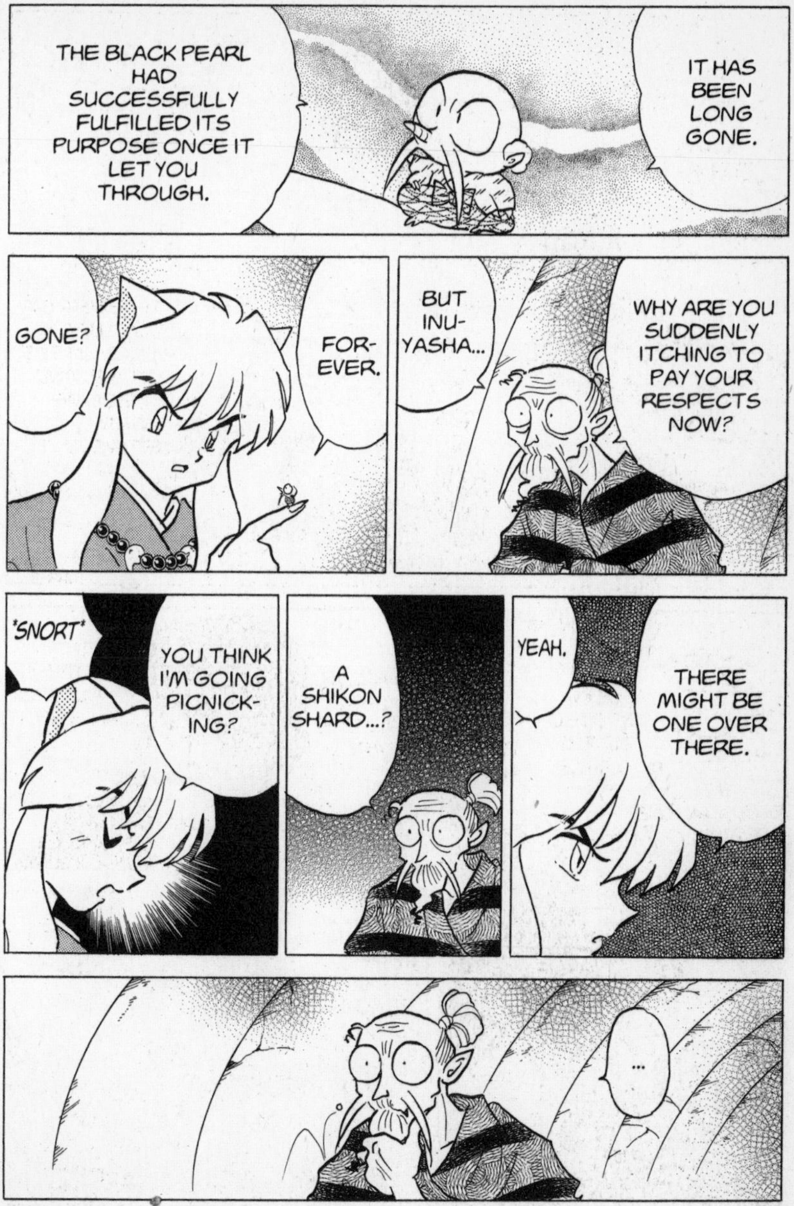
THE BLACK PEARL HAD SUCCESSFULLY FULFILLED ITS PURPOSE ONCE IT LET YOU THROUGH.
IT HAS BEEN LONG GONE.
GONE?
FOR-EVER.
BUT INU-YASHA...
WHY ARE YOU SUDDENLY ITCHING TO PAY YOUR RESPECTS NOW?
SNORT
YOU THINK I'M GOING PICNICK-ING?
A SHIKON SHARD...?
YEAH.
THERE MIGHT BE ONE OVER THERE.
...

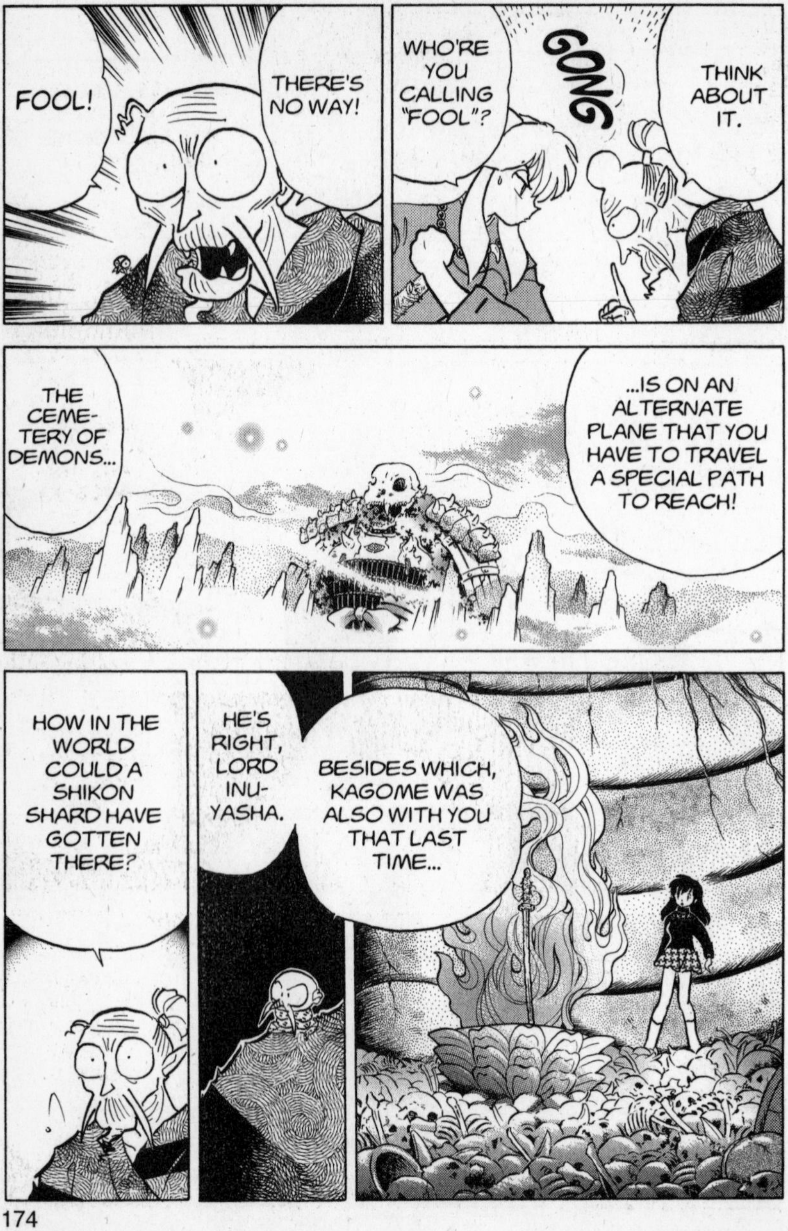
FOOL!
THERE'S NO WAY!
WHO'RE YOU CALLING "FOOL"?
GONG
THINK ABOUT IT.
THE CEME-TERY OF DEMONS...
...IS ON AN ALTERNATE PLANE THAT YOU HAVE TO TRAVEL A SPECIAL PATH TO REACH!
HOW IN THE WORLD COULD A SHIKON SHARD HAVE GOTTEN THERE?
HE'S RIGHT, LORD INU-YASHA.
BESIDES WHICH, KAGOME WAS ALSO WITH YOU THAT LAST TIME...

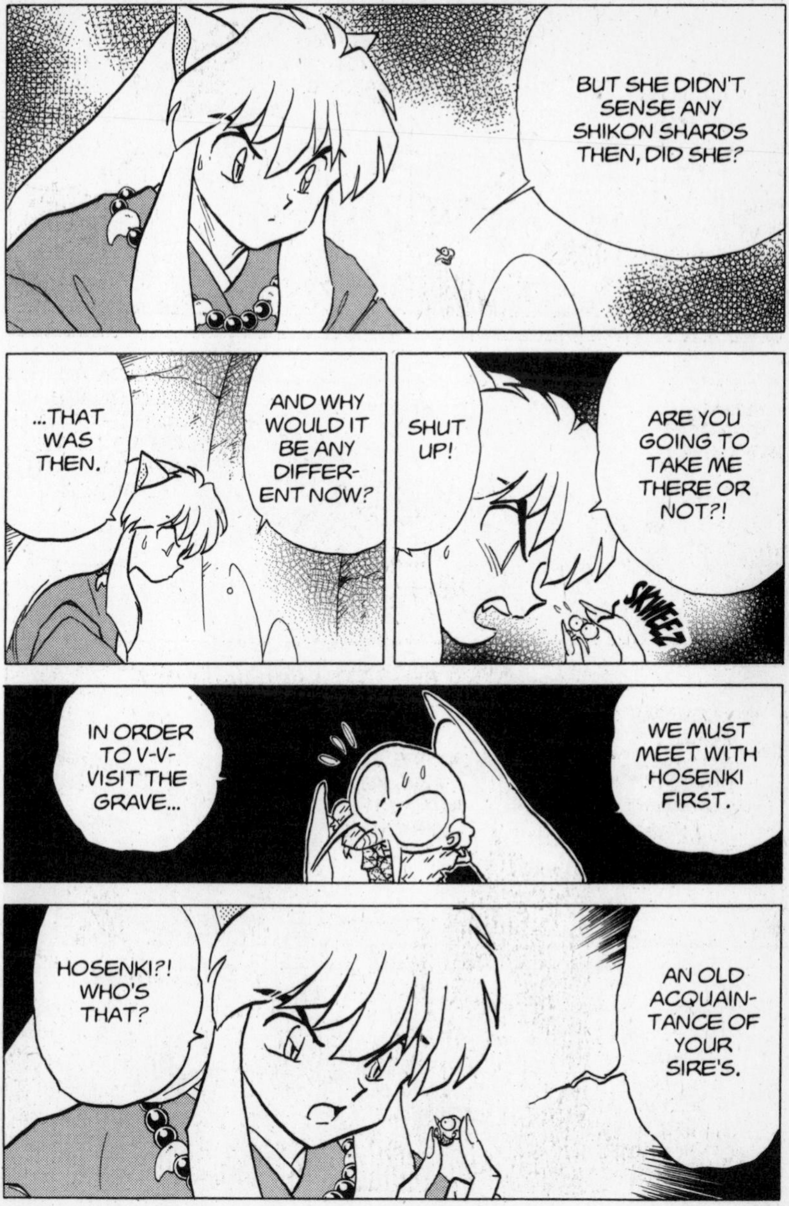
BUT SHE DIDN'T SENSE ANY SHIKON SHARDS THEN, DID SHE?
...THAT WAS THEN.
AND WHY WOULD IT BE ANY DIFFERENT NOW?
SHUT UP!
ARE YOU GOING TO TAKE ME THERE OR NOT?!
SKWEEZ
IN ORDER TO V-V-VISIT THE GRAVE...
WE MUST MEET WITH HOSENKI FIRST.
HOSENKI?! WHO'S THAT?
AN OLD ACQUAINTANCE OF YOUR SIRE'S.

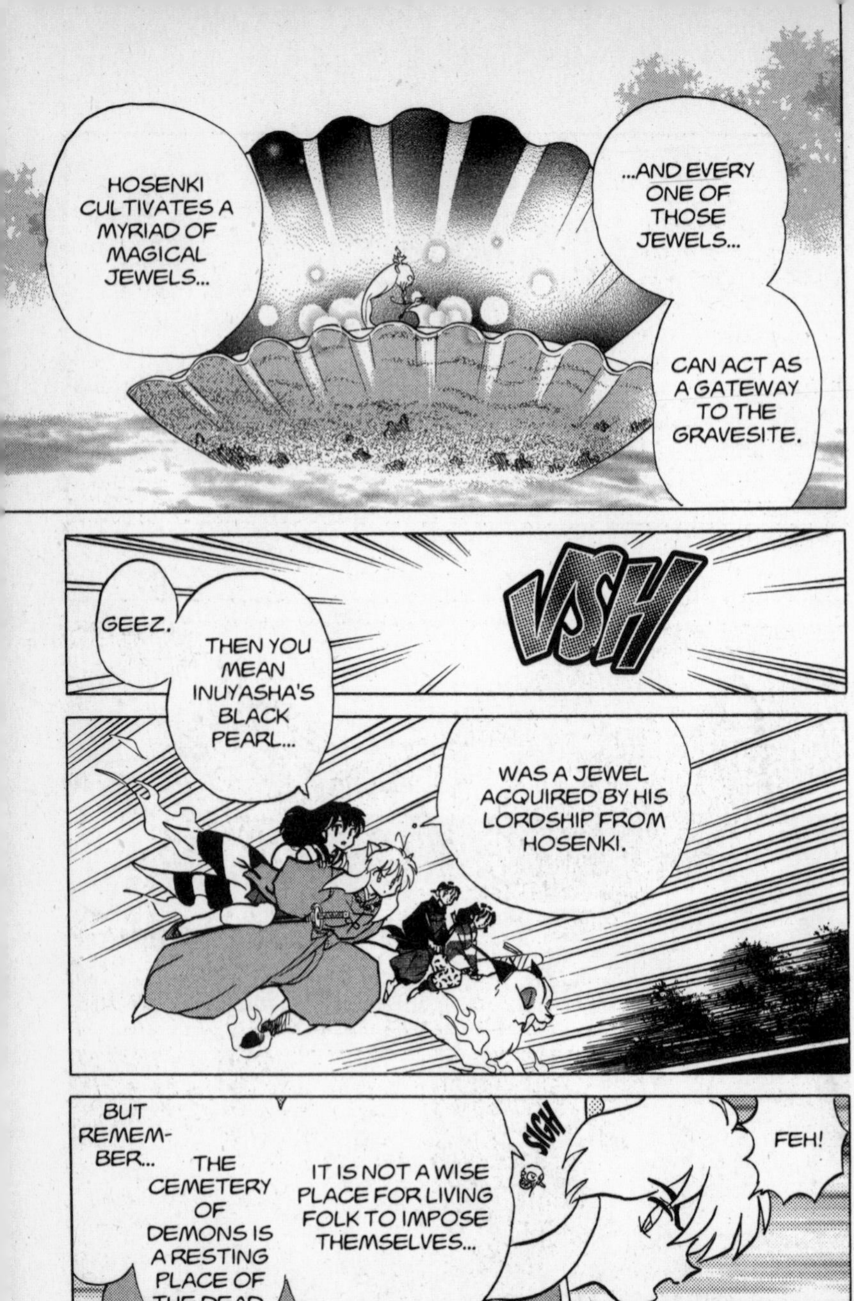
HOSENKI CULTIVATES A MYRIAD OF MAGICAL JEWELS...
...AND EVERY ONE OF THOSE JEWELS...
CAN ACT AS A GATEWAY TO THE GRAVESITE.
GEEZ.
VSH
THEN YOU MEAN INUYASHA'S BLACK PEARL...
WAS A JEWEL ACQUIRED BY HIS LORDSHIP FROM HOSENKI.
BUT REMEMBER...
THE CEMETERY OF DEMONS IS A RESTING PLACE OF THE DEAD.
IT IS NOT A WISE PLACE FOR LIVING FOLK TO IMPOSE THEMSELVES...
SIGH
FEH!

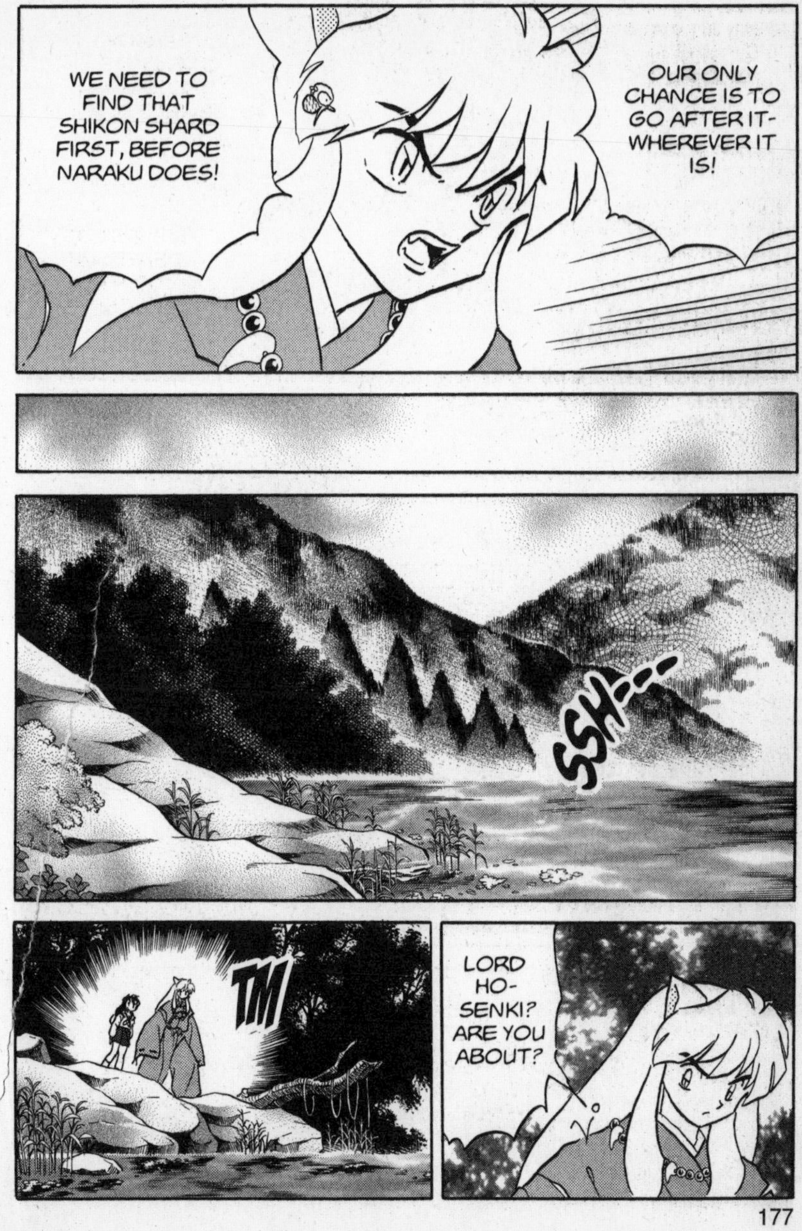
WE NEED TO FIND THAT SHIKON SHARD FIRST, BEFORE NARAKU DOES!
OUR ONLY CHANCE IS TO GO AFTER IT-WHEREVER IT IS!
SSH---
TM
LORD HO-SENKI? ARE YOU ABOUT?

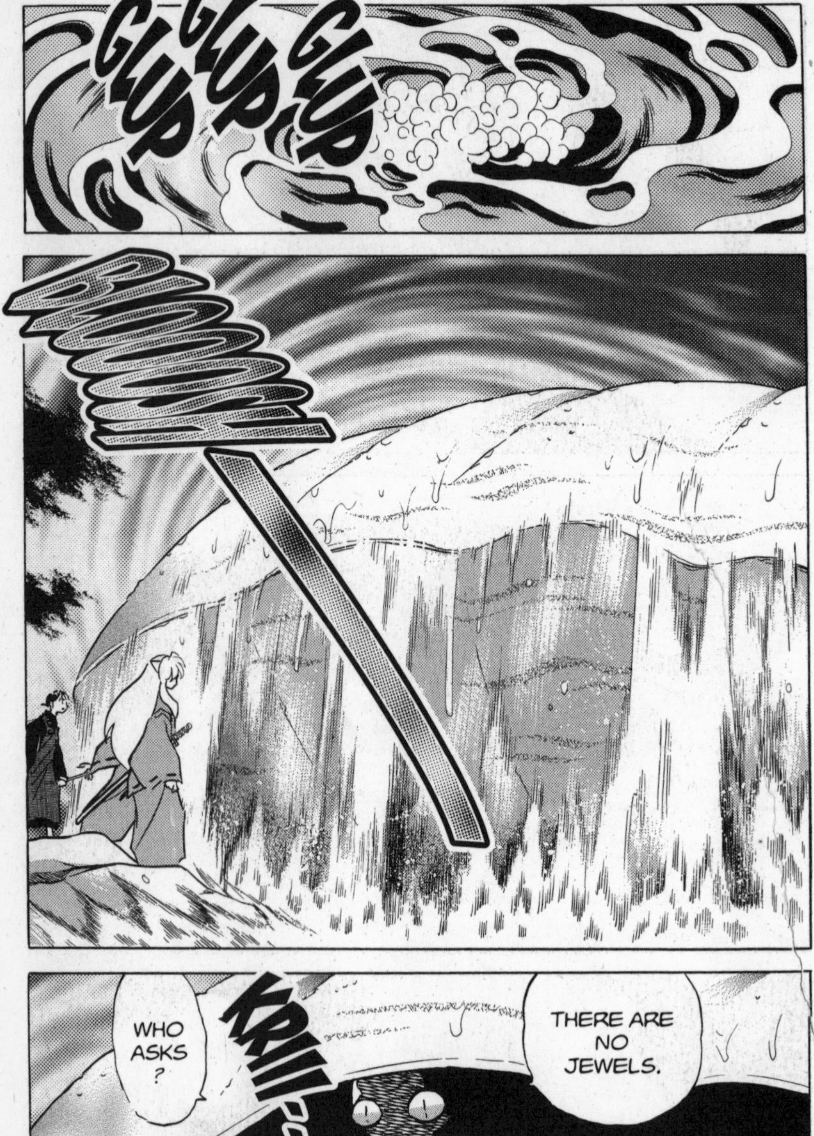
GLUP
GLUP
GLUP
WHO ASKS ?
THERE ARE NO JEWELS.

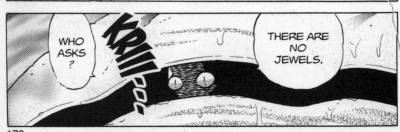

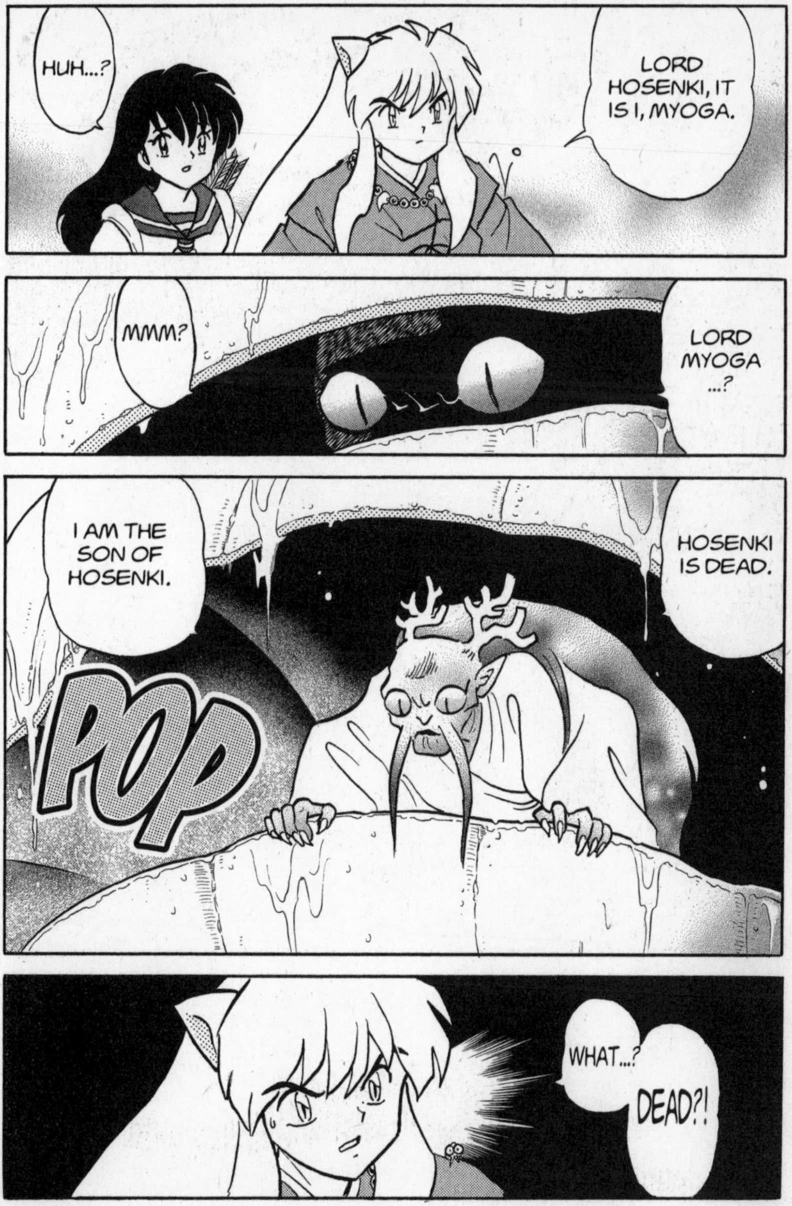
HUH...?
LORD HOSENKI, IT IS I, MYOGA.
MMM?
LORD MYOGA ...?
I AM THE SON OF HOSENKI.
POP
HOSENKI IS DEAD.
WHAT...?
DEAD?!

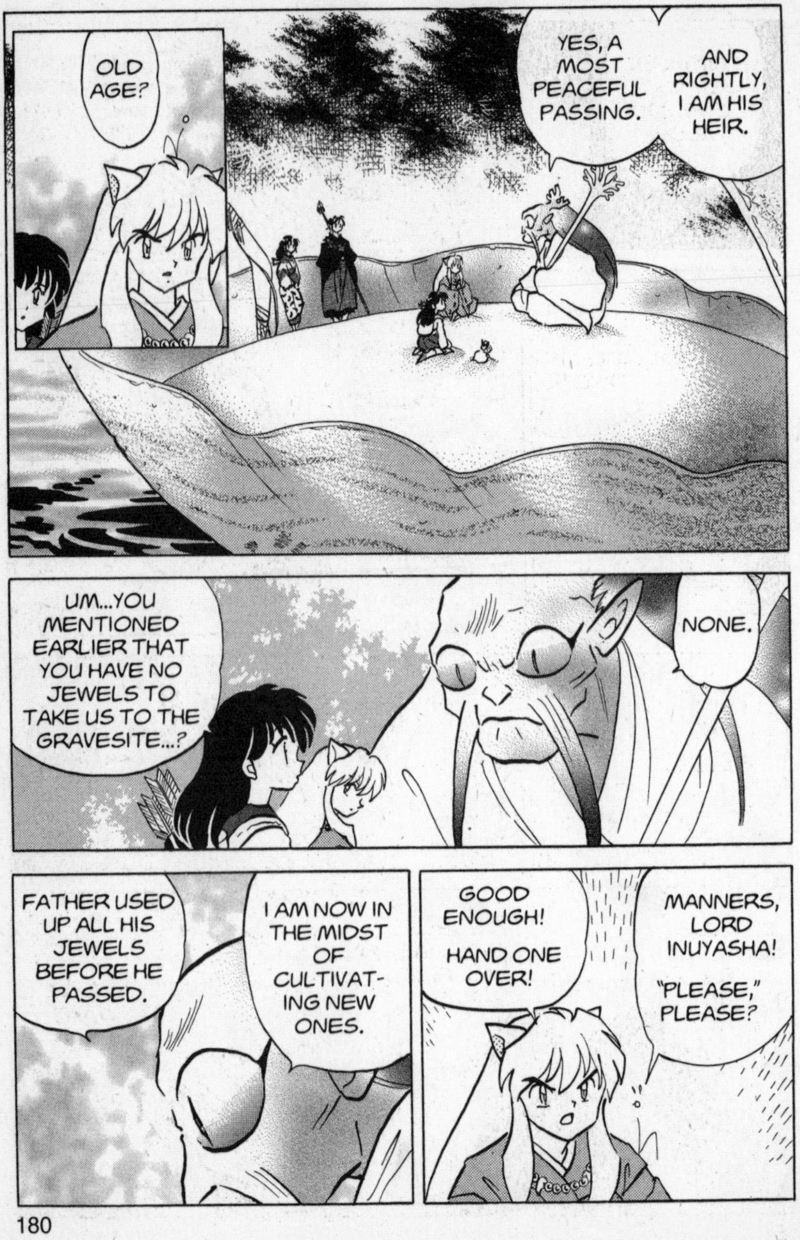
OLD AGE?
YES, A MOST PEACEFUL PASSING.
AND RIGHTLY, I AM HIS HEIR.
UM...YOU MENTIONED EARLIER THAT YOU HAVE NO JEWELS TO TAKE US TO THE GRAVESITE...?
NONE.
FATHER USED UP ALL HIS JEWELS BEFORE HE PASSED.
I AM NOW IN THE MIDST OF CULTIVAT-ING NEW ONES.
GOOD ENOUGH!
HAND ONE OVER!
MANNERS, LORD INUYASHA!
"PLEASE," PLEASE?

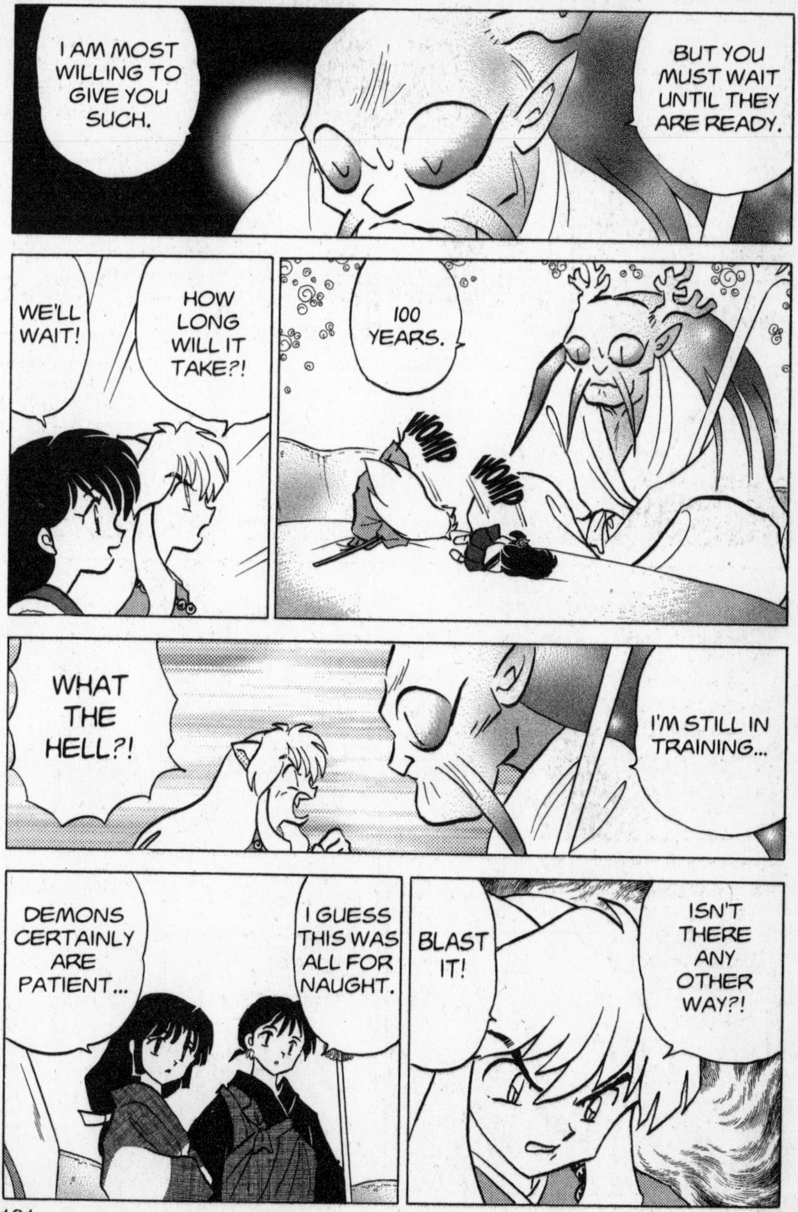
I AM MOST WILLING TO GIVE YOU SUCH.
BUT YOU MUST WAIT UNTIL THEY ARE READY.
WE'LL WAIT!
HOW LONG WILL IT TAKE?!
100 YEARS.
WOMP
WOMP
WHAT THE HELL?!
I'M STILL IN TRAINING...
DEMONS CERTAINLY ARE PATIENT...
I GUESS THIS WAS ALL FOR NAUGHT.
BLAST IT!
ISN'T THERE ANY OTHER WAY?!

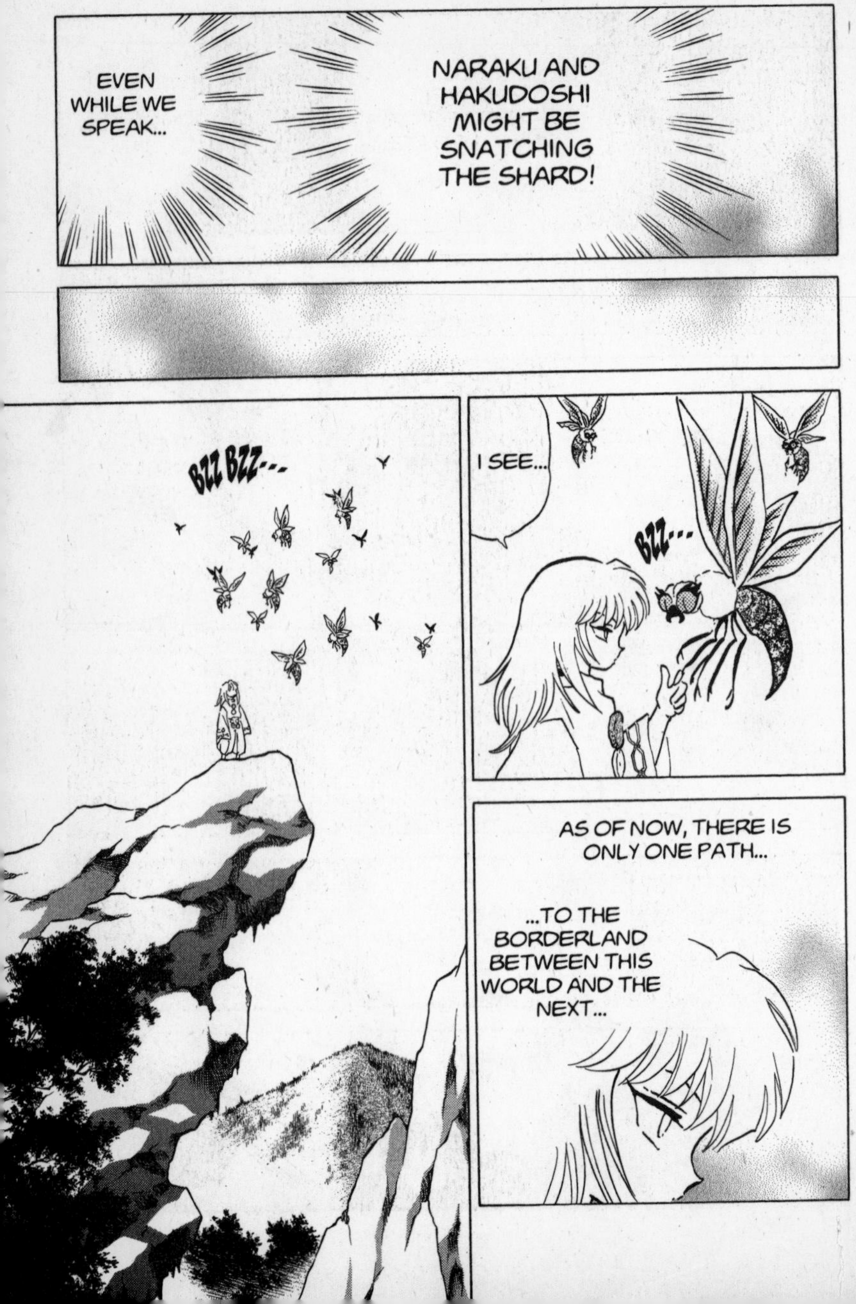
EVEN WHILE WE SPEAK...
NARAKU AND HAKUDOSHI MIGHT BE SNATCHING THE SHARD!
BZZ BZZ...
I SEE...
BZZ...
AS OF NOW, THERE IS ONLY ONE PATH...
...TO THE BORDERLAND BETWEEN THIS WORLD AND THE NEXT...

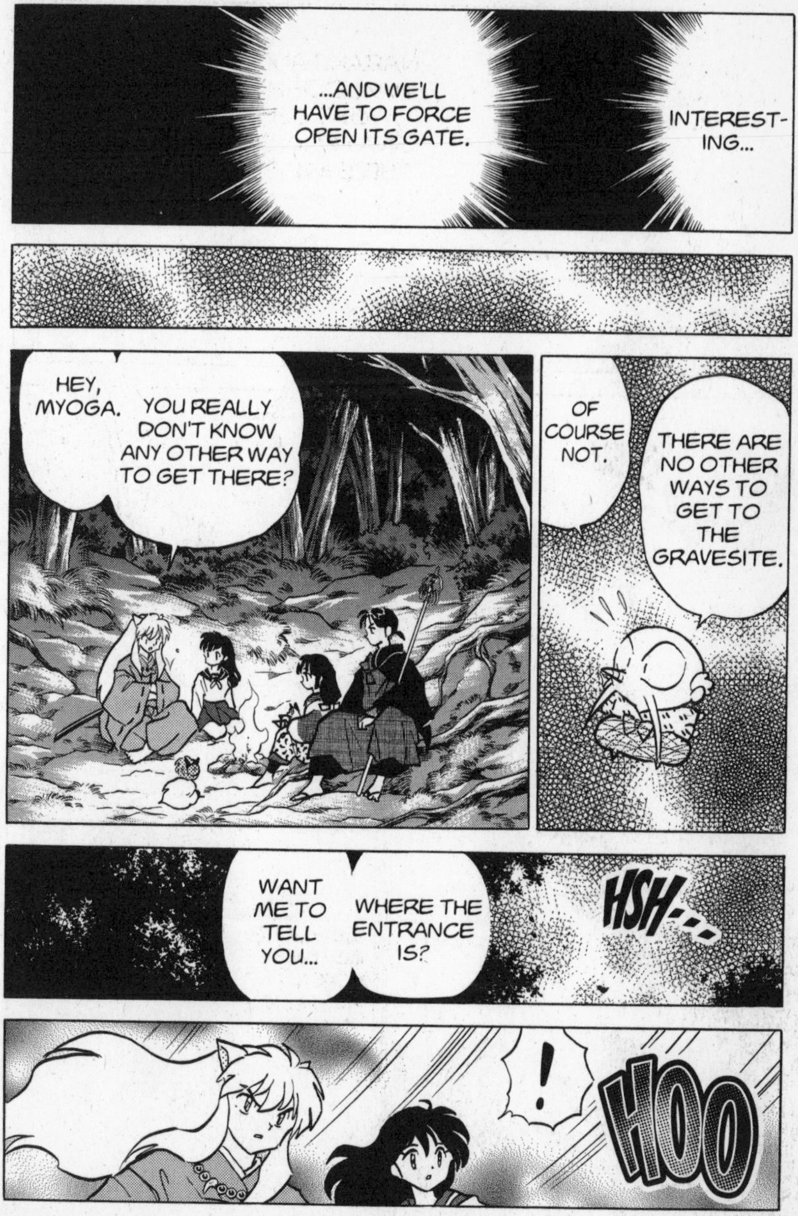
...AND WE'LL HAVE TO FORCE OPEN ITS GATE.
INTEREST-ING...
HEY, MYOGA.
YOU REALLY DON'T KNOW ANY OTHER WAY TO GET THERE?
OF COURSE NOT.
THERE ARE NO OTHER WAYS TO GET TO THE GRAVESITE.
WANT ME TO TELL YOU...
WHERE THE ENTRANCE IS?
HSH...
!
HOO

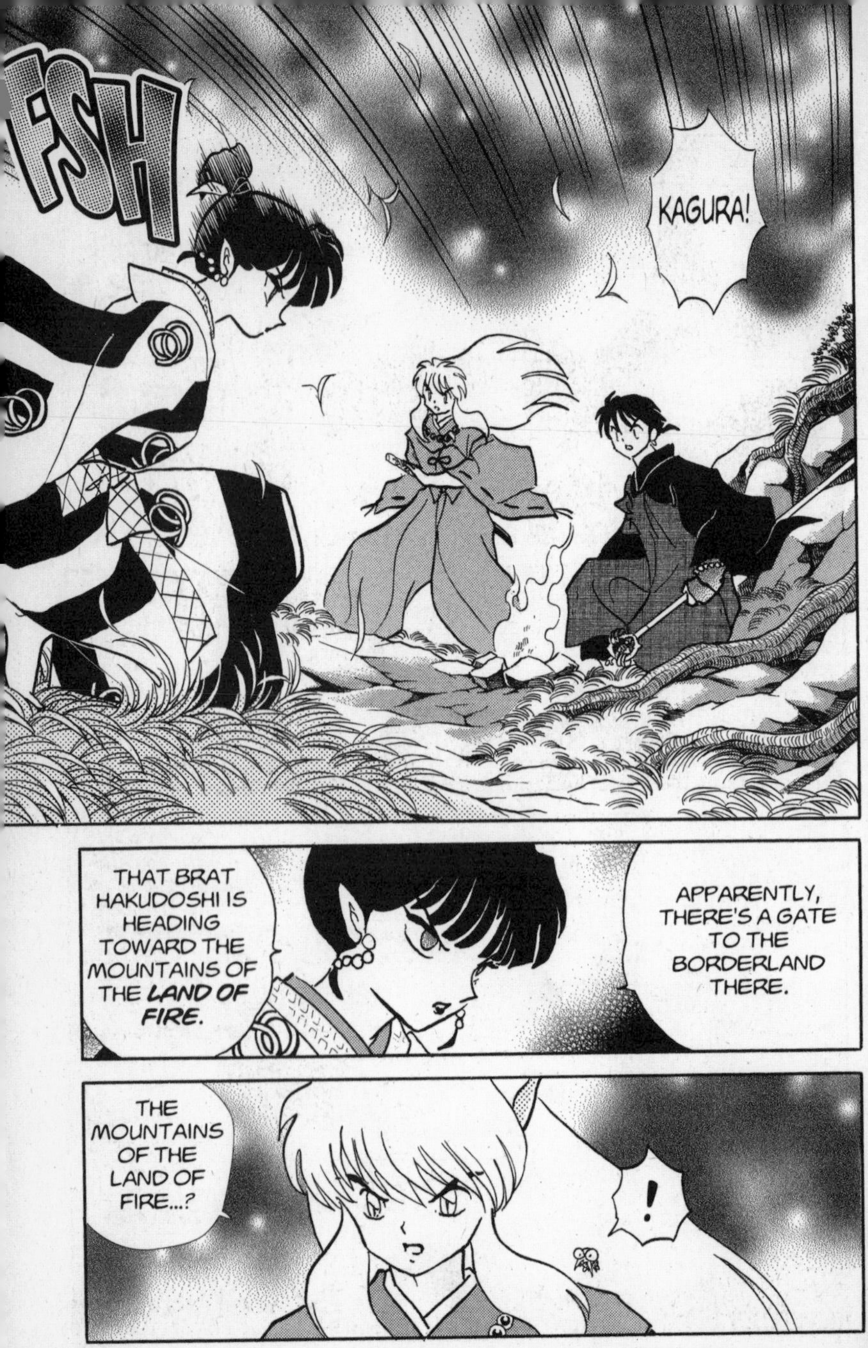
KAGURA!
THAT BRAT HAKUDOSHI IS HEADING TOWARD THE MOUNTAINS OF THE ***LAND OF FIRE***.
APPARENTLY, THERE'S A GATE TO THE BORDERLAND THERE.
THE MOUNTAINS OF THE LAND OF FIRE...?
!

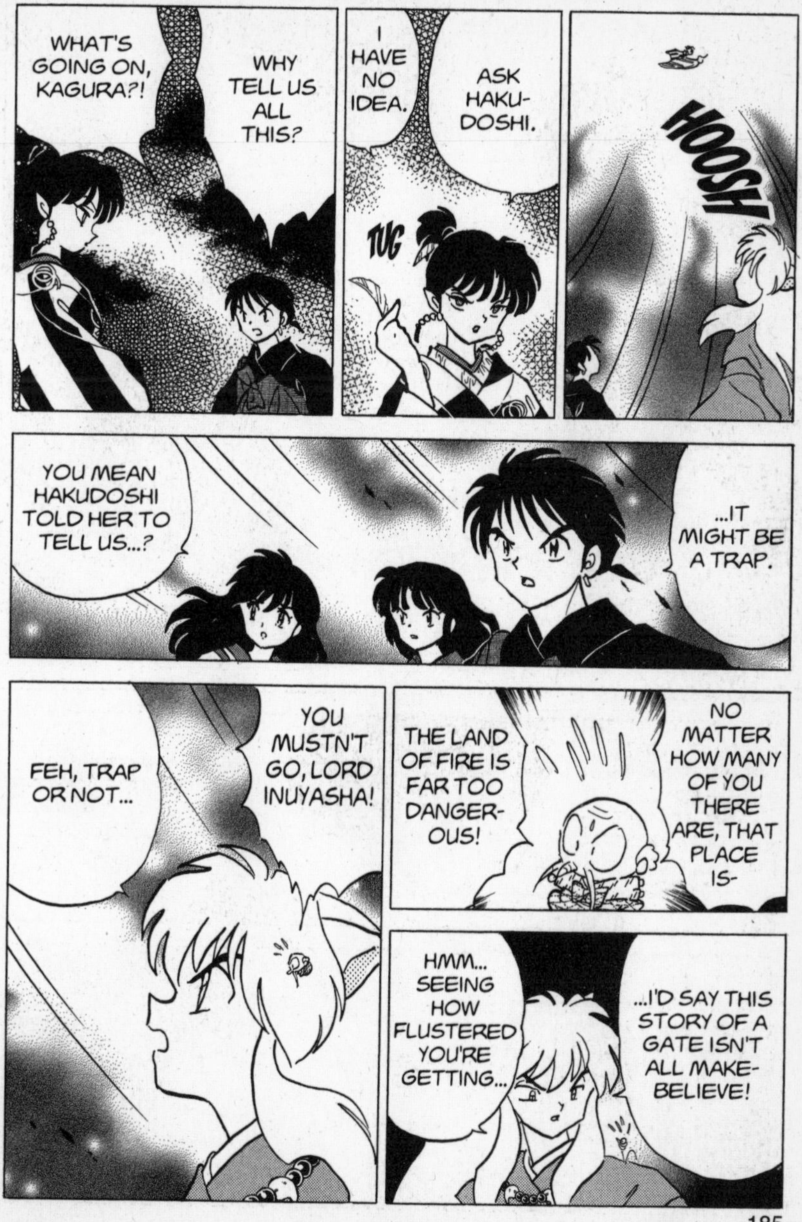
WHAT'S GOING ON, KAGURA?!
WHY TELL US ALL THIS?
I HAVE NO IDEA.
ASK HAKU-DOSHI.
TUG
HOOSH
YOU MEAN HAKUDOSHI TOLD HER TO TELL US...?
...IT MIGHT BE A TRAP.
FEH, TRAP OR NOT...
YOU MUSTN'T GO, LORD INUYASHA!
THE LAND OF FIRE IS FAR TOO DANGER-OUS!
NO MATTER HOW MANY OF YOU THERE ARE, THAT PLACE IS-
HMM... SEEING HOW FLUSTERED YOU'RE GETTING...
...I'D SAY THIS STORY OF A GATE ISN'T ALL MAKE-BELIEVE!

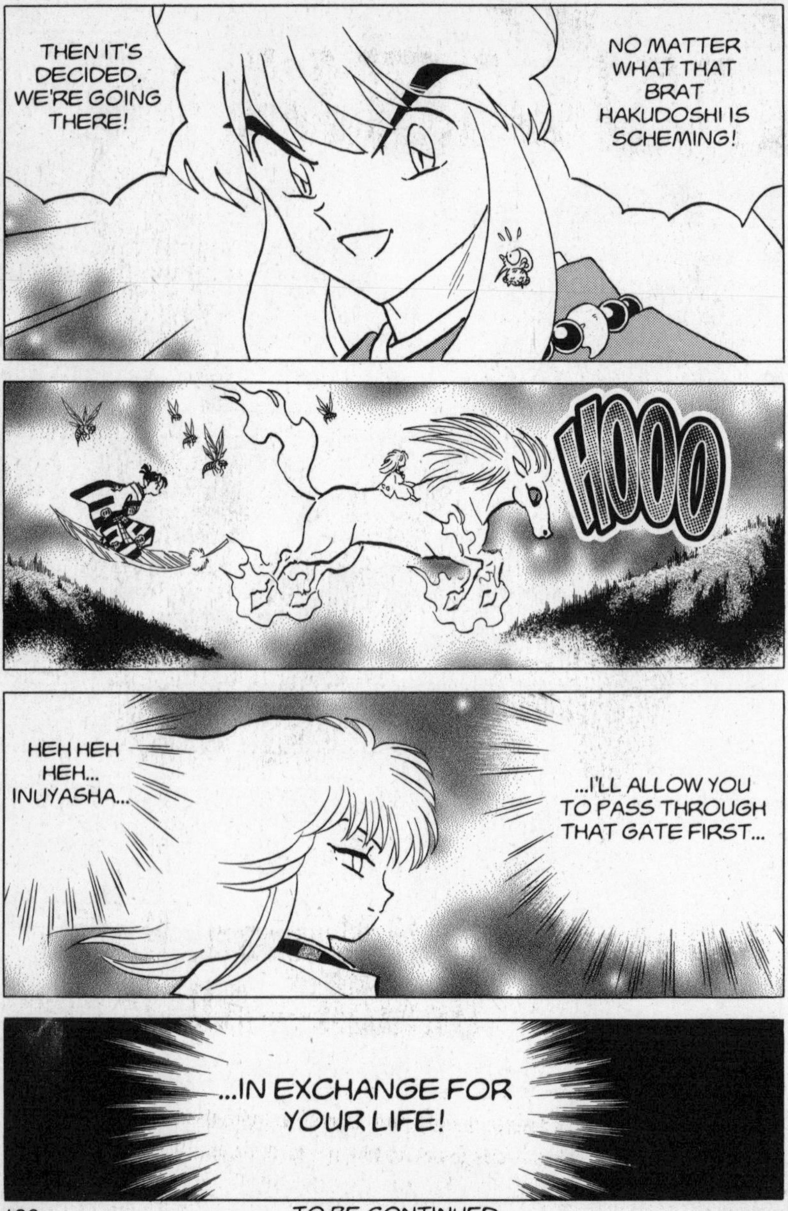
THEN IT'S DECIDED. WE'RE GOING THERE!
NO MATTER WHAT THAT BRAT HAKUDOSHI IS SCHEMING!
HOOO
HEH HEH HEH... INUYASHA...
...I'LL ALLOW YOU TO PASS THROUGH THAT GATE FIRST...
...IN EXCHANGE FOR YOUR LIFE!

TO BE CONTINUED...

INUYASHA

Read the action from the start with the original manga series

Full color adaptation of the popular TV series

The Art of INUYASHA

Original Illustrations by Rumiko Takahashi

Art book with cel art, paintings, character profiles and more

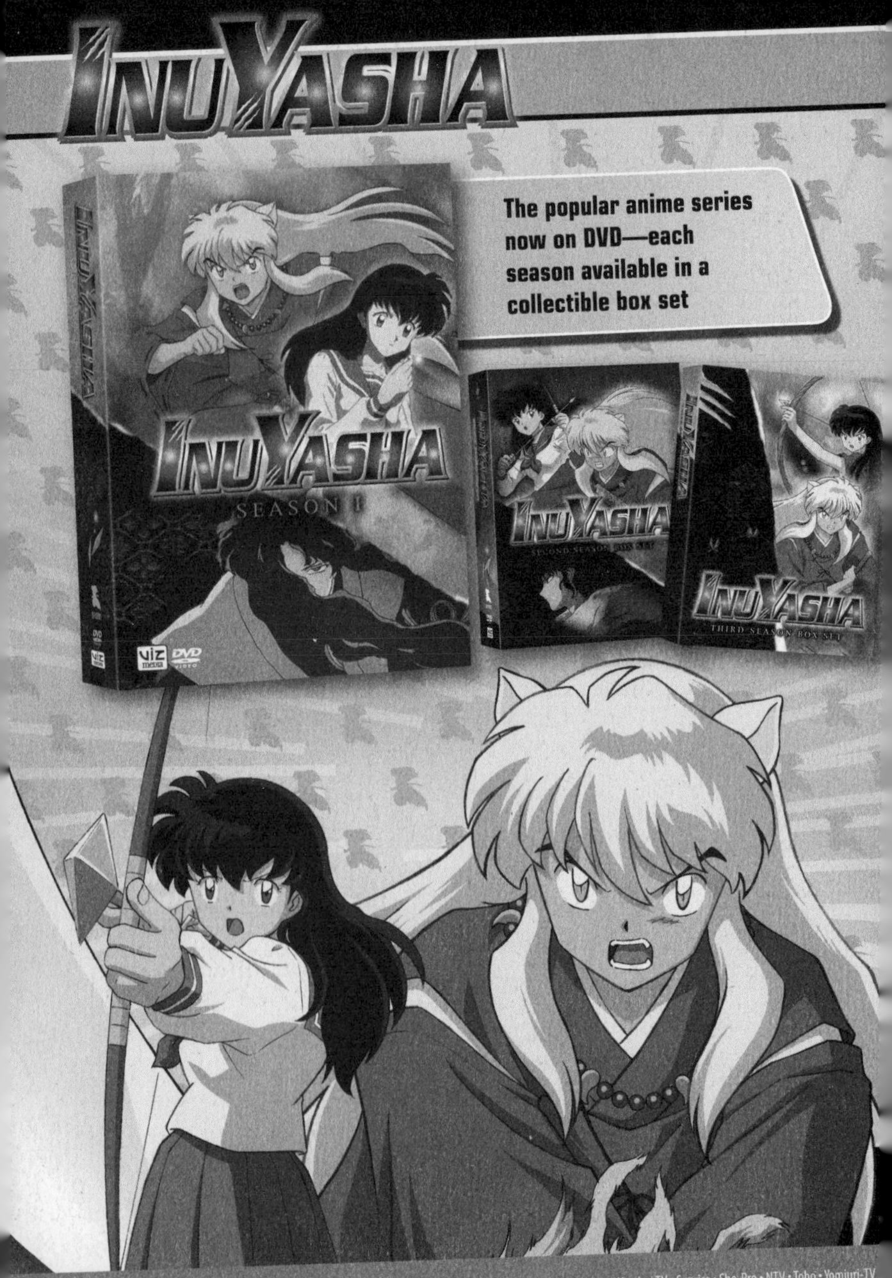
InuYasha
The popular anime series now on DVD—each season available in a collectible box set
InuYasha
Season 1
InuYasha
Second Season Box Set
InuYasha
Third Season Box Set